Justice, gender, and the politics of multiculturalism

D0743946

Justice, Gender, and the Politics of Multiculturalism explores the tensions that arise when culturally diverse democratic states pursue both justice for religious and cultural minorities and justice for women. Sarah Song provides a distinctive argument about the circumstances under which egalitarian justice requires special accommodations for cultural minorities while emphasizing the value of gender equality as an important limit on cultural accommodation. Drawing on detailed case studies of gendered cultural conflicts, including conflicts over the "cultural defense" in criminal law, aboriginal membership rules, and polygamy, Song offers a fresh perspective on multicultural politics by examining the role of intercultural interactions in shaping such conflicts. In particular, she demonstrates the different ways that majority institutions have reinforced gender inequality in minority communities and, in light of this, argues in favor of resolving gendered cultural dilemmas through intercultural democratic dialogue.

SARAH SONG is Assistant Professor of Law and Political Science at the University of California, Berkeley.

Contemporary Political Theory

Series Editor
Ian Shapiro

Editorial Board
Russell Hardin
Stephen Holmes
Jeffrey Isaac
John Keane
Elizabeth Kiss
Susan Okin
Phillipe Van Parijs
Philip Pettit

As the twenty-first century begins, major new political challenges have arisen at the same time as some of the most enduring dilemmas of political association remain unresolved. The collapse of communism and the end of the Cold War reflect a victory for democratic and liberal values, yet in many of the Western countries that nurtured those values there are severe problems of urban decay, class and racial conflict, and failing political legitimacy. Enduring global injustice and inequality seem compounded by environmental problems, disease, the oppression of women, racial, ethnic, and religious minorities, and the relentless growth of the world's population. In such circumstances, the need for creative thinking about the fundamentals of human political association is manifest. This new series in contemporary political theory is needed to foster such systematic normative reflection.

The series proceeds in the belief that the time is ripe for a reassertion of the importance of problem-driven political theory. It is concerned, that is, with works that are motivated by the impulse to understand, think critically about, and address the problems in the world, rather than issues that are thrown up primarily in academic debate. Books in the series may be interdisciplinary in character, ranging over issues conventionally dealt with in philosophy, law, history, and the human sciences. The range of materials and the methods of proceeding should be dictated by the problem at hand, not the conventional debates or disciplinary divisions of academia.

Justice, Gender, and the Politics of Multiculturalism

Sarah Song

CAMBRIDGE UNIVERSITY PRESS

CAMBRIDGE UNIVERSITY PRESS
Cambridge, New York, Melbourne, Madrid, Cape Town, Singapore, São Paulo, Delhi

Cambridge University Press
The Edinburgh Building, Cambridge CB2 8RU, UK

Published in the United States of America by Cambridge University Press, New York

www.cambridge.org
Information on this title: www.cambridge.org/9780521697590

First published 2007
Reprinted 2009

Printed in the United Kingdom at the University Press, Cambridge

A catalogue record for this publication is available from the British Library

Library of Congress Cataloguing in Publication data
Justice, gender, and the politics of multiculturalism / Sarah Song.
    p.   cm. – (Contemporary political theory)
  Includes bibliographical references and index.
  ISBN 978-0-521-87487-8 (hardback)
  ISBN 978-0-521-69759-0 (pbk.)
1. Sex discrimination against women.   2. Women's rights.   3. Minorities – Civil
  rights.   4. Multiculturalism.   5. Pluralism (Social sciences)   6. Culture
  conflict.   7. Social Justice.   I. Song, Sarah, 1973–   II. Title.   III. Series.
HQ1237.J87   2007
305.48′8 – dc22   200700749

ISBN 978-0-521-87487-8 hardback
ISBN 978-0-521-69759-0 paperback

For my parents

Contents

Acknowledgments

I have acquired many debts to people and institutions while writing this book, and it is a pleasure to acknowledge them here. I am thankful for the generous funding and support that enabled me to revise and complete this book, from the Woodrow Wilson National Fellowship Foundation, the Visiting Scholars Program at the American Academy of Arts and Sciences, and the Department of Political Science at MIT.

I presented earlier versions of parts of this book at conferences and colloquia, and I thank the audiences at the following places for their thoughtful comments and suggestions: at Yale, the Department of Political Science, the political theory workshop, and the Center for Race, Inequality, and Politics; at MIT, the political philosophy workshop, the Workshop on Gender and Philosophy, and the Women's Studies Intellectual Forum; the Harvard political theory colloquium; the University of Maryland Democracy Collaborative; the Brandeis colloquium on democracy and cultural pluralism; the University of Wisconsin political philosophy colloquium; Annual Meetings of the American Political Science Association and the Western Political Science Association; and the American Academy of Arts and Sciences research presentation series.

An earlier version of chapter 4 was published in *Critique internationale* 28 (2005) and several passages of chapters 2, 4, 5, and 6 were first published in the *American Political Science Review* 99, no. 4 (2005). I thank Presses de Sciences Po and Cambridge University Press for permission to reprint these.

Several people deserve special thanks. Rogers Smith read many versions of the manuscript and offered judicious guidance; I am deeply grateful for his generosity of spirit and for his steadfast support throughout this project. Ian Shapiro's keen insights compelled me to stay focused on concrete problems while making my arguments about justice and democracy. Jennifer Pitts asked some of the hardest and most important questions, which challenged me to make fruitful connections and expansions. Seyla Benhabib read an early version of the manuscript and offered helpful suggestions for its improvement. I am also grateful to her for inspiring my interest in political theory while I was an undergraduate in Social Studies at Harvard. Joshua Cohen, Daniel Sabbagh, and Jeff Spinner-Halev read different versions of the manuscript and offered many thoughtful suggestions for its improvement. My debt to all of them is profound.

At the earliest stages of this project, I benefited from the constructive criticism and friendship of my fellow graduate students at Yale: Alissa Ardito, Mayling Birney, Rebecca Bohrman, Brenda Carter, Elizabeth Cohen, Raluca Eddon, Chinyelu Lee, Serena Mayeri, Naomi Murakawa, Amy Rasmussen, Dara Strolovitch, and Dorian Warren.

I found a congenial intellectual home at MIT in the Political Science Department and in the Women's Studies Program. I am grateful to Suzanne Berger, Adam Berinsky, Chris Capozzola, Kanchan Chandra, Rebecca Faery, Chappell Lawson, Daniel Munro, Melissa Nobles, Jonathan Rodden, Emma Teng, Lily Tsai, Elizabeth Wood, and especially Joshua Cohen and Sally Haslanger for their intellectual camaraderie and support. I thank the Political Science Department for their generosity with leave time and research funding.

I am also indebted to a community of political theorists and philosophers who think and write about identity, ethnicity, nationalism, and multiculturalism. Seyla Benhabib, Avigail Eisenberg, Vicki Hsueh, Will Kymlicka, Anne Phillips, Rob Reich, Ayelet Shachar, Rogers Smith, and Jeff Spinner-Halev have all read and commented on parts of the book. I am also thankful to David Miller, whose scholarship and seminars fostered my interest in political theory during my time at Oxford.

I am especially grateful to friends, colleagues, and teachers who have commented on parts of the manuscript and with whom I have had valuable conversations about its themes: Karim Abdul-Matin, Brooke Ackerly, Seyla Benhabib, Richard Boyd, Kanchan Chandra, Chip Colwell-Chanthaphonh, Joshua Cohen, Michaele Ferguson, Hawley Fogg-Davis, Erik Freeman, Sally Haslanger, Vicki Hsueh, Chris Lebron, Theresa Lee, Eric MacGilvray, Jane Mansbridge, Daniel Munro, Tamara Metz, Ethan Nasr, Melissa Nobles, Frank Pasquale, Anne Phillips, Jennifer Pitts, Jennifer Ratner-Rosenhagen, Nancy Rosenblum, Daniel Sabbagh, Ayelet Shachar, Ian Shapiro, Marion Smiley, Rogers Smith, Verity Smith, Jiewuh Song, Jeff Spinner-Halev, Dara Strolovitch, Robin West, Elspeth Wilson, and Bernard Yack.

At Cambridge University Press, I wish to thank my editors John Haslam and Carrie Cheek and my production editor Rosina Di Marzo for their patient guidance, Jacqueline French for scrupulous copyediting, and Marie MacCullum for preparing the index.

For encouragement I thank my parents, my brother Samuel Song, and Gabriel Schnitzler, whose love and good humor enrich my life in immeasurable ways.

This book is dedicated to my parents, Byoung Hyuk Song and Young Il Song, my first teachers of justice.

1   Introduction

A Muslim girl seeks exemption from her school's dress code policy so she can wear a headscarf in accordance with her religious convictions. Newly arrived immigrants invoke the use of cultural evidence in defense against criminal charges. Over one hundred years after the Church of Jesus Christ of Latter-day Saints renounced polygamy, Mormon fundamentalists continue to practice it and argue for its decriminalization. Aboriginal groups insist on the right of self-government, including the right to determine their own membership rules. These claims are not simply demands for the enforcement of anti-discrimination law; they are also demands for positive accommodation of particular beliefs and identities. In practice, democratic governments in the West already grant a variety of accommodations to religious and cultural minorities, including exemptions to generally applicable law, support for the pursuit of cultural practices, and limited self-government rights.

By the term "accommodation" I mean to include measures involving both redistribution and recognition. In some cases, minority groups seek remedies for material disadvantages they suffer on the basis of their minority status. Such remedies include compensation for past discrimination, ensuring equal access to educational and employment opportunities, or economic restructuring of some sort. But many claims of minority cultural groups are not reducible to economic claims. Behind these claims is the view that material goods are not sufficient to ensure people's well-being; another crucial condition is the possession of self-respect, and this is tied to the respect others express or withhold. In addition to material claims, then, cultural minorities demand measures aimed at countering social and political marginalization and disrespect, including revaluing disrespected identities and transforming dominant patterns of communication and representation, or in the case of aboriginal groups, granting collective self-government rights. Political theorists have used the term "recognition" to capture these sorts of claims.[1] The demand for

---

[1] Taylor 1994; Galeotti 2002; Fraser and Honneth 2003.

1

recognition is for others to respect what James Tully has called people's longing for self-rule, "to rule themselves in accord with their customs and ways."[2]

Group claims for recognition and positive valorization are not a new political phenomenon nor are they specific to ethnic or religious minority groups. Feminists have long struggled not only for economic measures that abolish the gender division of labor, but also for measures that replace institutionalized androcentric values privileging attributes historically associated with masculinity with values expressing equal respect for women. Like gender claims, the claims of ethnic and national minority groups are matters of both redistribution and recognition. On the one hand, ethnic and national minority groups can be economically defined: they tend to experience higher rates of unemployment and poverty and are overrepresented in poorly paid menial work. Ethnic and national minority groups can also be defined in terms of a status hierarchy that values some groups as more worthy of social respect than others. Patterns of cultural valuation privilege attributes associated with "whiteness" or European identities while those coded as black, brown, or yellow experience cultural devaluation and social and political marginalization.

Virtually all axes of subordination (e.g. race, gender, class, ethnicity, sexuality) implicate both maldistribution and misrecognition in forms where each of those injustices has some independent weight, whatever their ultimate source. To be sure, some axes, such as class, tilt heavily toward the distribution end of the spectrum while others, such as sexuality, tilt toward the recognition end. Nancy Fraser has suggested that in contrast to class and sexuality, race and gender cluster closer to the center and are matters of both recognition and redistribution to a similar degree.[3] I think ethnicity is like race and gender in this regard. Of course the extent to which the injustices ethnic and national minorities experience stem from economic disadvantage or status subordination must be determined empirically in each case. Insofar as ethnicity and nationality implicate both maldistribution and misrecognition, the appropriate response will require both material and symbolic remedies.

The problem of internal minorities

Different types of groups have made different sorts of accommodation demands, and in response, states have in practice granted a great many of them. Catching up to the practice of accommodation, political theorists

---

[2] Tully 1995: 4–5.   [3] Fraser and Honneth 2003: 25.

have offered different principled arguments for accommodations for minority cultural groups. Many liberal defenders of multiculturalism have focused on inequalities *between* cultural groups, arguing that treating cultural minorities as equals requires special protections to secure liberties and opportunities that members of the majority culture already enjoy. Yet, as critics of multiculturalism have stressed, accommodation of minority group traditions can exacerbate inequalities *within* minority groups. Some ways of protecting minority groups from oppression by the majority make it more likely that these groups will be able to undermine the basic liberties and opportunities of vulnerable members. Indeed, representatives of minority groups may exaggerate the degree of consensus and solidarity within their groups to present a united front to the wider society and strengthen their case for accommodation. This tension has been characterized as the problem of "internal minorities" or "minorities within minorities."[4] The term "minority" here refers not to a group's numerical strength in the population but to groups that are marginalized or disadvantaged in some way. Vulnerable subgroups within minority groups include religious dissenters, sexual minorities, women, and children. Focused on the effects of group accommodations on women within minority groups, feminist theorists, including Susan Moller Okin and Ayelet Shachar, have characterized the problem of internal minorities as "multiculturalism v. feminism" or "multicultural accommodation v. women's rights."[5]

It is important to point out that this dilemma arises most clearly in liberal democratic societies committed to the value of equality. The basic dilemma emerges from conflicting demands that arise in the pursuit of equality for all. A core commitment of liberal democracies is that citizens treat one another as equals. On the one hand, as I'll argue, treating members of minority groups with equal respect requires special accommodations under certain circumstances. On the other hand, such accommodations cannot be permitted to violate the basic rights and liberties of individual members of minority groups. This dilemma raises questions that every multicultural liberal democracy must face. Why should special accommodations to members of minority groups be granted, if at all? What are the limits of accommodation? How might tensions between the pursuit of justice for cultural minorities and the pursuit of gender justice be addressed? These are the questions I explore in this book, focusing on a range of specific cases in which women are made more vulnerable through multicultural accommodation. To pursue these questions, we

---

[4] Green 1995; Eisenberg and Spinner-Halev 2005.
[5] Okin 1998 and 1999; Shachar 2002.

must explore philosophical arguments for multiculturalism, as well as look closely at the actual practice and politics of multiculturalism.

Reframing the debate

Before addressing these questions, it is crucial to examine how the dilemmas of multiculturalism have been framed. The interpretive framework underlying many analyses of multiculturalism provides an insufficient understanding of what is at stake in many contemporary cases. The normative solutions offered by political theorists fall short more because they have too narrowly defined the problem than because of the shortcomings of their normative theories. The problem of internal minorities has largely been understood as a problem with deeply illiberal and undemocratic minority cultures. For instance, recent formulations of the problem as "multiculturalism v. feminism," "group rights v. women's rights," or "culture v. gender" suggest that minority cultures are the source of minority women's subordination. These accounts of the problems of multiculturalism rely on a conception of cultures as well-integrated, clearly bounded, and self-generated entities. For instance, feminist critics of multiculturalism seem largely to accept the prominent multiculturalist view of cultures as largely unified and distinct wholes, even while recognizing gender as a cross-cutting social cleavage. In her critique of multiculturalism, Susan Okin suggests an account of cultures as monolithically patriarchal with minority cultures being generally more patriarchal than surrounding Western cultures.[6] Such an account overlooks the polyvocal nature of all cultures and the ways in which gender practices in both minority and majority cultures have evolved through cross-cultural interactions. This oversight prevents Okin's approach from recognizing the ways in which the majority culture is not always less but rather differently patriarchal than minority cultures.

While she is much more sympathetic to cultural accommodations than Okin, Ayelet Shachar also adopts a conception of culture that is similarly monolithic. She equates "identity groups" with "nomoi communities," defining both as "religiously defined groups of people" who "share a comprehensive and distinguishable worldview that extends to creating a law for the community," as well as a "distinct culture."[7] Shachar does not provide a normative defense of religious and cultural accommodations; we are left to infer a defense from her definition of cultures as "nomoi communities": that religious and cultural communities provide

---

[6] Okin 1999: 12–13, 17.   [7] Shachar 2001: 2, n. 5.

comprehensive worldviews is sufficient reason for institutional measures aimed at protecting them. But members of the same ethnic, racial, tribal, or national groups, all of which are included in her definition of "identity groups," do not necessarily share a comprehensive worldview. Shachar's definition makes the mistake of conflating culture and religion and of assuming the coherence and comprehensiveness of both sorts of communities. While religious groups and aboriginal groups with shared life forms may constitute "nomoi communities," many cultural communities do not. In contrast to Okin and Shachar and prominent defenders of multiculturalism, I adopt a view of cultures that is more attentive to the *politics* of cultural construction and contestation and develop an egalitarian approach that makes deliberation central to addressing gendered dilemmas of culture.[8]

A constructivist conception of culture, I argue, better captures the complex sources of the problem of internal minorities. As I discuss in chapter 2, on a constructivist account cultures are the product of not only internal contestation but also complex historical processes of interaction with other cultures such that the modern condition might more appropriately be characterized as intercultural rather than multicultural. Once we recognize that cultures are interactive and interdependent, we must also recognize that the starting point for intercultural dialogue over contested cultural practices is a terrain of already overlapping intercultural relations and practices. This allows us to be attentive to interconnections between majority and minority groups that have shaped cultural conflicts. Sometimes the experience of crossing cultures has fueled movements toward greater equality, but in other cases, intercultural interactions have reinforced unequal and oppressive norms and practices across cultures. Viewing cultures as well-integrated, bounded entities has led many observers to overlook how gender statuses are shaped by intercultural interactions, which in turn has lent support to a false dichotomy between egalitarian majority cultures and oppressive minority cultures. Although the United States, like other Western democracies, publicly supports gender equality in many respects, struggles to transform social norms and practices to make such equality a reality are incomplete and ongoing. Far from being neutral, mainstream norms – in some cases, patriarchal mainstream norms – have shaped both the practices at the heart of cultural conflicts and the normative frameworks within which claims for accommodation are evaluated.

---

[8] I will examine Okin's and Shachar's approaches to resolving the problem of internal minorities in greater depth in later chapters. See chs. 3, 4, and 6 for discussion of Okin and ch. 6 for discussion of Shachar.

Attention to intercultural interactions is crucial to addressing the problem of internal minorities for at least three reasons. The first has to do with the majority culture's influence on the gender norms of minority cultures. In some cases, the dominant culture's own patriarchal norms have offered support for patriarchal practices in minority cultures – what I call the *congruence effect*. In the past, the state directly imposed mainstream gender biases onto minority communities, as in the 1887 Dawes Act, which subverted Native American women's roles in agricultural work by making Native American men heads of households, landowners, and farmers.[9] More common today are the indirect ways in which mainstream norms support gender hierarchies within minority communities, as we'll see in examining the case of the "cultural defense" in American criminal law and the membership rules of the Santa Clara Pueblo. In these cases, it is the congruence of patriarchal norms, rather than respect for difference, that has informed state accommodation of minority practices. Some defenders of multiculturalism have suggested that when it comes to immigrants, as opposed to cultural groups that enjoy self-government rights or legal jurisdiction over certain social arenas, there really is no problem of internal minorities since immigrants are expected to integrate into the dominant culture and such integration entails the adoption of egalitarian values.[10] But this position overstates the gender egalitarianism of the dominant culture, as well as the extent to which immigrants embrace egalitarian values. We need to be careful not to equate the actual process of Americanization with ineluctable progress toward gender equality. Instead, we should ask to what values and norms immigrants are actually integrating. In some cases, patriarchal practices in minority cultures may find support from mainstream norms such that the process of assimilation involves an affirmation of patriarchal traditions within minority cultures.

A second reason for being attentive to majority–minority interactions in evaluating cultural claims has to do with the minority culture's influence on the gender norms of the majority culture. There are serious consequences for America as a whole in tolerating policies that permit gender subordination within minority cultures. Given that the struggle for gender equality within the majority culture is incomplete, tolerating patriarchal norms and practices within minority cultural communities may allow such norms to boomerang back and threaten struggles toward

---

[9] Cott 2000: 123.

[10] See, e.g., Jeff Spinner-Halev's claim that "most immigrant communities become more Americanized, take on more egalitarian values, and support autonomy for both their sons and daughters after one or two generations" (2001: 90).

gender equality within the wider society. Call this the *boomerang effect*. As we'll see in examining the "cultural defense," permitting reduced punishment for immigrant defendants who commit crimes against women may threaten advances toward gender equality within the wider society by establishing precedents that mainstream defendants can invoke.

A third reason to be attentive to majority–minority interactions is to discern the *diversionary effects* of the majority's condemnation of minority practices. Even where accommodation is denied, by focusing on the patriarchal practices of minority cultures, the majority can divert attention from its own gender hierarchies. In the past, European governments justified intervention into "other" (usually non-European and non-white) cultures in the name of liberating women from the oppression of "other" men. But often the result was not only the oppression of other cultures by Western powers but also the failure to challenge the subordination of women in both Western and non-Western contexts. Such intervention, fueled by a discourse of binary oppositions between an enlightened West and a traditional barbaric rest, reinforced gender inequality in colonial contexts by subverting women's historical sources of power. It also helped deflect criticism away from gender inequality in Western societies by emphasizing gender oppression in non-Western societies. Similarly, the US government justified interventions into Native American and Mormon communities out of a concern for women within these communities. Yet, American reformers and government officials opposed the ideas of feminism when applied to the dominant culture, even while they deployed the language of feminism in the service of its assault on the religions and cultures of "other" men.[11] Such rhetoric not only provided them with a ready justification for intervention into minority communities, but also helped divert attention from gender inequality within the majority culture by focusing on the gender relations of minority communities. Scrutinizing the majority culture's motivations behind its responses to minority cultural claims can help guard against political actions that reinforce not only gender inequality but also inequality across

---

[11] Claiming that "other" men oppress their women to justify intervention into "other" cultures is, of course, not unique to the United States. Numerous scholars have documented how representations of the oppression of non-Western women by non-Western men were used to justify British and French imperialism. For example, in examining the conduct and rhetoric of the British colonial establishment toward Islamic societies, Leila Ahmed (1992) demonstrates how British officials appropriated the language of feminism in the service of colonialism. The result was the fusion of the issues of women's oppression and the cultures of "other" men such that improving the status of women was thought to entail abandoning native customs. She also argues that the focus on "other" men helped Western colonial governors combat feminism within their own societies. See also Lazreg 1994 and Narayan 1997.

cultural and racial lines. A key issue here is how to reframe discourses of gender equality without fueling discourses of cultural and racial superiority.

Broadening our analysis of multicultural politics to include these interactive dynamics has important implications for normative debates on multiculturalism. First, it shifts the focus of debate from asking what cultures *are* to what cultural affiliations *do*. That is, we move away from trying to define and accord value to whole cultures toward evaluating the meaning and impact of particular practices. On this reformulation of the dilemma, "culture" is not the problem; oppressive practices are. Minority women engaged in the cultural conflicts I examine seek *both* equality for cultural minorities *and* equality for women. They don't seek to do away with cultural accommodations, but rather challenge aspects of cultural traditions that support women's subordination.[12]

A second implication of adopting this broader interactive view of cultural conflicts is the need to develop context-sensitive and democratic approaches to evaluating the claims of minority cultures. Evaluations of minority claims should be based on examination of particular practices in particular contexts with an eye toward interconnections between majority and minority practices. I argue that such contextual inquiry is best taken up through democratic deliberation. This book examines a range of cases to illustrate how the interactive dynamics discussed above have shaped the practice of multiculturalism. It is crucial to have these dynamics in mind in order to properly identify and address the complex sources of the problem of internal minorities.

Justice and the claims of culture

While I devote much attention to how cultural accommodations have worked in practice, the approach I take in this book is not merely contextual. Peering at context, no matter how closely, will not provide a normative framework for thinking about and responding to multicultural dilemmas, including the problem of internal minorities. Instead, I take a semicontextual approach. In chapter 3, I offer and defend a conception of justice in relations of culture and identity as a framework for evaluating

---

[12] Here I follow the lead of many scholars who have stressed the importance of recognizing that minority women are situated at the intersection of multiple social identities such that they are marginalized not just in terms of gender but also race, ethnicity, class, sexual orientation, and other social identities. Such intersectionality gives rise to problems that cannot be addressed by a movement focused solely on any single identity. See hooks 1981; Moraga and Anzaldúa 1981; Jayawardena 1986; Harris 1990; Crenshaw 1991; Mohanty, Russo, and Torres 1991.

cultural claims and addressing cultural conflicts. This framework is not offered as a comprehensive or definitive account, but rather as part of the ongoing conversation about how to understand and respond to the challenges raised by cultural diversity. Its aim is to demarcate the range of morally permissible institutions and practices with respect to the claims of culture in liberal democratic societies. At the same time, my approach recognizes that particular solutions and arrangements must be decided through deliberation by affected parties in particular contexts. I explore the implications of my normative arguments in the context of particular cases in Part II.

A key problem that emerges from the case studies is that majority cultures in liberal democratic societies often fall short of the egalitarian ideals they publicly espouse. As we'll see, what often drives the politics of cultural accommodation and conflict has not been concerns about justice, but the political dynamics of congruence, imposition, and diversion I discussed above. This is precisely why it is important to have some normative ideals in mind in approaching the case studies, to provide a basis for critique. Liberal democracies need guiding norms for intercultural dialogue, and the justice arguments developed in chapter 3 are intended to provide a normative framework from which to evaluate not only minority practices at the center of cultural conflicts but also majority responses to them.

The normative approach I develop, what I call *rights-respecting accommodationism*, is committed to both the pursuit of justice for cultural minorities and the pursuit of justice for women. I argue that justice requires special accommodations for cultural minorities under certain circumstances. My case for accommodation is grounded in a core value of liberal democracy, the idea that citizens should treat one another with equal respect. Citizens express mutual respect for one another not simply by accepting a set of basic rights and opportunities that apply equally to all. Under certain circumstances, uniform treatment must give way to differential treatment. I examine three circumstances that are especially relevant to multicultural societies, asking whether each supports a case for cultural accommodation: present discrimination, historical injustice, and state establishment of culture. What form accommodation will take and whether they should ultimately be granted will depend on context, and this is why I elaborate my approach in the context of specific cases. But in all cases, the egalitarian basis of my case for accommodation suggests the limits of accommodation: the protection of the basic rights of individual members of minority groups.

I contend that a rights-respecting accommodationist approach best expresses the idea of equal respect for persons under conditions of cultural diversity. It is offered as a middle way between the contention by some liberal theorists that multiculturalism is inconsistent with individual freedom and equality, on the one hand, and multiculturalist calls for cultural preservation, on the other. Some prominent liberal theorists maintain that justice should be culture-blind; what justice requires is a common set of rights and opportunities for all individuals, regardless of religious or ethnic affiliation. Brian Barry's critique of multicultural- ism and defense of a "unitary republican model" of citizenship is one prominent and lively example, and I examine his arguments closely in chapter 3. In contrast to this culture-blind approach, the egalitarian approach I defend is open to differential treatment under certain circumstances.

Yet, my egalitarian argument does not go as far as many multicul- turalists do. Many multiculturalists argue that any law or policy that disparately impacts minority cultural groups supports a claim for accom- modation on the grounds that cultural membership is a basic good to which all citizens are entitled. The claim here is that since the state unavoidably privileges members of the dominant culture while burdening cultural minorities' access to their own culture, it must somehow make it up to citizens who are native speakers of minority languages and bearers of minority cultural identities.[13] While I share multiculturalists' concern about differential impact, I do not think this fact alone is sufficient to support a claim for accommodation. Many multiculturalists seem to assume that all burdens on cultural attachments are always too severe to be borne by individuals. Yet, as I discuss in chapter 2, there is reason- able disagreement about the meaning and value of cultural membership. Rather than assuming that cultural membership is a basic good, we must ask about the kinds of interests that are at stake in claims for accommo- dation in order to assess whether differential impact of law and policy does indeed constitute unfairness.

My aim in making these arguments from justice is to provide a justifi- cation for cultural accommodation and a framework for addressing the problem of internal minorities while leaving the choice of specific policies and resolutions to be decided through democratic deliberation. A deliber- ative approach to particular cultural dilemmas has several advantages over approaches that give little or no role to the participation of those affected by the dilemmas in question. It comes closer to treating members of minority groups as equals by giving them a voice in the governance of cultural conflicts. It is also more attentive to the particularities of context than non-deliberative approaches. By drawing on the voices of affected

---

[13] See, e.g., Kymlicka 1995: 111; Carens 2000: 77–78. I examine this argument in ch. 3.

parties, a deliberative approach can help clarify the nature of the interests at stake, as well as help identify the complex sources of cultural conflicts. In some cases, the source may be internal to the culture and stem from contestation over long-standing traditions and internal power struggles. In other cases, it may not be minority practices alone but intercultural congruence between majority and minority practices that threatens the basic rights of vulnerable members, and this can be exposed through deliberation.

Outline of the book

Part I of the book explores key concepts and theoretical arguments in the contemporary debate about multiculturalism and group rights with a focus on finding common ground between what groups demand and what liberal democracy requires. Chapter 2 examines how culture has been conceptualized and used to defend minority group rights by prominent theorists of multiculturalism, including Charles Taylor and Will Kymlicka. I then discuss and defend an alternative conception of culture, a constructivist view. The constructivist view allows us to see that cultures are not only internally contested but also interactive, mutually constitutive, and loosely jointed. It also acknowledges the contingency and variability of individuals' experience of cultural membership. A key normative implication that follows from adopting a constructivist view is a shift in the basis for evaluating group claims from inherent features of cultural groups to their social and political effects. The question then is not whether whole cultures should be preserved on the basis of inherent features they possess, but whether the particular claim made in the name of culture merits protection.

Chapter 3 develops an egalitarian approach to evaluating the claims of minority cultures and addressing the problem of internal minorities, what I call rights-respecting accommodationism. I consider whether each of the following circumstances that tend to characterize culturally diverse societies supports a prima facie case for accommodation: present discrimination, historical injustice, and state establishment of culture. I argue that these circumstances support a presumption in favor of accommodation, but this presumption may be overridden by liberal democracy's commitment to protecting people's basic rights. I suggest a two-part deliberative inquiry to investigate the stakes involved in cultural claims and conflicts and demonstrate how such inquiry has been carried out in the context of religion cases in the United States.

In Part II of the book, I examine a range of cases that illustrate the problem of internal minorities – in particular, cases in which tensions between cultural accommodation and gender equality arise: "cultural defense" cases in American criminal law (chapter 4), aboriginal sovereignty and tribal membership rules (chapter 5), and the fundamentalist Mormon practice of polygamy (chapter 6). The aim of these chapters is to elaborate the conceptual and normative arguments made in Part I in the context of specific cases.

I should note here that the book's main empirical focus is on historical and contemporary cases from the United States, with a few brief comparative examples from England, Canada, South Africa, and France. One advantage of such focus is that it allows us to explore how one polity has approached issues of diversity and toleration with respect to a range of different religious and cultural groups. While my normative arguments are discussed mainly in the US context, they can be brought to bear on cultural conflicts in any culturally pluralistic liberal democratic society. The questions that remain constant have to do with the proper bases and limits of toleration in culturally diverse liberal democratic societies and how the limits are connected to liberal democracy's commitment to gender equality. My claim that liberal democracy's commitment to equal respect for all individuals provides both the basis and limits of cultural accommodation, as well as my claim about the key role of deliberation in addressing cultural conflicts, is intended to apply to all liberal democratic contexts. The intercultural dynamics of congruence, imposition, and diversion are not unique to the US context, nor are the normative implications that follow from such dynamics, including the importance of developing context-sensitive and deliberative approaches to cultural conflicts. But the particular way in which the limits of accommodation are drawn will depend on the particularities of context, including, among other things, the contingencies of national political culture, demographics, and the particular commitments and practices of specific groups within a polity. Thus, my approach does not suggest global answers to particular cultural dilemmas, such as the issue of veiling among Muslim girls or the membership practices of aboriginal groups. What is constant is a commitment to protecting the basic rights of women and girls, but what such a commitment requires with respect to the practice of veiling or a membership tradition will depend on context and what individuals at the center of these controversies are themselves saying. A key strength of the normative approach I defend is its recognition of the importance of close attention to the particularities of context and the inclusion of the voices of those affected by particular dilemmas in their resolution.

While I am by no means an expert on the particular communities involved in the specific cases I examine, by drawing on legal case materials and detailed secondary scholarship on these communities, as well as interviews I conducted in the Santa Clara Pueblo membership case, I believe I offer sufficiently detailed analyses of the cases to explore the dilemmas they present. I focus on the cases I do, not because they are representative of the vast range of claims in the politics of multiculturalism but rather because they illustrate the problem of internal minorities, the central focus of this book. The cases offer evidence for my claim that cultural traditions and practices at the center of cultural conflicts are made and re-made through both internal contestations and intercultural interactions. The cases also highlight a key theme of this book, one that has not received as much attention in the scholarly debate on multiculturalism: the role of intercultural interactions in shaping the problem of internal minorities – in particular, the different ways in which majority norms and institutions are implicated in sustaining gender inequality within minority communities. With a view of the ways in which cultures are already overlapping and interconnected, we will be better equipped to identify and respond to the dilemmas of cultural diversity.

Part I

2 The concept of culture in political theory

Evaluation of the claims of minority cultural groups and responses to the problem of internal minorities turn in part on how one thinks about culture and its value. Indeed, some political theorists directly derive normative prescriptions for a politics of multiculturalism from their conceptions of culture. This chapter examines three accounts of culture and cultural identity that are at the forefront of debates about multiculturalism: culture as an "irreducibly social good," culture as a "primary good," and culture as a constructed framework of meaning. The third constructivist view of culture raises a powerful challenge to the first two views, which conceive of culture as distinct stable wholes. In particular, the constructivist view recognizes that there is reasonable disagreement about what culture is and why it is valuable. After examining these three accounts of culture, I discuss the normative implications of adopting the critical insight of the constructivist challenge to set the stage for my normative arguments about multiculturalism and the problem of internal minorities.

Culture as an "irreducibly social good"

On one prominent conception of culture developed by Charles Taylor, culture is understood as an "irreducibly social" and intrinsic good. Following Herder, Taylor views culture in the idiom of language: "Language does not only serve to *depict* ourselves and the world, it also helps *constitute* our lives." Each culture, like each language, is the expression of the authentic identity of a *Volk*. It is language that shapes people's worldviews and experiences, and it is through language that individuals become who they are. While cultures are internally heterogeneous and change over time, they are nonetheless taken to be integral, discrete wholes, characterized by a set of attributes that distinguish each from the rest.[1] The Herderian conception of culture is echoed by the

---

[1] Taylor 1985: 10, 230–34 and 1994: 31, 42.

conception of culture that became dominant in anthropology in the early twentieth century and is now widely contested among anthropologists. On this view, cultures are well-integrated, well-bounded, and largely self-generated entities, defined by a set of key attributes, including a shared language, history, and values. As William Sewell has observed, culture, on this view, is a "concrete and bounded world of beliefs and practices."[2] My aim here is not to provide a genealogy of this view of culture, but rather to examine the normative work that Taylor's view of culture as an irreducibly social good is expected to do.

Taylor has argued that cultures belong to a class of goods that is "irreducibly social," which he defines in two distinct but overlapping ways: first, as goods that make conceivable actions, feelings, and valued ways of life, and second, as goods that incorporate common understandings of their value. On the first way of defining irreducibly social goods, culture is an irreducibly social good because it is a locus of goods we value. That is, the things and pursuits we value and find good can only be valuable or good "because of the background understanding developed in our culture." He moves from this premise to the following conclusion: "If these things are goods, then other things being equal so is the culture that makes them possible. If I want to maximize these goods, then I must want to *preserve* and *strengthen* this culture. But the culture as a good, or more cautiously as the locus of some goods (for there might be much that is reprehensible as well), is not an individual good."[3] Taylor emphasizes that the nature of the good of culture is importantly different from the nature of merely "public goods," such as street lamps, public parks, and dams, which are "public" in that they cannot be provided for one without being provided for a whole group. Street lamps and dams stand in causal relation to the goods they produce; these goods could come from some other means. In contrast, "a culture is related to the acts and experiences it makes intelligible in no such external way." Public goods, such as public parks and street lamps, can be reduced to individual goods – *my* enjoyment of the park, *your* illuminated walk home – but the good of culture cannot. Culture, Taylor stresses, is "not a mere instrument of the individual goods," a merely contingent condition of individual goods. Rather, it "is essentially linked to what we have identified as good. Consequently,

---

[2] Sewell 1999: 39. The preanthropological notion of culture is singular in connotation and was used interchangeably with "civilization" to connote phenomena that are present to a higher or lower degree in all peoples, whereas the modern anthropological notion of culture is plural and connotes the different ways of life of human groups. Stocking contends that the plural form originated in the work of anthropologist Franz Boas and the first generation of his students (1968: 203).

[3] Taylor 1995: 136 (emphasis mine).

it is hard to see how we could deny it the title of good, not just in some weakened, instrumental sense ... but as intrinsically good."[4]

The second way of defining irreducibly social goods is as an "irreducible feature of the society as a whole" or a good whose goodness is "the object of common understanding." A public good, such as a dam, is not a feature of society at all; it is not "inherently social" since a different range of technologies might provide another solution to the problem the dam is designed to fix. In contrast, a way of life characterized by honest and equal relations (Taylor's example) is an irreducibly social fact, and its goodness is an object of common understanding. Such relations are not merely the combination of individual facts (say, each individual's disposition toward others), but rather they rely on some common understanding about our way of life. Such common understandings are "undecomposable" because "it is essential to their being what they are that they be not just for me and for you, but for us."[5]

What follows for politics from defining culture as an irreducibly social and intrinsically valuable good? Taylor suggests that cultures should be "preserved" and "strengthened," a normative position that we might call *strong multiculturalism.* That the culture of Quebec – which in practice, Taylor says, means the French language – is an irreducibly social good in the first sense and sometimes in the second sense leads to a politics of defending the language as a common good. We should not understand the nature of the good of culture in a purely subjectivist way: that they are goods to the extent people desire them. To say that the Québécois have a mere "taste" for the preservation of the French language is to misunderstand the nature of the good as an irreducibly social good. The French language is a good, in Taylor's view, regardless of its popularity. Neither is it merely a "public good," available for individuals who choose to make use of it. Rather, it is an intrinsically social or common good: "the nature of the good requires that it be sought in common."[6]

What is required then is ensuring conditions for the success and flourishing of diverse cultures. The claim here is that justice requires not only providing equal liberties and opportunities for individuals but also *recognition* of the equal worth of diverse cultural identities and languages. This strong sense of recognition requires, as K. Anthony Appiah discussing Taylor remarks, that we "be acknowledged publicly as what [we] already really are."[7] Proper relations of recognition are based on accurate mutual knowledge among the individuals and groups involved. As Taylor puts it, "The thesis is that our identity is partly shaped by recognition or its

---

[4] Ibid. 137.   [5] Ibid. 139.   [6] Ibid. 140. See also Taylor 1994: 59.
[7] Appiah 1994: 149.

absence, often by the *mis*recognition of others, and so a person or group of people can suffer real damage, real distortion, if the people or society around them mirror back to them a confining or demeaning or contemptible picture of themselves." Drawing upon Herder, among others, Taylor stresses the notion of authenticity. Each of us has "an original way of being human," an "inner nature" or "inner voice." Given the crucial importance of recognition, Taylor argues, "The struggle for recognition can find only one satisfactory solution, and that is a regime of reciprocal recognition among equals."[8]

While appealing, the ideal of mutual recognition and cultural preservation is vulnerable on both metaphysical and moral grounds. First, neither the fact that culture is inherently social nor the fact that members of a cultural community value certain goods made possible by their culture is an argument for its preservation. As James Griffin has suggested, causal propositions that certain goods can only exist and be enjoyed through social interactions should not be conflated with claims about the value of those goods.[9] In addition, the boundaries of culture can be porous and shifting, so it is not clear that cultures can always be pinned down as clearly identifiable entities to be preserved.

The politics of recognition suffers from a deeper, metaphysical difficulty. The pursuit of recognition as knowing who others already really are overlooks crucial facts about social and political life (that human action is open-ended, unpredictable, self-surprising) and also facts about the relationship between human action and identity (that identities do not exist prior to and independent of human action and interaction but are constituted through them). As Patchen Markell has argued, there are two senses of recognition at work in Taylor's discussion, recognition as knowing and recognition as doing, and there are serious tensions between the two. In its cognitive sense, recognition refers to an expression of respect based on accurate knowledge of independently existing identities. In its second, constructive sense, recognition is treated as "a doing, which – like the chairperson's recognition of the speaker – actively constitutes the identities of those to whom it is addressed."[10] Taylor oscillates between these two senses of recognition. While the second sense of recognition as doing highlights the contingent and unpredictable nature of social and political life, the first sense of recognition as knowing obscures this crucial fact. Insofar as the politics of recognition pursues recognition as knowing, it is bound up, as Markell argues, with a "fundamental *ontological* misrecognition, a failure to acknowledge the nature and circumstances of our

[8] Taylor 1994: 25, 30–31, 50.   [9] Griffin 1986: 387–88.   [10] Markell 2003: 41, 58–59.

own activity" – in particular, the openness and unpredictability of our social and political life.[11] Acknowledging this crucial fact suggests a different understanding of the relationship between identity and action. Who we are is not something that is fixed prior to our actions but rather is constituted in and through our interactions with others – a point that a constructivist view of culture and identity acknowledges. The dominant mode of the politics of recognition, recognition as knowing, overlooks these crucial facts about the human condition.

Finally, as Taylor himself acknowledges in distinguishing culture as "a good" from culture as "a locus of some goods," cultures may contain "reprehensible" conventions and practices. While one member might value a particular practice and desire its preservation, another might find it "reprehensible." Aiming at the preservation of cultures can conflict with respecting the basic rights of individual members of minority cultural groups and may risk reinforcing intra-group hierarchies. In struggles for recognition in the Canadian context, what groups demand, as Taylor emphasizes, is "to maintain and cherish distinctness, not just now but forever." They demand "measures designed to ensure survival through indefinite future generations."[12] What is at stake for aboriginal groups and French-speaking Canadians is "*la survivance.*" Not simply the survival of *individuals* within these communities but the survival of *particular identities* and *languages*, francophone and indigenous, for future descendants. This preservation argument is troubling for at least two reasons. First, it would coerce members of the present generation in the name of the interests of future generations. But much more needs to be said about what the interests of future generations are and how we are to get at them. Just as there is reasonable disagreement about the value of cultural attachments among living members of a culture, there is sure to be disagreement between present and future generations about the value of cultural preservation. Second, individual members of minority groups may define their identities in various and conflicting ways based on their different social positions within the group. Whose narratives of group identity and traditions should be preserved? The political strategy of cultural preservation runs the risk of privileging certain members' – usually a group's more powerful members' – narratives of group identity, shoring up the self-respect of some at the expense of the self-respect of others. Indeed, powerful group members may quash dissent in order to

---

[11] Ibid. 59, 4–5.
[12] Taylor emphasizes that respecting such claims is what distinguishes his theory of multiculturalism from Kymlicka's (1994: 40, 41, n. 16).

present a unified front in seeking measures to ensure survival of their preferred narratives.

My aim here is not to refute a collectivist account of culture, but rather to point out its limits. Even if cultural and social relations are ontologically prior to individuals, as Taylor's account of culture suggests, it would not follow that they are morally prior. Taylor's distinction between culture as a good and culture as a locus of some goods opens the way for an individualist account of culture, which may better respect individual liberties and better resist intra-group domination. A culture may be the locus of certain goods, such as an ethos of honor or the virtue of honesty, but this fact alone does not provide a reason for granting special protections. We need an account of the value of such goods for individuals. This idea of culture as a locus of some goods, a context in which other goods become intelligible and meaningful, is one that is developed by Will Kymlicka, who argues that although cultures lack a "moral status of their own" they are instrumentally valuable to individuals.[13] I should stress that my criticism of the strong recognition suggested by Taylor's ideal of mutual recognition should not lead us to dismiss the idea of recognition altogether. Recognition in the second constructive sense, of constituting the identities of those to whom it is addressed, is an important part of the egalitarian ideal of multiculturalism I develop in chapter 3.

Culture as a "primary good"

Building on John Rawls's account of primary goods, Kymlicka argues for viewing cultural membership as a primary good and develops what we might call a theory of *weak multiculturalism*. It is weak in the sense that liberal commitments to freedom and equality constrain the cultural protections that are permitted. In his initial account and in some parts of the revised edition of *A Theory of Justice*, Rawls says that primary goods are things that all rational persons desire. Primary goods, he says, "normally have a use whatever a person's rational plan of life." The chief primary goods include liberty and opportunity, income and wealth, and "the social bases of self-respect."[14] To Rawls's list of primary goods, Kymlicka adds access to culture or cultural membership.

---

[13] Kymlicka 1989: 165.

[14] Rawls [1971] 1999: 54. In his revised account, Rawls suggests that primary goods are dependent on a *political* conception of the person. That is, primary goods are "what persons need in their status as free and equal citizens, and as normal and fully cooperating members of society over a complete life" ([1971] 1999: xiii; see also 1999: 417).

Kymlicka conceptualizes culture as "societal culture," which "provides its members with meaningful ways of life across the full range of human activities, including social, educational, religious, recreational, and economic life, encompassing both public and private spheres." Societal cultures have the following features. They are "encompassing" in the sense that they cover most areas of human activity. This feature is meant to distinguish societal cultures from the various "subcultures" of many other social groups. Other features include territorial concentration, a shared language, and the institutional embodiment of values and practices. On Kymlicka's account, there are two different ways in which access to such cultures is a 'primary good.' The first has to do with its connection to freedom and the second with self-respect.[15] It is worth considering both sets of connections as they are central to Kymlicka's normative theory of multiculturalism.

Kymlicka devotes more attention to linking culture and individual freedom. Cultures provide "contexts of choice" necessary for the exercise of individual freedom. If we believe that a good life is one that people choose for themselves, then we should also be concerned that individuals have an adequate range of options from which to choose. What provides an adequate range of options and renders them meaningful, argues Kymlicka, is one's culture. Consequently, liberals should also be concerned about cultures.[16] As Kymlicka puts it, "liberals should be concerned about the fate of cultural structures, not because they have some moral status of their own, but because it's only through having a rich and

---

[15] Kymlicka 1995: 76.

[16] A key premise of Kymlicka's theory is that only "societal cultures" can serve as contexts of choice. But Kymlicka never fully explains why this is so. He contrasts societal cultures with various "subcultures," which he characterizes as "the distinct customs, perspectives, or ethos of a group or association, as when we talk about 'gay culture' "; examples include "the various lifestyle enclaves, social movements, and voluntary associations" (Kymlicka 1995: 18). The key difference between societal cultures and subcultures seems to be that the former are "encompassing" of most areas of life and are "institutionally embodied," whereas the latter are neither. But the cultural practices of many social groups, including ethnic immigrants – who, in Kymlicka's account, do not have and are not capable of having societal cultures – are institutionally embodied. There is a long tradition in North America of immigrant communities building institutions that serve important functions, including schools, hospitals, nursing homes, media outlets, and voluntary associations (see Choudhry 2002). The point about the scope or comprehensiveness of societal cultures is undeniable, but why should this difference matter? It may be that "subcultures" don't provide enough or the right kind of options to serve as contexts of choice, but some of the "subcultures" that Kymlicka refers to, especially the cultures of ethnic minorities, may serve this role. Hereafter I use the more general term "cultures" that includes the ways of life of both ethnic and national minorities. I will discuss other ways of justifying a stronger set of entitlements for national minorities over ethnic minorities that rely less on political sociological claims about culture and more on normative arguments about oppression and historical injustice in ch. 3.

secure cultural structure that people can become aware, in a vivid way, of the options available to them, and intelligently examine their value."[17] In other words, cultures enable individual autonomy by offering narratives or scripts that we can use in fashioning our projects, evaluating our pursuits, and telling our life stories.

Cultural membership is also seen as crucial for individual self-respect. Kymlicka posits a deep and general connection between a person's self-respect and the respect given to the cultural group of which she is a part. He adopts Rawls's idea of primary goods, arguing that cultural membership is one of the "social bases of self-respect." Because of its crucial importance, parties in Rawls's original position have, Kymlicka argues, "a strong incentive to give cultural membership status as a primary good." Rawls takes cultural membership for granted, but, as Kymlicka puts it, "Rawls's own argument for the importance of liberty as a primary good is also an argument for the importance of cultural membership as a primary good."[18] Just as liberty is a social basis of self-respect, so, too, is cultural membership. In a later account, Kymlicka endorses the premise articulated by other multiculturalists, foremost Charles Taylor in his seminal essay, "The Politics of Recognition": individuals "can flourish only to the extent that [they] are recognized." This is because culture serves as an "anchor for [people's] self-identification and the safety of effortless secure belonging."[19] Failure to provide adequate respect to a cultural group threatens the self-respect of its members. As Kymlicka puts it, "people's self-respect is bound up with the esteem in which their national group is held. If culture is not generally respected, then the dignity and self-respect of its members will also be threatened."[20] It seems then that Kymlicka shares with Taylor a key premise of the position I characterized as *strong multiculturalism*: that cultural membership is an integral component of people's lives on account of its connection to individual self-respect.

There are two additional features to Kymlicka's account of cultural membership that we should note. First, it is not simply membership in *any* culture but in *one's own* culture that must be secured. Having access to "their own culture" is "something that people can be expected to want, whatever their more particular conception of the good." Kymlicka observes that most liberals have implicitly accepted as reasonable

---

[17] Kymlicka 1989:165. Kymlicka reiterates this view in his later work: "Put simply, freedom involves making choices amongst various options, and our societal culture not only provides these options, but also makes them meaningful to us" (1995: 83).

[18] Kymlicka 1989: 166.

[19] Taylor 1994: 50; Margalit and Raz 1990: 447–49 (both cited in Kymlicka 1995: 89–90).

[20] Kymlicka 1995: 89.

people's "expectation to remain in their culture." This is because of the great difficulty of giving up one's culture. As he puts it, "the ties to one's culture are normally too strong to give up, and this is not to be regretted."[21] Second, Kymlicka is careful to stress that what counts as a "context of choice" is the "cultural community, or cultural structure itself" and not "the character of a historical community." The latter consists of "the norms, values, and their attendant institutions in one's community (e.g. membership in churches, political parties, etc.)." The former is the existence of the culture itself, and "[i]t is the existence of a cultural community viewed as a context of choice that is a primary good, and a legitimate concern of liberals."[22]

That access to one's own culture is of fundamental importance – indeed a "primary good" to which all are entitled – is a key premise in Kymlicka's case for minority group rights, and it merits further scrutiny. The connections between culture, on the one hand, and individual freedom and self-respect, on the other, are not as straightforward as Kymlicka suggests.

The first difficulty has to do with the distinction between cultural structure and character. Kymlicka argues that it is the cultural structure, not character, that serves as the "context of choice" that enables individual freedom. One way to understand the idea of a cultural structure is as the bare existence of culture, that each person should have a cultural community. But then the defense of culture seems trivial. As John Tomasi has argued, "If it is the mere existence of 'one's own' cultural structure that is the good, then each individual person . . . has that good, and each has it equally."[23] In other words, it is not clear what special rights the premise that we each need a cultural structure (as existence) generates since we each already have access to a culture. Culture is whatever we already do or believe at any given time. Kymlicka might respond that he is concerned with cultural structures that are threatened with extinction. But it is hard to make sense of cultural structures on the verge of extinction without some account of the particular character or content of cultures. If a cultural structure is nothing more than the existence of a cultural community, then it seems that threats to its survival would be threats to the survival of *persons* who are members of the cultural community, and this threat could be addressed by liberalism's commitment to protecting the basic rights and liberties of individual persons without any reference to the value of cultures. Moreover, the view of cultural structure as existence may be too thin to do the work that Kymlicka assigns to it. To

---

[21] Ibid. 84, 86–87.   [22] Kymlicka 1989: 166–67, 169 and 1995: 104–105.
[23] Tomasi 1995: 589. See also Johnson 2000.

serve as a "context of choice" that provides real options necessary for the exercise of individual autonomy, cultures must carry some particular content – a sufficiently rich set of customs, rituals, norms, and practices.

Kymlicka does sometimes suggest that culture is more than the bare existence of a cultural community. Cultures, he says, provide their members with "meaningful ways of life across the full range of human activities, including social, educational, religious, recreational, and economic life."[24] Presumably these meaningful ways of life include a variety of cultural norms and customs rich enough to serve as "contexts of choice." But this move toward a general definition of culture in terms of particular content raises its own set of difficulties. If what gets protected through a regime of group rights is some particular content, there is the danger of freezing cultures in time and space. As Jeremy Waldron puts it, "To *preserve* a culture is often to take a favored 'snapshot' of it, and insist that this version must persist at all costs, in its defined purity, irrespective of the surrounding social, economic, and political circumstances."[25] Such a strategy of preserving specific cultural norms and practices may destroy or at least diminish the very thing we value most about cultures – their ability to change and adapt. In addition, the strategy of preservation fails to ask, "Whose version of culture?" Preserving minority cultures may mean protecting not only practices that enable individual freedom and enhance the self-respect of their members but also oppressive practices that do the exact opposite. Cultures can enable individual freedom by providing members with a range of meaningful options, but it can also radically constrain individual freedom. This Janus-faced nature of culture challenges the view that cultures straightforwardly serve as "contexts of choice" for all members.

One way Kymlicka responds to these concerns about the relationship between culture and freedom is by emphasizing that his view of culture is not defined in "a very thick, ethnographic" sense but "a very different and thinner" sense that includes what is essential to cultural survival (common language and societal institutions) and excludes illiberal norms and practices. So the definition of culture would be thick enough to serve as a "context of choice" but still minimal and unobjectionable in that what is essential to the culture's survival does not overlap with what is oppressive or reprehensible. Kymlicka makes this move in addressing the question of what liberals ought to do when the cultural structure and illiberal ways of life are tied together such that liberalization of the culture will undermine the "cultural structure." His answer: such situations "do not arise nearly

---

[24] Kymlicka 1995: 76. See also 1989: 135, 165 and 2001: 25.   [25] Waldron 1995:109–10.

as often as liberal critics of minority rights claim."[26] When discussing immigrants or ethnic minorities, he tells us that what they want is "inclusion and full participation in the mainstream of liberal-democratic societies." Immigrants "accept the principle of integration into common institutions: they are simply seeking fairer terms of integration." Most of the demands made by immigrants "are evidence that members of minority groups want to participate within the mainstream of society."[27] Not all demands or expressions of cultural identity are acceptable, but that is not a problem since what immigrants want is no threat to liberalism. But what if groups do not want what Kymlicka says they do? What if members of a minority group demand recognition of not just their language but also a "thicker, ethnographic sense" of culture that includes patriarchal and other oppressive norms and practices on the grounds that these particular customs are the sine qua non of their cultural identity? Some groups may value culture for reasons very different from the reason why liberals value culture: not because they serve as "contexts of choice" that enable individual autonomy but because their customs and rituals are their own and they have deep affective attachments to them.

Just as the connection between culture and individual freedom is contingent, so, too, is the connection between culture and self-respect. Kymlicka takes it as given that "most people, most of the time, have a deep bond to their own culture," noting that a full explanation of this bond would involve aspects of psychology, sociology, linguistics, the philosophy of mind, and neurology.[28] Many people do have "deep bonds" to groups and rely on them for self-respect, but are they bonds to *cultural* groups? People have affective bonds to a range of communities – family, friends, fellow hobbyists and partisans, co-workers and co-religionists. So the choice is never between being a fully integrated member of a cultural group and being a detached, free-floating individual. Arguments for political recognition of cultural affiliations have tended to rely on the premise that there is one single community – one's nation or "societal culture" – to which individuals are deeply attached. But people have bonds to smaller, larger, and cross-cutting communities, and it's not clear why any one particular community should take priority above the others. To be sure, some people have strong attachments to *cultural* groups, such as attachments to their nation.[29] But the assertion that *most* people have strong attachments to their own ethnic or national culture needs more support than multiculturalists tend to provide, and its truth cannot be established by philosophical argument alone. In the

---

[26] Kymlicka 1989: 198–99.   [27] Kymlicka 2001: 20, 169; 1995: 177–80; 1998: ch. 3.
[28] Kymlicka 1995: 90.   [29] See Spinner-Halev and Theiss-Morse 2003.

absence of such support, alternative speculations seem just as plausible in the context of liberal democratic societies: that people have multiple communal attachments and other communal attachments besides ethnic or national ones may be more highly valued by individuals, or more radically, that the aspiration of individualism and economic globalization is slowly remaking the nature of cultural group attachments.[30] Rather than assuming that people have strong attachments to *cultural* identity, we need to recognize that people have multiple identities with differing degrees of attachment to different identities. To do otherwise would arbitrarily privilege *cultural* attachments over people's other communal attachments.

The work of sociologists who study ethnic and cultural identity suggests that the nature and strength of individuals' identification with groups varies across groups and across individuals within groups and is deeply affected by social, political, and economic conditions. Proponents of multiculturalism need to be attentive to these differences. In her study of ethnic identity among white middle-class Americans, sociologist Mary Waters finds that white ethnic identity is often symbolic and voluntary. When asked what was distinctive about their ethnic identity, many of her Irish, Italian, and German American respondents stressed what we might call middle-class American values, such as valuing family, education, and patriotism.[31] To be sure, to say an identity is symbolic is not to say that it is shallow or without consequence. As Waters points out, while Irish American or Italian American ethnic identity may lack much distinctive content, many take pride in their ethnic identities and seek to pass this sense of identity to their children. "Symbolic ethnicity" fulfills people's desire to belong to a collective.[32] Yet, insofar as ethnic or cultural identity is adopted and altered under conditions of diversity, the convergence and mixing of the content of identities and individual identification with multiple identities seem just as plausible as a strong bond to a single identity. Under such conditions, we will find great variety in the strength of people's identification with cultural identity and its connection to self-respect. For some, strong identification with cultural identity may be crucial for self-respect, but for others, the experience of cultural membership may be stifling and damaging to self-respect. We'll see in Part II that there are many cases that challenge the view that cultural membership is straightforwardly supportive of individual freedom and self-respect.

The upshot of this discussion is to challenge the premise that posits a single value to cultural membership as a matter of general theory. The nature and extent of belonging and the value of cultural membership are

---

[30] On the latter, see Kateb 1994: 521.   [31] Waters 1990: 134.
[32] See Gans 1979 and Waters 1990: 134, 150.

not matters that can be determined at the level of theory once and for all. There is reasonable disagreement over the meaning and value of cultural membership. In contrast to Kymlicka's theory, which values cultural membership in terms of its role as a "context of choice" enabling individual autonomy and its connection to individual self-respect, we need to be open to the possibility that cultural membership may be differently valued by different members.

The structure of identity

The meaning and value of cultural attachments vary not just across groups but also from individual to individual. It is not just cultures that are characterized by multiplicity, but individuals themselves hold multiple social identities. We may identify with being female or male, black or white, Irish or Mexican American, gay or straight. Of course, we may also identify with being shy or clever or kind. But in contemporary democratic societies, it is the former set of identities based on shared social markers, such as gender, race, ethnicity, nationality, religion, and sexuality, which have important social and political consequences. These markers carry expectations about how a person will think and act and with whom they will associate, and those who identify with particular social markers look to them in forming and pursuing their life plans. It is important to have the following structure of social identities in mind.[33]

First, there must be available in public discourse some *criteria of ascription*. Before there can be "blacks" or "Mexican Americans" there must be a social conception of blacks or Mexican Americans. People must know that these labels exist and there must be some degree of consensus about how to identify those to whom they should be applied. Usually this consensus is organized around a set of attributes and stereotypes. Skin color and hair type are physical attributes that have long been associated with racial identity. A common language and shared history are attributes associated with ethnic and national identity. Descent has been a central feature of racial and ethnic identity. The content of these social conceptions have varied over time, but long-standing stereotypes that associate certain attributes with a particular social identity are neither easily overturned nor within the exclusive control of those to whom the identity is ascribed.

A second dimension of social identity is *treatment by others*. Who we take ourselves to be is shaped by the regard of others. As Taylor puts it, we

---

[33] The following discussion draws on Appiah 2004: 66–69.

define our individual identities "always in dialogue, sometimes in struggle against, the things" others want to see in us.[34] To treat individuals as members of group X is to do or say something to them in part because they are an X. This treatment may take the form of invidious discrimination, or it may take more benevolent forms, such as offering them special treatment because they are X, perhaps in part to counter negative treatment they have experienced as an X. Even if individuals resist identifying as an X, patterns of behavior toward them may compel them toward such identification. This dimension suggests why identity is a matter for politics: treatment by others on the basis of one's social identities can profoundly shape one's life prospects. I will say more about political responses to identity-based claims in the next chapter.

A third dimension of social identity, one which multiculturalists have not given sufficient attention to, is *individual identification*. Certain attributes may mark me as a member of group X, but this third dimension is missing unless I internalize the labels associated with X available in the public discourse. This is akin to Marx's observation about working-class identity. In his view, unlike workers under previous modes of production, workers under capitalism constitute not just a class "in itself," but as their consciousness of their place in history grows, they will come to see themselves as a class "for itself."[35] This third dimension suggests why social identity is of ethical significance: it can provide rich materials for people to draw upon in fashioning their lives. In telling the story of who you are, you draw on larger social narratives. Your family's escape from Nazi Germany or communist North Korea is a central part of the story you tell about yourself. Your connection to social identities can heighten your sense of accomplishment. You are the first woman president of your professional association, the first African American editor in chief of the Harvard Law Review, or the first widely acclaimed Asian American woman comedian. Through their internalization, social identities can play a central role in how people live and evaluate their own lives.

Typically, people can and do identify with many different groups. You may be a woman of Mexican ancestry who is Catholic, politically left, fluent in Spanish and English, and works as a human rights lawyer. Within the range of identities we can have, we can choose to some extent what priority to give to one or another. Which collective identities we embrace and to what extent depends on context – who we are with, what the circumstances are, who's asking and defining the identities and labels. This third dimension suggests the need to be attentive to the *experience of*

---

[34] Taylor 1994: 32–33.   [35] Marx [1845–46] 1972.

identity, to ask whether and how someone identifies with a collective identity and what role that identity plays in her life. This is crucial if those who are sympathetic to claims for cultural accommodation want to take seriously the freedom of individuals to identify (or not) with the range of social and cultural identities available to them. If the importance of a social identity to an individual is assumed and some singular value is attributed to that identity, then an individual's freedom in relations of identity is diminished.

The constructivist challenge

Recent criticism of normative theories of multiculturalism has focused on the conception of culture upon which many of these theories are premised. Influenced by the "Geertzian moment" in anthropological discourse, many scholars have embraced a conception of culture as a shared framework of meaning that emerges in and through social interactions.[36] What these scholars have challenged is the popular, deeply entrenched assumption that ethnic and national groups are primordial in foundation and map neatly onto distinct cultures. As many scholars of nationalism have emphasized, nations are imagined communities.[37] On a constructivist account, cultures are narratively constituted through the stories people tell about themselves and the rituals and practices they perform. Cultural communities have long interacted and shaped one another in their interactions, and they have been internally heterogeneous from the start. The experience of cultural belonging varies across age, gender, class, kinship, and occupation. Cultural norms and practices reflect power differentials and struggles over who can speak and which of the multiple stories will achieve relative dominance. This means that understanding culture requires constant work from participants and observers, not settling on a "fixed encyclopedia of supposed cultural essentials."[38] We must attempt to understand cultural differences in particular contexts and from different points of view. So while cultural diversity is an undeniable fact about the world, the particular constellation of cultural identities and communities in the world is fluid and contested.

I think there are four elements to the constructivist account of culture that are worth drawing out. First, cultures are the product of specific and complex historical processes, not fixed primordial entities. Second, as

---

[36] For constructivist accounts of culture, see Geertz 1973; Ortner 1974, 1996, 1999; Said 1989; Narayan 1997; Johnson 2000; Benhabib 2002; Wedeen 2002.
[37] Anderson 1983.   [38] Sollors 1989: xv.

critics of multiculturalism have stressed, cultures are internally contested, negotiated, and reimagined by members, who are sometimes motivated by their interactions with outsiders. Third, cultures are not isolated but rather overlapping and interactive. Cross-cultural interactions have long been an important source of cultural change.[39] Such interactions have been heightened in the contemporary age through massive migrations of people across borders. And fourth, cultures are loose-jointed and therefore more resilient than multiculturalists suggest. That is, the different strands of a culture are loosely coupled such that the loss or change of one strand does not necessarily bring down the entire culture, leading to cultural extinction or collapse.

Prominent theories of multiculturalism downplay the extent to which cultures are internally contested, interactive, and loose-jointed. A conception of culture as coherent, self-contained, and tightly knitted wholes is at the heart of multiculturalists' case for cultural preservation. As Margalit and Halbertal put it, a culture is a "comprehensive way of life" that "affects everything people do: cooking, architectural style, common language, literary and artistic traditions, music, customs, dress, festivals, ceremonies." Cultures are "pervasive" and "encompassing."[40] One gets the sense that the pieces of a culture hang so tightly together such that unraveling one piece threatens the entire structure. In the background is the specter of cultural extinction and collapse. Cultural preservation is the goal of group-specific rights and protections.

But the point about extinction is questionable as a statement of empirical fact. Multiculturalists have not produced evidence that cultural change or deviation from particular cultural traditions necessarily threatens the existence of entire cultures. At times this point about extinction is presented as an a-priori claim: that all cultures form a tight seamless web such that deviation from any part will necessarily induce collapse. This assumption calls to mind Lord Devlin's discussion of the relationship between public morality and the preservation of society. He was writing about sexual morality, and he defended the legal enforcement of sexual morality on the grounds that a society should preserve or safeguard whatever is essential to its existence.[41] His central premise was that a "recognized morality," including moral principles pertaining to sexual relations, is necessary for a society's existence. The analogous claim in the

---

[39] See Wolf 1982 who suggests that cultures have evolved through cross-cultural encounters for a millennium.

[40] Margalit and Halbertal 1994: 498–99. See also Margalit and Raz 1990: 444; Kymlicka 1995: 80.

[41] Devlin 1965: 11. See also Hart 1963.

debate on multiculturalism is that any unraveling of the seamless web of culture is bound to produce cultural collapse. But as in the debate on sexual morality, the claim rests on thin empirical ice.

If cultures are more dynamic and loose-jointed than multiculturalists suggest, how can group-specific rights be based on the goal of cultural preservation? One way to argue for cultural preservation without the premise of cultural collapse would be through the bare assertion of cultural conservatism, that insulation from any cultural change is a value in itself and justifies regulation. As far as I know, few multiculturalists take up this line. Instead, multiculturalists have tended to resolve the issue by sharply demarcating inside and outside forces. Margalit and Halbertal argue that people have an "overriding interest" in a right to cultural survival, protected from outside forces. Kymlicka recognizes the fact of cultural interchange, but he, too, seeks to insulate minority cultures from external influences while leaving them open to internally induced cultural change. His theory aims to protect cultural distinctness while rejecting the desirability of cultural isolation or purity. As he puts it, "It should be up to each culture to decide when and how they will adopt the achievements of the larger world. It is one thing to learn from the larger world; it is another thing to be swamped by it, and self-government rights may be needed for smaller nations to control the direction and rate of change."[42]

But the inside–outside boundary is difficult to pin down. Cultures do not correspond in any neat way to national or societal boundaries, and many cultures have long interacted and influenced one another through relations of trade, warfare, and conquest. Today, due in part to interactions through the global economy, transnational communications networks, and the increasing migrations of peoples across borders, people in many parts of the world live in multicultural contexts and possess multiple identities. If this is true, then claims about cultural extinction may not apply to a great many cases. It may make sense to speak of cultural endangerment or "swamping" only in certain cases, such as in some cases of aboriginal contact with European culture.

The history of the Pueblos in what is now the American Southwest suggests that while the concern about swamping applies to much of the history of their relations with colonial powers, overall theirs is a story of cultural adaptation rather than extinction. The arrival of the Spaniards in 1540 threatened demographic disaster among the Pueblos. Population decline was the result of warfare with Spaniards and nomads,

---

[42] Margalit and Halbertal 1994; Kymlicka 1995: 104–105.

epidemic disease, and drought and famine. It was not until after 1750 that a gradual recovery and increase of the Pueblo population began. But even in the face of these injustices, their cultural traditions did not become extinct; rather, they evolved through intercultural encounters and inter-marriage. Miscegenation began from the Spaniards' first appearance among the Pueblos, including the Santa Clara Pueblo. The number of mestizos grew steadily throughout the colonial period. Black servants brought from New Spain by Spanish settlers also intermarried with the Pueblos.[43]

By the time Anglo-Americans assumed control of the Southwest in 1846, they discovered Pueblo culture had preserved the underpinnings of indigenous culture while having incorporated a significant degree of Hispanic folkways during Spanish and later Mexican rule. Pueblos them-selves came to identify many Spanish elements as part of the Pueblo cultural framework, especially in the face of Anglo-American pressures to assimilate. The Pueblos claimed certain aspects of Spanish dress as their own and fused Catholic religious practices with traditional Pueblo ceremonies. Until the turn of the twentieth century, Spanish was the lingua franca, and the system of government inherited from the colonial period was retained. Pueblo culture adapted once again under Anglo-American rule. By 1950, English had replaced Spanish as the major second language; indeed, many children in less conservative Pueblos spoke only English and understood Indian languages only a little or not at all.[44] The history of the Pueblos suggests that even in the face of colonial conquest and coercion, cultural change without wholesale cul-tural extinction is possible. As historian Marc Simmons describes in writing about the Pueblos, "[W]hile many traditional practices will dis-appear, others will be reworked and adjusted to fit a changing scene, permitting each of the Pueblos to retain its identity and maintain pride in a lifeway that is distinctly its own."[45]

In many cases, it may make more sense to speak of the adaptation of cultural identity rather than its extinction. Consider the cultures of con-temporary Native peoples. In the United States, the 1990 census found that 56 percent of Native Americans lived in urban areas. In Canada, Australia, and New Zealand, the corresponding figures for aboriginal peoples in the 1990s were 70, 73, and 83 percent. Native people have moved to cities in search of education, jobs, and adequate health care. Some were forced by assimilationist government policies; others chose to move. The reality is that the majority of indigenous citizens of these four countries now live in

---

[43] Simmons 1979a: 192–93.   [44] Simmons 1979b: 209, 211–12, 221.   [45] Ibid. 222.

multiethnic settings, and they have taken marriage partners from different cultural backgrounds.[46] This multicultural experience has led to the adaptation of old cultural forms into new cultural forms, but the generation of new cultural forms does not necessarily mean that Native American identities have been lost. In the Arizona borderlands, musicians of the Tohono O'odham Nation issue CDs featuring tunes such as "Juan Rios Mazurka" and "Cheek to Cheek Polka," a fusion of Native, Mexican, and European music. The writer Sherman Alexie, a Coeur d'Alene Indian, plays in a blues band. When asked about his appropriation of an African American musical form, he says his music is "Indian blues" or "Crazy Horse with a slide guitar." Such hybridity is not limited to music but applies to visual arts, dance, architecture, agriculture, healing practices, and religion.[47] Does this process of musical fusion and change constitute the loss of Native American identities? While we can say that something of value – a particular Native musical tradition or a particular Native language – has been lost, it is not clear that Native American identities have been lost. Rather, it seems just as plausible to say that they have been adapted and reinvented through ongoing cross-cultural encounters.

To be sure, cultures are not only characterized by change and flux. The extent of interchange and interpenetration of cultures varies across contexts, and to say that cultures are constructed is not to say that they are infinitely malleable or of little significance for individual members of cultural communities. What the constructivist challenge suggests is the need for greater attention to the *politics* of cultural construction, change, and maintenance. A constructivist view of culture is more attentive to internal contestation and intercultural dynamics than the two prominent views of culture discussed above. Some political theorists have recognized that intercultural interactions are an important source of cultural change. James Tully has emphasized that cultures are not only "overlapping, interactive and internally negotiated," but also "densely interdependent in their formation and identity." Similarly, Bhikhu Parekh contends, "[C]ultures are not the achievements of the relevant communities alone but also of others, who provide their context, shape some of their beliefs and practices, and remain their points of reference. In this sense almost all cultures are multiculturally constituted." Both Seyla Benhabib and Monique Deveaux have highlighted the permeability of boundaries between cultures.[48] Ayelet Shachar stresses that groups are always

---

[46] Statistics cited in Brown 2003: 221. Native Americans have the highest rate of intermarriage of any ethnic or racial group in the United States (Gould 2001: 759).
[47] Weber 1999: A1; "Questions for Sherman Alexie" 1997: 8.
[48] Tully 1995: 10; Parekh 2000: 163; Benhabib 2002: 7; Deveaux 2003: 790.

reacting to the effects of state power, and her "joint governance" approach, which calls for ongoing interaction between the state and minority groups in the governance of different spheres of minority group life, clearly recognizes that minority and majority cultures are interconnected.[49]

While these theorists have recognized the role of intercultural interactions in cultural construction, they stop short of examining how intercultural interactions have shaped the identities and practices of minority cultures, as well as how they have fueled cultural conflicts. Many cultural conflicts may indeed be *intra*cultural; conflicts over female circumcision, polygamy, and customary marriage may primarily be struggles within particular cultural communities over the meaning and importance of particular practices.[50] But many cultural conflicts arise out of *inter*cultural interactions; what appear to be intracultural conflicts may have been fueled by intercultural interactions. In some cases, intercultural interactions may provoke hardening of hierarchies within minority groups, as in cases where group leaders shore up traditional decision-making structures within the community in the face of external challenges to those structures. In other cases, the state may be more directly implicated in supporting hierarchies within minority communities: the practices being contested within minority communities may themselves have been introduced or reinforced by the state. Cultures vary in the degree of fluidity, contestation, and permeability, but even in relatively closed societies the content of cultures is not determined purely "from the inside." Rather, cultures are shaped by interactions and struggles with other cultures. This suggests the need to examine more closely the processes by which cultural identities are constructed.

Cultures are shaped not just in the course of ordinary social interactions but also by concerted state action. The state's role in constructing identity may be starkest with respect to racial identity. The American state has long marked people out on the basis of race, sometimes to exclude and marginalize and at other times to address racial discrimination. Many scholars point to the fact that individuals with the same bloodline and phenotype have been defined in radically different ways

---

[49] While Shachar develops institutional designs aimed at promoting interaction between states and minority groups in the governance of minority affairs, her analysis does not explicitly examine the role that states have played in shaping and reinforcing minority group identities and practices at the center of cultural conflicts. Rather, as I discussed in the Introduction, she takes "identity groups" which she equates with "nomoi communities" as a given (Shachar 2001: 2, 88–92, 117–45).

[50] For the claim that the challenges posed by traditional minority cultural groups stem primarily from intracultural conflicts, see Deveaux 2003.

at different points in time as evidence that "race" is constructed out of prevailing norms, beliefs, movements, laws, and institutions.[51]

Ethnic and cultural identities have also been shaped by state action. As David Laitin argues, the three major tribes in Nigeria were recent creations. The idea that there was a single "Hausa-Fulani" tribe was "largely a political claim by the leadership of the NPC in their battle against the South," and the notions of "Yoruba" and "Igbo" were created from nineteenth-century political experience.[52] Similarly, in the United States, indigenous identities are intimately connected with state recognition. As James Clifford recounts in his essay on the Wampanoag Indians of Mashpee, government has played a crucial role in defining what counts as a tribe. The Mashpee plaintiffs sought recognition as a tribe in order to secure restitution of lands taken by non-Indian residents, developers, and local governments over the course of two centuries. The 1977 case hinged on whether the Mashpee Wampanoags constitute a tribe as defined by federal law, and this turned on questions of the continuity of cultural traditions and identity. Although they resided in what had been known as an "Indian town" on Cape Cod, they lacked institutions of tribal governance for much of their history, they owned no tribal lands (other than the 55 acres acquired just before their trial), the Mashpee language ceased to be spoken since about 1800, and residents had intermarried over the centuries with other Indian groups, whites, blacks, Hessian deserters from the British Army during the Revolutionary War, and Cape Verde islanders.

Anthropologists for the tribe focused on the concept of culture, but they struggled to define it. Culture appeared to lack any essential features. As Clifford puts it, "Neither language, religion, land, economics, nor any other key institution or custom was its *sine qua non*. It seemed to be a contingent mix of elements. At times the concept was purely differential: cultural integrity involved recognized boundaries; it required merely an acceptance by the group and its neighbors of a meaningful difference, a we–they distinction."[53] Many elements of what they identified as Mashpee culture had been combined with elements from external sources. The Mashpee plaintiffs were compelled to present culture as continuous, well-integrated wholes; any sharp contradictions or mutations that may have been a part of everyday life had to be left out, as winning

[51] See Omi and Winant 1994; Hollinger 1995; Smith 1997; Haney Lopez 1998; Nobles 2000.
[52] Laitin 1986: 7–8.
[53] Clifford (1988: 278, 323) recounts the trial, *Mashpee Tribe* v. *New Seabury et al.* (1977), by consulting the trial record.

state recognition depended on it. In other words, the Mashpee had to mute the constructed and dynamic character of their identity.[54]

The constructivist view allows us not just to examine critically the role of the state in constructing culture but also to acknowledge the variability of the value and experience of cultural membership for different groups and different members within groups. Cultural identity is about far more than simply possessing the attributes associated with a particular cultural group. It also involves varied ways of identifying with and participating in collective life – how you present yourself physically to the world, with whom you keep company, what motivates you to get involved in politics. Some people may attach great importance to some aspects of cultural identity or none at all, and the specific value people attach to cultural membership can vary greatly. Whether individuals are identified with or themselves identify with particular social identities is shaped in part by state action, as well as the constraints and options provided by the larger environment of different identity groups. As long as racial or ethnic identity is used to assign opportunities and rewards in society, these social identities will continue to be much more complex than a matter of individual choice and selective personal enjoyment of tradition. This is precisely why identity-based claims are a proper subject for politics.

We should be careful not to overstate the critical insight that emerges from the constructivist challenge to holistic conceptions of culture. To say that cultures are narratively constructed frameworks of meaning is not to make the stronger claim that cultures are always radically heterogeneous and contested, hybrid and porous. To assert this stronger claim would be to make the same mistake as those who adopt an essentialist view of cultures as coherent bounded wholes, albeit in the name of anti-essentialism. As the anthropologist David Scott puts it, "*For whom* is culture partial, unbounded, heterogeneous, hybrid, and so on, the anthropologist or the native? Whose claim is this, theory's or that of the discourse into which theory is inquiring?" Scott rightly urges a critical stance toward culture's own conceptual history, which would yield an appreciation of the conditions and possible limits of the anthropological notion of culture for political theory. The constructivist view of culture is a product of anthropology, social theory, and philosophy, and the culture concept's history is not "natural," something that is "simply

---

[54] The Mashpee Wampanoag Indian tribe finally received federal recognition as a sovereign American Indian nation in February 2007, thirty-two years after it began its struggle for recognition. See Weber 2007.

there, unfolding."[55] Recognizing that the culture concept has evolved within a particular discourse and in response to particular political demands of the day should lead us to be wary of viewing all cultures as radically contested and heterogeneous just as it should lead us to be wary of viewing all cultures as holistic and homogeneous. Cultures vary in the degree of fluidity, contestation, and permeability. Some cultures are more closed and bounded than others. The more modest claim of the constructivist challenge is that cultures are not entities that exist prior to social and political interactions but rather are created in and through them. This suggests the need to be attentive to how cultural traditions are created and sustained, and by and for whom.

A key normative implication that follows from adopting the constructivist view of culture is to shift the basis of evaluation of group demands from *inherent features of groups* to the *social and political effects* of cultural identity groups. The question is not whether cultures should be preserved on the basis of inherent features they possess, but whether the particular claim made in the name of culture should be accommodated. This means focusing on the content of minority group claims (their goals and actions), as opposed to determining what the groups really are (bona fide cultures or cultural imposters).

Focusing on the political claims of culture allows for making distinctions between desirable and reprehensible elements of culture rather than bracketing the reprehensible elements as content and not structure, as Kymlicka suggests, or labeling whole cultures as reprehensible gender-wise, as some feminist critics have. This opens up a third way for minority women at the center of gendered cultural conflicts, who are committed to both equal justice for cultural minorities and equal justice for women. Justice sometimes requires accommodating the claims of minority cultural groups for reasons I discuss in the next chapter, and such accommodation may have the effect of supporting a group's efforts to preserve its collective identity, a goal that many multiculturalists defend. On my approach, however, the reason for granting the group claim does not rely on claims about cultures being an "irreducibly social good" or a "primary good." Rather, the focus is on what cultural affiliations and practices do, not what cultures are. A constructivist view of culture recognizes that there is reasonable disagreement about the meaning and value of cultural affiliation, and this suggests the need to take a case-by-case approach in determining whether and how particular affiliations and practices are

---

[55] Scott 2003: 101–102.

valued by members of a group seeking accommodation and what the effects of accommodation would be.

The constructivist view also allows us to be attentive to how cultures change, for better or worse, in interactions with one another. We must look at the borderlands between cultures and be attentive to resonances between the norms and practices of the majority culture and those of minority cultures. Close attention to interactions between cultures can help us see not just cross-cultural differences but also cross-cultural similarities. Before turning to examine particular cases, we need a normative account of why the claims of cultural identity groups should be given a fair hearing in the first place. As I have argued, a normative case for cultural accommodation cannot rest on the premise that cultures are "irreducibly social goods" or "primary goods." Why then should the claims of cultural minorities be given a fair hearing at all?

3 Justice and multiculturalism: an egalitarian argument for cultural accommodation

Liberal democracies committed to both justice for cultural minorities and justice for women face a genuine dilemma when these commitments conflict. This chapter accepts the feminist contention that the pursuit of gender equality is a crucial and valuable goal of liberal democratic societies. As Susan Okin put it, feminism means "the belief that women should not be disadvantaged by their sex, that they should be recognized as having human dignity equal to that of men, and that they should have the opportunity to live as fulfilling and as freely chosen lives as men can."[1] The other half of the dilemma, justice for cultural minorities, requires greater elaboration since there is greater disagreement about what this requires. This chapter offers an argument for why liberal democracies should grant special accommodations to minority cultural groups and what the limits of accommodation should be, a position I call rights-respecting accommodationism, which provides a framework for addressing the problem of internal minorities.

I start from a value fundamental to liberal democracy, the idea of equal respect, and offer an interpretation of what equal respect in relations of culture and identity might entail. I argue that differential treatment through a range of accommodations is sometimes required to treat members of minority cultural groups with equal respect. Citizens express mutual respect for one another not simply by accepting a set of basic rights and opportunities that apply equally to all. Under certain circumstances, equal respect requires going beyond uniform treatment toward differential treatment. I explore three kinds of circumstances that are especially relevant to multicultural societies and that arise out of histories of interaction between majority and minority cultures, and consider whether each supports a prima facie case for special accommodation: (1) present discrimination, (2) historical injustice, and (3) state

---

[1] Okin 1999: 10. I share Okin's feminist commitments, although I disagree with her, as will become clear in both this chapter and in the case study chapters, on how gender equality is best pursued in the context of cultural conflicts.

establishment of culture. What form accommodations will take and whether they should ultimately be granted will depend on contextual inquiry taken up through democratic deliberation, and I will consider specific cases in detail in later chapters. In all cases, however, the basis of my argument for cultural accommodation suggests the limits of accommodation: protecting the basic rights of members of minority cultural groups. I will say more about this below.

My aim in this chapter is to provide a general argument for why liberal democracies should grant fair hearing to the claims of minority cultures in the first place and to offer a normative framework for public deliberation to address gendered dilemmas of culture. I offer these normative arguments not with the hope of solving such dilemmas but to suggest the starting terms for democratic contestation through which citizens themselves choose specific policies and take action to address specific dilemmas. The approach I develop is semicontextual in that it aims to provide normative principles for addressing cultural conflicts while being attentive to the particularities of context.[2]

As I indicated in the Introduction, my egalitarian argument is offered as a middle way between the long-standing liberal contention that cultural accommodation is inconsistent with respecting individual freedom and equality, on the one hand, and multiculturalist calls for cultural preservation, on the other. Against Barry's culture-blind "unitary republican model," I argue that the claim that uniform treatment constitutes just treatment must be tested in light of possible kinds of injustices that tend to characterize multicultural societies. On the other hand, while my egalitarian approach is open to differential treatment under certain circumstances, it does not aim at cultural preservation as some prominent multiculturalists do. The concern for cultural preservation has led some multiculturalists to argue for redress for any law or policy that disparately impacts religious and cultural minorities. This argument assumes that most if not all burdens imposed by laws on religious and cultural commitments threaten the survival of cultural communities and are therefore too severe to be borne by individual members. As we saw in chapter 2, a

---

[2] My approach shares with Joseph Carens's "justice as evenhandedness" the conviction that justice requires attention to context, but it differs in that Carens's approach, as I understand it, does not provide a clear set of liberal or democratic principles by which to evaluate cultural conflicts. In contrast, the approach I develop here aims to make explicit a set of principles by which to approach contextual considerations, and in this sense, is semicontextual. So while I agree with Carens that "history matters, numbers matter, the relative importance of the claims to the claimants matters," we need some principles with which to think about how these contextual factors should be brought to bear on addressing cultural dilemmas (Carens 2000: 12).

prominent multiculturalist presumption is that a good of fundamental importance is at stake. While I share multiculturalists' concern about differential impact, I do not think this fact alone is sufficient to support a claim for accommodation. Not all burdens imposed by state laws and policies are burdens on fundamental interests since there is reasonable disagreement about the meaning and value of cultural affiliations. Rather than assuming that all burdens on cultural practices constitute burdens on fundamental interests, we need to ask whether they do.

Why equality?

At the core of liberal democracy is the presumption that no person is intrinsically superior to another, that all persons are of equal moral worth. In his observations about America, Alexis de Tocqueville presented this presumption as fact when he commented on its "eminently democratic" social conditions – equality of wealth and "to some extent" equality of mental endowments largely owing to reforms in inheritance laws and the spread of public education.[3] Echoing Tocqueville, Robert Dahl observes that in democratic societies "the idea of intrinsic equality" is "an assumption so fundamental that it is presupposed in moral argument."[4] As Tocqueville did, Dahl is, in part, making an empirical point about the persistent and widespread influence of the idea of equality in democratic societies. He points to its historical roots in religious doctrines that we are equally God's children, as well as to Bentham's dictum, "everybody is to count for one, nobody for more than one."[5] Of course, the idea of equality is not a perfect mirror of the actual state of affairs but rather the basis of an ideal that democratic societies have aspired to. The demand for equality has been at the core of many social and political movements, mobilized in opposition to various forms of hierarchy and oppression, from the American Revolution to the civil rights and women's movements. The demand has been for a democratic social and political order, an order in which people regard one another as equals.

Echoing this demand, political theorists and philosophers have offered different substantive conceptions of equality. Indeed, the idea of equality seems to be a central feature of many normative theories of social and political arrangements that have withstood the test of time. These theories do not aim to answer the question "why equality?" so much as "equality of what?" Theories that are otherwise at odds with each other demand equality of something.[6] Utilitarians insist on equal weights on everyone's

---

[3] Tocqueville 1966: 50, 55.   [4] Dahl 1989: 84–85.   [5] Ibid. 86.
[6] See Sen 1992: 12–13, 16.

utility gains in the utilitarian objective function; libertarians have demanded the equal right to liberty as such; liberal egalitarians have focused on equal basic liberties and resources; and democratic theorists argue for conditions that would ensure citizens' equal opportunity to influence collective decision-making. These are distinct conceptions of equality, and each provides a different answer to the question "equality of what?" Yet, they all express the idea that individuals are owed equal respect in the design of political institutions under which they live.

The idea of equal respect figures prominently in Rawls's theory of justice. Although "justice as fairness" is not a theory of democracy and says little about democratic politics, it is a contribution to democratic theory in that it argues that a democratic political regime is required by justice. Rawls intends his theory "for a democratic society"; it is addressed to a society of equals, and treating individual members with the equal respect they are owed requires democratic political arrangements.[7] Rawls distinguishes between two conceptions of equality: "equality as it is invoked in connection with the distribution of certain goods, some of which will almost certainly give higher status or prestige to those who are more favored, and equality as it applies to the respect which is owed to persons irrespective of their social position." He states that equality of the first kind is defined by his second principle of justice regarding the distribution of resources. Equality of the second kind, defined by his first principle of justice and by such natural duties as mutual respect, is "fundamental" – "it is owed to human beings as moral persons."[8] For Rawls, the basis of this more fundamental equality lies in people's moral powers – in particular, a capacity for a sense of justice. Each person in virtue of possessing this capacity is owed respect, regardless of natural endowments or social position.[9] When he says that his theory of justice is intended "for a democratic society," he means a

---

[7] See Cohen 2003.

[8] Rawls [1971] 1999: 447. Here Rawls draws on Bernard Williams, who distinguished between the conception of equality of opportunity that is "invoked in connection with the distribution of certain goods, some at least of which are bound to confer on their possessors some preferred status or prestige" and "equality of respect ... which urges us to give less consideration to those structures in which people enjoy status or prestige, and to consider people independently of those goods" (Williams [1962] 1997: 101).

[9] Rawls 1971: xviii; 1993: 302. In *Theory*, Rawls sees the moral powers in Kantian terms: they are the essential capacities for moral and rational agency. It is in virtue of these capacities that we see ourselves and each other as free and responsible agents. Rawls provides another account, suggested in *Theory* and developed in *Political Liberalism*, which characterizes moral powers less ambitiously: they are the capacities of democratic citizens. Here the basis of equality does not lie in a capacity for self-regulation or in a generic moral capacity, but specifically in the capacity to understand, offer reasons in support of, and act on principles of justice (Freeman 2003: 5; Cohen 2003: 107). Rawls's political, not

society whose members are understood in the political culture as entitled to equal respect. For Rawls, then, the idea of equal respect is fundamental, and conceptions of distributive equality can be understood as derivative principles.

Ronald Dworkin also accepts the idea of equal respect as fundamental, and derives two different rights from it. The first is the right to *equal treatment*, which is "the right to an equal distribution of some opportunity or resource or burden." For example, every citizen has a right to an equal vote in a democracy, as expressed by the Supreme Court's decision that one person must have one vote even if a different arrangement would secure the common good. The second is the right to *treatment as an equal*, which is "the right to be treated with the same respect and concern as anyone else" or "the right to equal concern and respect in the political decision about how these goods and opportunities are to be distributed."[10] I agree with Dworkin and Rawls that on the liberal conception of equality the right to *treatment as an equal* must be taken to be fundamental and the right to *equal treatment* as derivative.[11] That is, the latter holds only in those circumstances where it follows from the more fundamental right of treatment as an equal. Sometimes providing equal treatment is the only way to treat people as equals, but sometimes not. In some cases, treating people as equals requires special or differential treatment.

The conception of justice in relations of culture and identity I develop in this chapter builds on the idea of equal respect. Citizens show respect for one another by accepting that certain constraints have to be embodied in political institutions. These constraints include not only the familiar freedoms of religion, expression, and political participation, but also equality of opportunity and fairness in the social and economic structure of society. When it comes to the claims of minority cultural groups, there are, I'll argue, certain circumstances under which they have a prima facie claim to special treatment. Whether claims are ultimately granted and

---

metaphysical, conception of the person aims to avoid endorsing any particular religious or comprehensive moral doctrine about intrinsic moral worth. To consider whether he does so avoid relying on any comprehensive doctrine would take me away from my main inquiry. I do want to note that there are a variety of comprehensive grounds for the idea of equality, which are not incompatible with the political grounds that Rawls offers as a basis of equal respect. Comprehensive grounds include theological claims (God created us as equals), Kantian and earlier Rawlsian accounts (we possess rational agency), or species-centered accounts (we possess unique capacities to ensure one another's survival). On the latter, see Smith 2003: 164–69.

[10] Dworkin 1978: 227, 272–73. At times, Dworkin writes as if it is government, as opposed to all citizens, that is the agent providing equal treatment or treatment as equals. I intend the notion to apply not just to state action but also to the ethos and actions of citizens.

[11] See Dworkin 1985: 190.

what specific form they take will depend on public deliberation by those affected by the practices in question.

Here I think it worth clarifying the relationship between the idea of treating people as equals and democratic deliberation. That so many different theories of justice share the feature of demanding equality of some kind may stem from the requirements of ethical reasoning, especially about social and political arrangements. If we accept that others are owed equal respect, we are led to accept that all those governed by the exercise of collective power must have the opportunity to participate in the exercise of that power. We must justify our claims and actions to others on grounds that they could reasonably accept. In short, if we accept that a democratic society is one in which citizens are owed equal standing and equal respect, then political democracy and the equal right to participate in collective decision-making is a natural concomitant. I will say more about the role of deliberation in addressing the problem of internal minorities after presenting my case for why minority claims should receive a fair hearing in the first place.

Rights-respecting accommodationism

If we accept that a liberal democratic society is one in which people treat one another as equals, what then is required in terms of the claims of culture? What does it mean for people to treat one another with equal respect under conditions of religious and cultural diversity?

Some claims by cultural minorities ask not for special or differential treatment but rather similar treatment. For example, cultural claims in criminal defenses that I discuss in chapter 4 are not claims for complete exoneration or exemption from the criminal law, but rather requests for the consideration of cultural evidence in the application of existing criminal defenses, such as "mistake of fact" and "provocation." Minority defendants, like mainstream defendants, want to be judged in light of considerations about what, for example, it would be reasonable to be provoked by or what it would be reasonable to take as constituting consent. Because such factors depend on and may vary across cultural contexts, cultural evidence is needed to raise a "mistake of fact" or "provocation" defense. In other cases, minority claims for accommodations are demands for differential treatment. I think equal respect for persons under conditions of cultural diversity sometimes requires differential treatment. But when? And why? In this section I examine three circumstances that are especially relevant to multicultural societies: present discrimination, historical injustice, and state establishment of culture.

I should emphasize here that the basis of my egalitarian case for cultural accommodation suggests the limits of accommodation: the protection of the basic rights of individual members of minority cultural groups. On my rights-respecting accommodationist approach, it is not sufficient that minority groups demonstrate that one of the three circumstances obtains; they also need to show that accommodation would not undermine the basic rights of individual members. I take *basic rights* to include those rights and liberties that have come to be associated with liberal democratic citizenship: freedoms of conscience, expression, and association, and the right to participate in the exercise of collective power to which one is subject. As I argued above, liberal democracy's commitment to treating people as equals requires that they have a voice in governing collective affairs. Ensuring the worth of these basic liberties requires certain basic opportunities, including adequate subsistence, education, and employment opportunities. I do not intend this list as an exhaustive account of basic rights, nor do I mean to suggest that the content of the basic rights of citizenship is not itself a proper subject for democratic contestation; it is. There is disagreement over which rights are basic in the relevant sense. Some defend an extensive set that includes all the rights mentioned above and more, while others defend a much more limited set, such as one that focuses on a right to freedom of association and a right against cruel, degrading treatment.[12]

The problem with the latter view is that it would permit more powerful members of a group to inflict injustice on more vulnerable members. But why should the right of free association take priority over the prevention of injustices that groups can inflict on their members? A defender of the minimal view might reply that a right of exit is implied by the right of association so that religious dissenters or women who experience discrimination within the group are free to leave if they wish, but as I argue in chapter 6, the best way to ensure a genuine right of exit is to protect a variety of other rights. So even if a right of association and exit were foundational to liberalism in that all other rights can be derived from it, it would not follow that they are the only basic rights. Furthermore, a more extensive set of rights may be necessary for democratic participation and dialogue to be possible in the first place. I will say more about this below in discussing the role of deliberation in addressing cultural conflicts. I suggest the list of basic rights above as the starting terms for democratic dialogue while recognizing that citizens themselves

---

[12] For example, Chandran Kukathas (1992, 1997, 2003) defends the right of freedom of association and a right against cruel, degrading treatment as the only basic rights. So long as a community respects these rights, it should be allowed to decide its own affairs.

must decide the precise content of rights and how they should best be protected through democratic dialogue.

To set the stage for a discussion of the circumstances in which special treatment for cultural minorities might be warranted, it is helpful to begin by way of contrast with the idea of *uniform treatment,* one prominent liberal response to cultural diversity. The idea of uniform treatment means treating people the same by providing a common framework of individual liberties and opportunities within which they can pursue their life plans and practice their beliefs. This approach is difference-blind. So long as there is a good rationale for the law or policy and the law lacks malevolent intent, the nature and distribution of the burdens imposed by the law are not of common concern. Individuals themselves are responsible for bearing the burdens of their beliefs and cultural affiliations.

Brian Barry's critique of multiculturalism and defense of "unitary republican citizenship" is a good example of the uniform treatment approach. He suggests that in the vast majority of cases, either the case for the law is strong enough to rule out an exemption, or the case made for the exemption is strong enough to defeat the law altogether.[13] In opposing the "rule and exemption approach," where the rule is kept and an exemption granted to religious or cultural minorities, he emphasizes that this approach is permitted in very rare cases and warns that this approach is "actually very hard to justify in any particular case" and requires "a great deal of finagling." Turning to specific cases, Barry opposes granting exemptions from Britain's animal slaughter laws to Jews and Muslims to use traditional methods of ritual slaughter, and he opposes Britain's exemptions for Sikhs from motorcycle helmet laws. He also thinks that the US Supreme Court made the right decision in denying Native Americans the sacramental use of peyote in exception to anti-drug laws.[14]

On Barry's argument, there is no need to inquire into the impact of laws upon people, so long as there is a good rationale for the law. It is "absurd," he says, to suggest that a law's differential impact constitutes unfairness since every law is more burdensome on some individuals than others.[15] He points to laws against rape and pedophilia to make his point. Such laws give priority to the interests of women over the interests of potential rapists and to the interests of children over the interest of potential pedophiles, and in doing so, the law has a more severe impact on potential rapists and pedophiles. There is nothing inherently unfair about the differential

[13] Barry 2001: 39, 321.
[14] Ibid. 33, 50, 41–46. The latter case is *Employment Division, Department of Human Resources of Oregon* v. *Smith*, 494 US 872 (1990), which I discuss below.
[15] Barry 2001: 34.

impact of these laws since the purpose of the law is to protect some interests at the expense of others when they conflict.

Barry is right that differential impact of laws on different individuals does not necessarily constitute unfairness, but he is too quick in suggesting that it almost never does. We have good reasons for laws against pedophilia and rape; it is difficult to come up with any reasons to grant exemptions to these laws. But the point about differential impact is not that all individuals should enjoy equal success and fulfillment, regardless of their aspirations and desires. As far as I know, very few egalitarians actually argue for equality of outcome for *individuals*; more often than not this view is a popular intellectual straw man in debates about equality. The clear problem with this view is that it makes no room for individual agency and responsibility. But there is an important point that comes from equality of outcome. The concern is with differential impact across different social *groups* that have suffered histories of discrimination and disadvantage on the basis of race, ethnicity, gender, religion, disability, and sexuality.

Under conditions of diversity, we cannot dismiss the claim that the differential impact of laws across social groups constitutes unfairness until we examine the claims and the circumstances under which they arise. The problem is not the mere fact that uniform treatment has differential impact across groups; as Barry rightly says, this will always be the case with any legal or social norm. Rather, the problem is that the claim that uniform treatment constitutes equal treatment is empty without attention to the circumstances that give rise to claims for accommodation. The claim that uniform treatment lives up to treating people with equal respect needs to be tested in light of possible kinds of injustices that tend to characterize culturally diverse societies. The point here is not that we should abandon uniform treatment altogether but that in some circumstances we may need to go beyond it and extend differential treatment.[16]

---

[16] Inquiry into the unequal burdens imposed by law may seem like a radical idea, but it is not new. The focus on differential impact is already used as a measure of equal opportunity in the context of American anti-discrimination law. On what legal scholars have called a "disparate impact approach," in the context of employment, an employer's practices of hiring, promotion, and compensation must benefit racial minorities according to their proportion in the relevant labor pool, unless the employer can show that it would be very costly to do so. Instead of inquiring into acts of discrimination and asking whether they were intentional, the disparate impact approach is based on outcomes on hiring and promotion and focused on numerical standards. For example, if women and members of minority racial groups are not employed in proportion to their percentage in the relevant benchmark population, then the presumption is that they have not enjoyed truly equal opportunities. The definition of the relevant benchmark population is contested; it may or may not be identical to the national population depending on the context. In US anti-discrimination law, it is normally considered to be the population of qualified job applicants living in the labor force area. See *Hazelwood School District* v.

What circumstances might warrant special protections for cultural minorities? Below I consider three different circumstances of minority cultural group disadvantage that may support a prima facie case for accommodation. To set the stage, I want briefly to contrast two different understandings of egalitarian justice in order to situate culture-based inequality in a broader context of social and political inequality. I think proponents of both conceptions would consider their views as following from the fundamental idea of equal respect I discussed above. On one prominent liberal understanding of egalitarian justice, what critics of the view have dubbed "luck egalitarianism" or "equality of fortune,"[17] individuals should be held responsible for inequalities that stem from their choices but not for inequalities that derive from unchosen aspects of their circumstance. The crucial issue is whether an inequality is chosen or not. Fairness requires assisting individuals for disadvantages stemming from factors beyond their control; such disadvantages should be borne collectively by all members of society. On this argument, the charge of unfairness by members of the majority culture to policies of accommodation for members of minority cultural groups is met with the following response: they must share in bearing the costs of accommodation, whether it takes material or symbolic form, since the fair thing to do is to assist others with unchosen inequalities. The category of unchosen circumstance has been taken to include inequalities stemming from physical disability, natural disasters, poor family background, and lack of talent that translates into high earning power in the market. To this category, Kymlicka's liberal egalitarian defense of minority group rights adds "inequalities of cultural membership." On his view, it is unfair that cultural minorities whose minority status is unchosen must devote more resources to fulfilling their cultural commitments than members of the dominant culture. Minority group rights are justified, Kymlicka argues, "within a liberal egalitarian theory ... which emphasizes the importance of rectifying unchosen inequalities."[18]

But I don't think the choice–circumstance distinction should be the decisive issue when it comes to considerations about inequality, including culture-based inequalities. "Bad luck" is a poor way to characterize the source of a great many disadvantages that people face mainly because this characterization overlooks or at least understates the role that social structures and human actions play in shaping disadvantage. To be sure,

---

United States, 433 US 299 (1977) at 308, n. 13. See also Strauss 1991. I will examine the question of whether differential impact of law and policy along ethnic/cultural lines constitutes injustice below.

[17] See Wolff 1998: 101, 106; Anderson 1999: 289; Scheffler 2003: 5–6.

[18] Kymlicka 1995: 109.

some inequalities that stem from bad brute luck are matters of justice – for example, being born with a disability or being a citizen of a country with few natural resources and a weak economy. For this reason, I wouldn't go all the way with some critics of luck egalitarianism who argue that we must choose between eliminating social oppression and neutralizing the effects of luck as the defining aim of egalitarianism.[19] I think it would be hasty to throw out the concern with addressing the effects of bad luck altogether. I don't think that most critics who are themselves committed to the pursuit of egalitarian justice would jettison what seems to be the core idea of luck egalitarianism: that people's prospects in life should not be determined by forces that are beyond their control. Both sources of inequality should be of concern for egalitarians.

But the critics have a point: we should differentiate bad brute luck, on the one hand, and unjust social relations and structures, on the other, as distinct sources of inequality and perhaps prioritize the latter over the former for several reasons. First, structural inequality may be more invidious and pervasive than bad brute luck inequality, and focusing on the choice–circumstance distinction may divert attention from considerations about the nature and extent of disadvantage and the nature of the interests and commitments that are burdened, which should be at the forefront of egalitarian debates. The question of whether an individual chose to convert to a minority religion or chose to embrace and assert his gay identity should not be relevant in thinking about whether the inequalities he faces are of collective concern; instead, we should ask about the nature and extent of disadvantage he experiences on the basis of group differences. It is also important to distinguish between different sources of inequality since they may require different kinds of response and be prioritized in different ways, as I discuss below. When it comes to inequalities stemming from minority group status, they seem to arise not through cosmic bad luck but through unequal social relations and structures sustained by the decisions and actions of individuals. This suggests that we should think of culture-based inequalities as an example of structural inequality rather than bad brute luck inequality. Consider the following three sources of culture-based inequality.

Present discrimination

First, there is present discrimination and prejudice that sustains inequalities across different groups. Before the civil rights movement and the

---

[19] See, for example, Anderson 1999 and Mendus 2002.

enactment of federal anti-discrimination laws in the United States, state discrimination was unconstitutional, but there was disagreement over what constituted discrimination (e.g. whether segregated schools were discriminatory), and in many states private discrimination against entire groups on the basis of race, gender, ethnicity, religion, and disability was legal. Today, through the enforcement of civil rights laws, such as the Civil Rights Act of 1964 and the Americans with Disabilities Act of 1990, categorical exclusions by the state or employers are less common. While blanket discrimination against entire groups by the state is relatively rare, discrimination persists in different social spheres from education, work, and housing to everyday interpersonal interactions. Discrimination has both material and symbolic dimensions, not just denial of equal access to education and jobs but also social marginalization and political exclusion on the basis of group identity. Any plausible conception of egalitarian justice must provide remedies to those who have suffered such discrimination. From the standpoint of egalitarian justice, such protection should apply not just to discrimination on the basis of race and gender but also ethnicity and religion.

The claim here is that individuals should be free to express their identities in part through cultural and religious affiliations and associations without fear of losing their jobs or risking social and political marginalization. This claim can be interpreted as demanding something more than negative liberty, freedom from persecution. It is also a demand for addressing what we might call structural or systemic disadvantage, something that only the broadest definitions of discrimination would capture. Racial and ethnic disadvantages remain pervasive in the United States and other Western democracies such that individual prosecutions of discriminators would not provide an adequate response. In addition to the enforcement of anti-discrimination law, remedies aimed at transforming social, economic, and political structures of inequality are required, including affirmative efforts in public and private employment, the expansion of educational opportunities, and transformation of mainstream institutions and norms.

Consider a world in which there is genuine equality of opportunity in education and employment. In such a world, not only would there be no overt or intentional discrimination against women or racial and ethnic minorities in hiring, pay, and promotions. There would also be no strong racial, ethnic, or gender patterns in the distribution of educational or employment opportunities. We would expect men and women to be equally distributed across all occupations and income brackets, and members of different racial and ethnic groups to pursue different kinds of work at similar rates. Skeptics might argue that women and ethnic minorities are themselves choosing to cluster in certain kinds of jobs in light of their preferences and skills – women in nursing and child-care work, Asian immigrants in convenience store and budget motel businesses – to explain the social division of labor. They might stress that different groups have different attitudes toward different kinds of work and toward material success more generally. Yet, it is by no means clear that inequalities in the distribution of educational and occupational attainment on the basis of race, ethnicity, or gender is the product of choice and not deeper structures and norms of inequality. In the absence of clear evidence that cultural or gender differences map onto existing patterns of stratification in education and the labor market, alternative explanations for group-based inequalities seem just as plausible: histories of discrimination and educational disadvantage, socialization and stereo-typing in favor of certain roles and jobs for certain groups of people, workplace policies modeled on the assumption that each worker has a wife at home, and inadequate child-care provision. Proponents of egali-tarian justice need to be attentive to such factors of structural injustice, not just intentional or overt forms of discrimination, in addressing the claims of ethnic minorities. Such systemic present disadvantage on the basis of race, ethnicity, or gender, usually linked to a long history of discrimination on the basis of group differences, supports a prima facie case for remedy.

Historical injustice

Another circumstance in which differential treatment for minority cul-tural groups is warranted arises from the persistence of the effects of historical injustice. It is plausible that historical injustice is partly causally responsible for the systemic disadvantages that members of some racial and ethnic minority groups suffer today. Despite the difficulty of counter-factual analyses and establishing clear causal links between past injustices committed against certain minority groups and the present disadvantages they suffer, we can explain the disadvantaged status of many aboriginal groups with reference to the long history of conquest, theft, and domi-nation they have suffered.[20] In some cases, the perpetrator of the injustice has been the state. In apologizing for the past policies and practices of the US Bureau of Indian Affairs (BIA), its Assistant Secretary Kevin Gover directly linked past government action with the present disadvantages that Native Americans face.[21] Disadvantages stemming from historical

---

[20] On the difficulties of conducting counterfactuals and making causal links, see Lyons 1977; Elster 1978; Sher 1979 and 1980; Waldron 1992.
[21] Gover 2000.

oppression are in many cases difficult to verify, but where they can be, justice requires special accommodation. This does not mean that members of historically oppressed groups deserve all the rights they currently have or all the claims they demand. Rather, it means that there are grounds for granting some kind of remedy.

As the BIA official's remarks acknowledge, it is hard to deny that historical injustices have ongoing effects on our institutions and social relations, even if it is difficult to make specific causal links. Past injustices committed against Native Americans helped create systemic inequalities, and by failing to rectify them, subsequent generations have helped sustain such inequality. In this sense, the injustice endures. Yet, historical injustice arguments that are based on claims about *causal responsibility* are difficult to make since they rely on establishing causal links between perpetrators and victims. On this strict model of responsibility, one assigns responsibility to a particular agent for a particular state of affairs if his action can be shown to have caused that state. Reparations claims are often grounded on attributing causal responsibility, as well as on moral appraisal of the agent's conduct – whether he intended the outcome, whether he foresaw it, or whether his action violated some standard of reasonable care. We can say that white settlers who expropriated Native American land are causally responsible and morally blameworthy for the harms caused to Native Americans at that time. But if the original white settlers and the Native Americans wronged by them are no longer alive, does anyone bear responsibility for remedying the injustice – what we might call, following David Miller, *remedial responsibility*?[22]

Where we can identify enduring collective agents, such as the state, that have perpetrated injustices, it becomes possible to assign remedial responsibility. Claims about collective responsibility require an account of how the collective is connected to the individuals who constitute it. We might say that the more individual members have the opportunity to shape collective decision-making and the more they are able to identify with the decisions, the more justified we are in assigning collective responsibility to them.[23] In the case of *democratic* political communities, because individual members share a common political culture and have opportunities to influence collective decision-making through a shared set of institutions, there is a stronger case for holding individual members collectively responsible for the actions of their state. On this account of collective responsibility, individual members are not held responsible in terms of their personal complicity with particular acts; rather, they are

---

[22] Miller 2001: 456.   [23] Miller 2004: 262.

held responsible in terms of their political membership for remedying the past wrongs of the state.

Even if we accept this account of collective responsibility, does it make sense to say that collective responsibility can be inherited from one generation to the next? One might object that the fact that no present individual members of a collective are themselves guilty of the past injustices in question gives them a reason to reject any claim for remedies of those injustices. As I emphasized above, holding an enduring collective entity responsible for past injustices does not mean attributing causal responsibility or moral blame to present members of the collective. Rather, it means that present citizens in virtue of their political membership bear collective responsibility for remedying the ongoing effects of past injustices. The rationale here is that present members of the political community should share not only the benefits of the common institutions and practices they have inherited, but also the costs, including responsibility for past injustices committed by those same institutions. In practice, we already honor obligations transgenerationally. States honor past obligations made through treaties and laws established through precedent. American citizens and public officials share a set of political arrangements and ideals established by the US Constitution, and while controversial, states also acknowledge past wrongs through public apologies, as in the BIA apology, or through compensation, as in the case of reparations to Japanese Americans interned during World War II.

I think concerns about historical injustice pervade much current thinking about multicultural politics, although it is not always made explicit. For instance, Kymlicka's distinction between "national minorities" and "ethnic groups" or "immigrants" seems to be based in part on considerations of historical injustice. National minorities are for the most part groups whose homelands were conquered and forcibly incorporated in the past, and their members are, therefore, seen to be entitled to a much more substantial set of rights than members of immigrant ethnic groups. These rights include the right of self-government, veto powers, and land claims. His primary example is aboriginal groups, although he also includes Puerto Ricans, Chicanos, Basques, Bretons, Scots, and Québécois, all of whom have also been victims of state-sponsored discrimination and assimilation.[24] In the case of Chicanos, whom Kymlicka distinguishes from voluntary migrants from Latin American countries, conquest and annexation of what was once their homeland is the

---

[24] Kymlicka 1995: 79, 108–15. As he puts it, the incorporation of national minorities "has typically been involuntary, due to colonization, conquest or the ceding of territory from one imperial power to another" (Kymlicka 2000: 221).

historical injustice that contributes to their status as a historically disadvantaged minority.[25] Although Kymlicka downplays the role of historical considerations in his "equality argument" for multiculturalism, he implicitly relies on backward-looking considerations – in particular, the fact of past oppression through conquest and forcible incorporation.

I think the equality argument's reliance on historical injustice should be made explicit. Focusing on the link between past oppression and present disadvantage allows us to distinguish between different types of claims made in the name of equality. As I discussed above, Kymlicka's luck egalitarian case for multiculturalism aims not only at rectifying structural inequalities stemming from past oppression but rectifying all "unchosen inequalities."[26] But focusing on all unchosen inequalities greatly expands the list of those seen to be entitled to special assistance: not just those born with physical disabilities and those who are religious and cultural minorities not by choice but also those with unchosen expensive tastes for fine wine and caviar and those dissatisfied with their other native endowments, including beauty and physical features or personality traits.[27] Present disadvantage stemming from past oppression is an especially urgent concern of justice. Indeed, I think oppressed groups have a stronger claim, all else being equal, than non-oppressed groups for special protections.[28] This is partly because the inequalities that oppressed groups face tend to be more systemic or pervasive, especially in contrast to the "disadvantages" faced by those with expensive tastes for fine wine and caviar, and it is also because, as I argued above, in democratic political communities citizens bear collective responsibility for systemic disadvantages stemming from past oppression by the state. Inequality that arises from unchosen expensive tastes appears frivolous in contrast to the systemic inequality that stems from past or present oppression. Insofar as individuals continue to suffer the effects of historical injustices on the basis of group membership, they are owed some form of remedy.

What form remedy will take depends on context, including the nature and extent of the present disadvantage linked to historical injustices, what

[25] As historian David Hollinger points out, since the 1970s Latinos have won recognition as a historically disadvantaged minority that has suffered injustices comparable to those suffered by black Americans. These injustices include discrimination by whites "but in the background is a slavery equivalent . . . the annexation of what is now the southwestern section of the United States from Mexico in 1848" (1995: 37).

[26] Kymlicka 1995: 109.

[27] See Anderson 1999: 302. For the argument that membership in minority cultural groups should be viewed as an expensive taste, see G. A. Cohen 1999.

[28] Here I agree with Spinner-Halev's claim that oppressed groups should be "provisionally privileged" over non-oppressed groups when it comes to claims for group rights (2001: 97).

the group actually demands, the extent to which the group's culture is institutionally embodied, and the social and political effects of granting accommodation, among other things. Remedy may take both material and symbolic forms. Symbolic remedies include *public acknowledgment* of historical injustices through apologies, memorials, monuments, and museums. Material remedies include *restitution* of the thing that was originally taken, as in the return of stolen property, or *compensation* through giving money or in-kind payments, such as affirmative action or special legal or constitutional provisions granting self-government rights, land claims, and language rights.[29] There is a symbolic dimension to material remedies in that granting the latter entails public acknowledgment of the past wrongs being remedied. The insistence behind all of these claims is that facing up to historical injustice is crucial to treating present-day members of historically oppressed groups as equals.

This historical injustice argument suggests that some claims of "cultural minorities" – ethnic and national minorities – share with the claims of many racial minorities a basis in histories of oppression and marginalization. The basis of claims for remedy in both cases is mistreatment within a social and political system. This is not to say that race maps neatly onto culture. It doesn't. Race is the product of a history of victimization based on what we now recognize to be biologically superficial differentiations of human groups, and race-based remedies are designed to correct race-based injustices. In contrast, culture, while also a product of historical and political processes, is a shared framework of meaning passed down from generation to generation. Cultural differences are more relevant and can be found more readily across ethnic lines than across racial lines.[30] In addition, the specific remedies sought by racial minority groups may differ markedly from those of ethnic or national minority groups: the former may seek abolition of racial distinctions and race-thinking, whereas the latter may seek increased ethnic or national consciousness and respect for their cultural differences. But we should be careful not to overlook the common ground underlying the demands of both types of groups: both demand remedies for material and symbolic

---

[29] For these and other forms of remedy for historical injustices, see Posner and Vermeule 2003.

[30] For discussion of the relationship between race, ethnicity, and culture, see Hollinger 1995: 3–37. I do not mean to suggest here that race is a category only defined in biological terms and ethnicity defined only in cultural terms, though many today may think of it this way. At different points in history, biology and culture were thought to be virtually indistinguishable, especially under Lamarckian beliefs that acquired characteristics were heritable. On the history of race-thinking and racial categorization in the context of US citizenship law, see Smith 1997.

injustices they have experienced on the basis of their group differences. This is the claim at the heart of the historical injustice argument.

People may suffer invidious discrimination more often on the basis of race than on the basis of ethnicity or nationality. For instance, although Japanese Americans were interned during World War II as Japanese rather than as Asians, it is arguably their Asianness that led to harsher treatment against them in contrast to German or Italian Americans.[31] But this should not lead us to overlook ethnicity- or religion-based discrimination. Many immigrants, including Arab Muslims in North America and Europe, are racial, ethnic, and religious minorities, and it is not always clear that the marginalization or disadvantage they experience is based on any one identity or group membership, as opposed to a combination of them. We can recognize the greater scope and severity of race-based discrimination in certain contexts without dismissing the reality of ethnicity- and religion-based discrimination.

These considerations about historical injustice suggest what is morally relevant about the distinction between aboriginal groups and immigrants such that the former are entitled to a more robust set of entitlements. Aboriginal groups have prima facie rights to self-government not because they happen to have maintained distinct "societal cultures" over time, whereas immigrants do not possess such cultures, as one of Kymlicka's arguments justifying the distinction between national minorities and immigrants suggests. On this political-sociological argument, it is the fact that immigrants have limited institutional capacities to sustain "societal cultures" that justifies denying them self-government rights. But this political-sociological argument ignores the extent to which some immigrant cultures are institutionally embodied.[32] It also arbitrarily excludes those indigenous groups who have suffered more cultural dislocation, such as the Chumash people of California, from political recognition while including those groups that have succeeded in maintaining an institutionally embodied culture, such as the Navajo.

Another argument that Kymlicka offers to justify stronger entitlements for aboriginal groups is an argument from choice: many immigrants chose

---

[31] See Hollinger for this argument (1995: 37).

[32] As Choudhry has argued, Kymlicka's mistake here is to take institutional capacities as factual givens and base his account of just institutions around them when these capacities are in fact highly contingent. In particular, Kymlicka assumes that sovereignty requires a defined territory, overlooking institutional arrangements of deterritorialized sovereignty. See Choudhry (2002: 69–70) for examples, including immigrant communities that run schools, hospitals, nursing homes, media outlets, and voluntary associations, and the proposal that aboriginal peoples who are interspersed in the general population govern themselves with respect to social services, housing, and primary and secondary education.

to migrate and want to integrate, and such consent cancels the option of self-government rights. But this argument suffers from several difficulties. First, as Kymlicka himself acknowledges, it is difficult to draw the line between involuntary refugees and voluntary immigrants in a world with massive economic inequalities and different levels of respect for human rights.[33] Second, even if immigrants have chosen to migrate, it is not clear that they are not, on Kymlicka's argument, entitled to access to their own culture, which he defines as a "primary good" that is ordinarily very difficult to give up and to which all people are entitled. Lastly, while many immigrants may choose to integrate, some may not. On the choice argument, if immigrants refuse integration, then their claim for stronger entitlements would have to be considered.

In contrast to both the political-sociological and choice arguments that Kymlicka offers, on my account, it is the long history of discrimination at the hands of the state that justifies stronger entitlements for aboriginal groups than for many ethnic minorities or immigrants. This approach does not rule out stronger entitlements for some ethnic minorities. Those that have suffered historical injustice would be entitled to special compensation, such as Japanese Americans who were interned during World War II.[34] Non-oppressed ethnic minorities may be entitled to special protections for other reasons, which I consider in the next section, but not by either the present discrimination or historical injustice arguments considered above.

Let us examine the historical injustice argument for aboriginal self-government rights more closely. Proponents of indigenous sovereignty emphasize the importance of viewing indigenous claims against the historical background of the denial of equal sovereign status of indigenous groups, the dispossession of their lands, and the destruction of their cultural practices.[35] This background calls into question the legitimacy of the state's authority over aboriginal people and provides support for

---

[33] Kymlicka 1995: 99.

[34] The US government has offered monetary compensation to Japanese Americans interned by the government during World War II. The compensation was intended less as compensation for material disadvantages that resulted from the internment and more as symbolic acknowledgment of the injustice of internment. Japanese Americans' claims for remedy were successful in part because the causal chain of harm was easy for Japanese Americans to demonstrate since the injustice occurred in the recent past. It also helped that the claimants were easily identifiable and many were still alive (all individuals living in mainland United States in 1942 who were perceived to be of Japanese origin, regardless of citizenship status), and the perpetrators of the wrong were also clearly identifiable (the US government had ordered the internment and its agents had carried out the order). See Howard-Hassmann 2004.

[35] See, e.g., Ivison, Patton, and Saunders 2000; Buchanan 2003: ch. 9; Moore 2005.

the claim that aboriginal groups should enjoy collective self-government rights. Proponents of tribal sovereignty also point to historical agreements, such as the treaty rights of indigenous peoples. But we should be wary of relying decisively on historical agreements since they may have been made under conditions of substantially unequal bargaining power with outcomes severely disadvantaging aboriginal groups.[36] What is central to the historical injustice argument is that indigenous peoples were once self-governing communities and that colonizing powers forcibly incorporated them, depriving them of their institutions of self-government. The claim is that such injustice should be remedied through the restoration of some form of political self-rule.

To call for such remedy based on historical injustices, however, is not to say that aboriginal groups should enjoy absolute sovereignty. On Kymlicka's blend of egalitarian and historical arguments, aboriginal groups are granted virtually unlimited self-government rights. Analogizing national minorities with nation-states, he argues in both cases there is "relatively little scope for legitimate coercive interference." Respecting national minorities' self-government rights may mean exempting them from federal bills of rights and judicial review. Indeed, on his view, the self-government rights accorded to national minority groups is so robust that intervention into these communities is justified only in the case of "gross and systematic violation of human rights, such as slavery or genocide or mass torture and expulsions, just as these are grounds for intervening in foreign countries."[37] This view has troubling consequences from the perspective of vulnerable internal minorities. On Kymlicka's view, religious dissenters within aboriginal groups or Native women who oppose the gender-biased membership rules of their tribes have little recourse other than to exit their tribes, and there is little that the state can do to ensure a genuine right of exit. Spinner-Halev's historical injustice argument for group rights is more explicitly absolutist when it comes to oppressed groups: "when an oppressed group uses its autonomy in a discriminatory way against women it cannot simply be forced to stop this discrimination."[38]

The difficulty here is that aboriginal sovereignty, as with any sovereign authority, cannot be assumed but rather requires defense. On an egalitarian account, political authority must be consistent with protecting the basic rights of individual members. Kymlicka's own egalitarian case for aboriginal sovereignty is contradictory: he holds that self-government

---

[36] On the limits of historical agreements as a basis for minority group rights, see Kymlicka 1995: 116–20.
[37] Ibid. 167–69.   [38] Spinner-Halev 2001: 97.

rights for aboriginal groups are justified on grounds that cultural membership is a crucial good that enables the freedom and supports the self-
respect of individual members, but then in applying his theory, he
defends self-government rights for groups that don't respect the freedom
and self-respect of some members.[39] It is hard to see how a group's
history of oppression can justify its own abuse of vulnerable members
within the group, especially when these vulnerable members appeal to
their rights as democratic citizens in the larger polity in challenging
particular abuses by their group.

In contrast, on my account, sovereignty is limited by a commitment to
protecting the basic rights of individual group members. I do not mean to
suggest that applying federal bills or charters of rights and judicial review
to address the problem of internal minorities is the best or only solution.
As Margaret Moore suggests, many indigenous people may not trust the
domestic court systems of the United States, Canada, and other countries
with aboriginal populations, and as a result, permitting members of
aboriginal groups to appeal to international legal bodies to determine
violations of basic rights and liberties may be more desirable.[40] But we
should not rule out the federal courts as a forum of appeal for members of
aboriginal communities. As we will see in examining the Santa Clara
Pueblo case, some Native Americans see themselves as members of
both their tribe and the United States, and they have sought protection
from abuse by tribal authorities by appealing to the federal courts. I will
pursue these questions further in discussing the Santa Clara Pueblo case
in chapter 5. My point here is that present disadvantage stemming from
historical injustice is one kind of circumstance that provides strong,
though not unlimited, support for claims of aboriginal sovereignty and
other accommodations for historically oppressed groups.

State establishment of culture

A third circumstance that may support a case for cultural accommodation
has to do with the differential impact of state action on different groups.
Even in the absence of present or past discrimination, culture endows
certain activities and experiences with value while putting constraints on
other pursuits. The laws and policies of a society tend to reflect the
dominant culture's values and constraints, and the resulting inequalities
are something short of discrimination in the sense that I have been using
the term. The idea here is that "cultural disadvantage" or marginalization

---

[39] Kymlicka 1995: 163–70.   [40] Moore 2005: 291.

resulting from state establishment of culture must be remedied in order to treat religious and ethnic minorities as equals and to foster their social and political inclusion. We need to consider more closely whether all such cases of cultural disadvantage or marginalization constitute injustice. In my view, cultural accommodation is owed only where state action imposes burdens on interests of fundamental importance.

In multicultural societies, we can easily find patterns of state *support* for some cultural groups over others. Defenders of multiculturalism have made much of this point. The differential impact of state action is a key feature of their case for minority group rights. As Kymlicka and others have stressed, the state can avoid having an established church, but it cannot avoid establishing one language for public schooling and other state services or privileging one religion when it comes to instituting days of rest or public holidays.[41] This "cultural advantage" can translate into economic and political advantage since members of the dominant linguistic and cultural community have a leg up in schools, the workplace, and politics. Cultural advantage also takes a symbolic form. When state action extends symbolic affirmation to some groups and not others in establishing the state language and public symbols and holidays, it has a normalizing effect, suggesting that one group's religion, language, and customs are more valued than those of other groups.

In addition to valuing certain cultures over others, legal and social norms place *constraints* on some cultural groups over others. Consider the case of dress code regulations in public schools or the workplace. Schools and workplaces might ban religious symbols and dress, or they might require certain types of dress. Take, for example, the case of Simcha Goldman, a US Air Force officer, who was also an ordained rabbi. He wore a *yarmulke*, which is part of the Orthodox tradition of covering one's head out of respect to an omnipresent god. Goldman's religious observance conflicted with an Air Force regulation banning the wearing of headgear indoors. When Goldman refused to remove his *yarmulke*, he was threatened with a court martial. He brought a First Amendment claim, alleging discrimination on the basis of religion. The Supreme Court rejected his claim.[42] The constraint that Goldman faced did not stem from the dictates of his religion alone, but rather from the intersection of the demands of religion and the rules of the workplace. Sometimes, the constraints imposed by religion can intersect with the laws or rules of the wider society such that members of some groups face additional constraints beyond direct constraints imposed by religion.

[41] Kymlicka 1995: 111; Carens 2000: 77–78; Patten 2001: 693.
[42] *Goldman* v. *Weinberger*, 475 US 503 (1986).

On Barry's uniform treatment approach, believers themselves are held responsible for bearing the consequences of their beliefs. That would mean that if Goldman wished to continue working as an Air Force officer, he would have to give up an aspect of his religious observance, or otherwise, look for another job. But it is important in such cases to distinguish burdens that are imposed by the religion itself (intrinsic) and burdens that are not essential dictates of religion (extrinsic).[43] Religion may command that believers dress in a certain way (intrinsic burden), not that believers refrain from attending school or going to work. The burden that believers face in such cases does not stem from religion alone, but from the intersection of religious beliefs and particular social and legal norms (extrinsic burden). While intrinsic burdens are not of collective concern (bearing the burdens of the dictates of religion – e.g. prayer, worship, particular dress code – comes with being religious), what about extrinsic burdens? Are they justifiable? They may be burdens that individual believers should bear, but maybe not.

Barry contrasts religious and cultural affiliations with physical disabilities and argues that culture and religion do not constrain us in the way physical disabilities do. In his view, a physical disability supports a strong prima facie claim to compensation because it limits a person's opportunities to engage in activities that others are able to engage in. In contrast, religion and culture may shape one's willingness to *seize* an opportunity, but they do not affect the question of whether one *has* an opportunity. There is, Barry argues, a critical distinction "between limits on the range of opportunities open to people and limits on the choices that they make from within a certain range of opportunities."[44] Justice is concerned only with ensuring equal opportunities and not with equal access to particular choices or outcomes. When it comes to cultural affiliations, they do not limit the *range of opportunities* people enjoy but rather the *choices* they can make within the set of opportunities available to all and, therefore, are not concerns of justice.

But opportunities are not objective in the strong physicalist sense suggested by Barry. The opportunity to do X is not just having the possibility to do X without facing *physical* encumbrances; it is also the possibility of doing X without incurring excessive costs or the risk of such costs.[45] This is not to say that opportunities are completely "subject-dependent." Bhikhu Parekh has argued that opportunity is "subject-dependent" in the sense that "a facility, a resource, or a course of action is just a mute and passive possibility and not an opportunity for an

---

[43] Peter Jones (1994: 38) makes this helpful distinction. See also Miller 2002.
[44] Barry 2001: 37.   [45] For further discussion on this point, see Miller 2002: 51.

individual if she lacks the capacity, the cultural disposition, or the necessary knowledge and resources to take advantage of it."[46] It is true that in
some cases individuals' ability to make use of the particular options
within a range of opportunities is influenced by dispositions and knowledge stemming in part from their religious and cultural backgrounds. But
the problem here is not only that cultural minorities may lack the capacity
or "cultural disposition" to take advantage of a particular opportunity but
also that the law and the cultural commitment conflict in such a way that
the costs for cultural minorities of taking advantage of the opportunity are
prohibitively high.

Where do these considerations about the connection between culture
and opportunity leave us? In contrast to Barry, many multiculturalists
suggest that every case in which a law or policy disparately impacts a
religious or cultural practice constitutes injustice. For instance, Kymlicka
points to the Goldman case and other religion cases, as well as to language
cases, as examples in which "group-specific rights" are required in light of
the differential impact of state action.[47] The argument here is that since
the state cannot achieve complete disestablishment of culture, it must
somehow make it up to citizens who are bearers of minority religious
beliefs and native speakers of other languages. Where complete disestablishment is not possible, one way to ensure fair background conditions is
by providing roughly comparable forms of assistance or recognition to
each of the various languages and religions of citizens. To do nothing
would be to permit injustice. But on the argument I'm developing here,
differential impact does not constitute injustice in every case. The fact of
differential impact alone is not enough to support a claim for accommodation. We need to consider the reasonableness of the claims being made,
and not just the burdensomeness of laws and policies on minority practices. Considerations of reasonableness will depend on what else is at
stake. I will return to this point about reasonableness below.

The prominent multiculturalist presumption that all burdens on religious and cultural affiliations are too severe to be borne by individuals
seems to stem from at least three sources. First is the premise about the
value of cultural membership. On one prominent view, cultural membership is taken to be a fundamental good in virtue of its role in enabling
individual freedom and supporting self-respect. But as I discussed
in chapter 2, these are not the only or even primary reasons that individuals may value culture. There is reasonable disagreement over the
meaning and value of cultural affiliation. For some individuals, cultural

[46] Parekh 2000: 241.   [47] Kymlicka 1995: 108–15.

membership may not only fall short of serving as a "context of choice" but may actually undermine individual self-respect. On Kymlicka's theory, culture's fundamental importance is presumed to be on a par with the unique value attributed to conscientiously motivated practices based on religion. Multiculturalists do not always distinguish religious from more purely cultural claims. For instance, all the examples of what Kymlicka calls "polyethnic rights" are *religious* examples.[48] One reason why culture and religion are easily conflated is that the distinction between them is often blurred in practice. Religious beliefs are shaped by cultural traditions, and cultures are informed by particular religious traditions. For example, the Amish way of life is informed by religion, and Native American religions are shaped by Native cultural practices.[49]

There is, however, an important sense in which religious beliefs and cultural attachments may be different. Both may be central components of people's identities, but the tenets of religion, unlike the demands of cultural affiliation, are matters of conscience and obligation and therefore might be viewed as being of more fundamental importance. One might argue that adherence to a religious belief entails accepting the belief as being of fundamental importance and embracing the commitment to live by its dictates, whereas being a member of a minority cultural group does not necessarily entail accepting one's cultural identity as being of fundamental importance or accepting any commitment to live according to whatever norms are associated with cultural identity. For instance, to be a Catholic is to take up the obligation to follow the tenets of Catholicism, whereas identifying as a Chicano may not entail acceptance of any particular set of norms or actions as matters of fundamental importance. One might counter that speaking Spanish is central to what it means to be Chicano, but there are many Chicanos who do not speak Spanish but express strong attachments to their cultural identity. A case can be made

[48] Most of Kymlicka's examples involve religious practices: Jews and Muslims in Britain who have sought exemptions from Sunday closing laws and humane animal slaughter laws; Sikh men in Canada who have sought exemption from motorcycle helmet laws and from official dress codes of police forces; Orthodox Jews in the United States who have sought the right to wear the *yarmulke* during military service; and Muslim girls in France who have sought exemption from school dress codes so they can wear the *hijab* (1995: 31, 114–15). Shachar also conflates cultural identity groups and what she calls, following Robert Cover, "nomoi communities"; both are defined as groups of people that "share a comprehensive world view that extends to creating a law for the community" (2001: 2, n. 5). But cultural communities do not always constitute comprehensive law-giving communities in the way many religious communities do.

[49] As Lawrence Sager (2000: 195–96) puts it, "[T]he normative distance between religion and culture may not be so very great" since culture often "sits just behind and – in public perception at least – dominates religious belief." He points to *Wisconsin* v. *Yoder*, 406 US 205 (1972) and *Employment Division* v. *Smith*, 494 US 872 (1990) as examples.

that in liberal democratic societies, citizens who view one another as free and equal would accept that matters of religion and conscience ought to be protected by the state. Not religious citizens but all citizens who have fundamental convictions that they take as imposing obligations on them can recognize the importance of state protection of freedom of religion and conscience.[50] This is because citizens would recognize that religious and other moral convictions impose especially demanding requirements on adherents, requirements that are seen as matters of fundamental obligation. In practice, many liberal democracies have accorded special protection to matters of religion and conscience. In the United States, protection of religious freedom is written into the Constitution. As a result, claims for religious accommodation based on disparate impact may enjoy a greater degree of success than more purely cultural claims, and cultural claims cloaked as religious claims may have greater success in gaining recognition.

Yet, we should be careful here about the work we expect the distinction between religion and culture to do, as the distinction is blurred in practice. Many people consider themselves Catholic without adhering to all the tenets of Catholicism, while some aspects of cultural identity may be felt by some as an obligation, something of great normative weight. For instance, speaking French or speaking Tewa may be felt as a duty or commitment by those who identify themselves as Québécois or Santa Claran. The key point here is that insofar as both religion and culture make a variety of demands of varying degrees of importance on members, we need to question rather than assume the importance of the practices – religious or more purely cultural – for which accommodation is sought. We cannot determine in advance of contextual inquiry whether something of fundamental importance is burdened.

A second source for the presumption that law's differential impact is always too much for minority groups to bear is the claim that any burden imposed by law on minority religions and cultures will lead to the extinction of cultural identities and communities. But as I discussed in chapter 2, in a great many cases, cross-cultural encounters lead to the adaptation, not extinction, of cultural identities.

A third, and in my view more convincing, reason for focusing on differential impact is the concern about the vulnerability of members of minority religious and cultural groups to discrimination. Here the focus is on the political and social effects of cultural affiliations, not the nature of cultures. As I argued above, there is a prima facie case for remedying disadvantages stemming from present discrimination or the enduring

---

[50] For elaboration of this argument, see Murray 1993 and Cohen 1998.

legacy of past discrimination. With regard to state establishment of culture, if state action has the effect of reinforcing the marginalized status of religious and cultural minority groups, endangering the basic liberties and opportunities of their members, there is a prima facie case for accommodation. Where possible, this may mean transforming prevailing social norms to incorporate the perspectives and contributions of marginalized groups, as in the case of revising the "canon" of school curricula or providing multilingual ballots and publication of bilingual bus schedules and notifications of public meetings. Where such transformation is not feasible, as in the case of the establishment of a day of rest and Sunday closing laws, there should be a presumption in favor of accommodation through exemption. This does not mean that all social conventions should be revised and all minority claims accommodated, but rather that there is a presumption for giving fair hearing to minority claims.

On the approach I'm defending, then, the question of whether differential impact constitutes injustice depends on additional considerations – about the *kinds of interests* that are burdened and the *purpose of the law* imposing the burden. It is not enough to focus on the burdensomeness of laws and policies on minority groups; we need to ask about the reasonableness of the burdens imposed. Reasonableness requires the willingness to seek fair terms of social cooperation and the acknowledgment that people disagree on fundamental matters of religion and morality which are differently burdened by generally applicable laws. To inquire into reasonableness, evaluation of cultural claims should proceed by a dual test that weighs the group's interest in the burdened practice against the state's interest in the law or policy. First, we must ask about the *impact* of the law or policy on the group. What is the nature of the burden imposed? What is the value of the tradition or practice in question, and what role does it play in defining the group's beliefs or identity? To what extent is this role contested? Does the law have the effect of denying basic liberties and opportunities to members of minority religions and cultures or reinforcing their marginalized status in society? The point of inquiring into differential impact is not to say that every citizen must be equally burdened by every law. Instead, the point is to ask whether the law impinges on something of fundamental interest to some individuals. The second part of the dual test asks about the *rationale* of the law or policy. Is it intended to privilege or burden a particular group? What interest or purpose does it serve? Is it merely a convention that no longer serves a purpose? If the rule serves no legitimate interest, then it should be revised or perhaps even repealed. If the law serves a compelling public interest, then it must be weighed against the group's interest in the tradition or practice that is burdened by the law.

The role of deliberation

This two-part inquiry is best taken up through democratic deliberation. I have offered the arguments from egalitarian justice above to suggest potential parameters and possibilities for public debate, but specific policies and solutions should be decided through deliberation among those governed by the particular rules and policies in question. As I argued above, treating people as equals requires ensuring that they have the opportunity to participate in collective decision-making. Deliberation takes place not only in a range of official political fora, such as legislatures, courtrooms, and electoral campaigns, but also in a range of informal settings in civil society, including political demonstrations, the media, local communities, and cultural associations. Individuals in a democratic society can participate through protest and petitions and speaking out at public hearings and in gatherings within their own communities. Informal deliberation is especially important when it comes to addressing conflicts over minority cultural traditions since members of minority cultural groups tend not to have the same levels of access to official political fora. The inclusion of a range of voices from minority communities is crucial for clarifying what is at stake in cultural conflicts and for devising contextually wise solutions.

Before fleshing out the role of deliberation in addressing cultural conflicts, I want to address some important objections to my attempt to connect democratic deliberation with liberal egalitarian commitments, as well as objections to the ideal of deliberation more generally. Some might interpret liberal and democratic commitments as being at odds. Simply put, a democratic conception of citizenship regards citizens as the ultimate source of political legitimacy, giving them the final say in determining the nature of the political system and the content of policies, whereas on a liberal conception of citizenship, citizens are typically understood as holding certain inalienable rights and liberties, which are not up for debate or reversal in the political process. Cast in these terms, liberalism and democracy are seen to conflict.[51] Many contemporary liberal theorists suggest a view of liberalism as a set of principles that possess a moral standing altogether independent of the democratic process, and when it comes to cultural conflicts, they have tended to evaluate

---

[51] This view has a long history within liberalism, from Madison, Tocqueville, and Mill to the libertarian liberalisms of Robert Nozick and William Riker. See Hamilton, Madison, and Jay 1961: nos. 10, 51; Tocqueville 1966: 246–61; Nozick 1974; Mill 1978; Riker 1982. Some democratic theorists have also emphasized tensions between liberalism and democracy. See, e.g., Wolin 2004: ch. 15.

the claims of culture in terms of their congruence with liberal principles and without any reference to democratic principles or procedures.[52]

Yet, the view of liberalism and democracy as conflicting political traditions masks commitments that are common to both: a commitment to opposing the exercise of arbitrary power and defending individuals against abusive intrusions of authority.[53] To be sure, liberals and democrats tend to diverge on what institutional implications follow from this commitment. Liberals, fearful of tyrannous majorities and viewing government as a key source of domination, typically aim to protect individuals from the realm of collective action. In contrast, democrats seek to structure political institutions to reflect the preferences of the governed; they see collective participation as the best way to protect individual freedom. We should, however, be wary of viewing the liberal and democratic traditions as dichotomous or opposed. As Judith Shklar observed, "liberalism is monogamously, faithfully, and permanently married to democracy."[54] If people cannot exercise their political freedoms, they cannot effectively resist domination and preserve their freedoms. The demands of liberalism and the pursuit of democracy are intimately linked. Some countries combine principles of individual liberty with principles of collective self-government and egalitarianism, and for this reason might properly be called liberal democracies.[55]

Some theorists of deliberative democracy have suggested a specific way of linking liberal and democratic commitments. For deliberation or any political process to contribute to democratic legitimacy, it must meet certain minimal conditions. Public deliberation requires a set of substantive rights and guarantees of the sort that liberal theorists view as fundamental.[56] On the model of deliberation I'm defending here, for deliberative outcomes to be legitimate, individuals must regard one another as free and equal: *free* in that they recognize that no particular comprehensive moral or religious view serves as the defining condition of participation or authorization of the exercise of political power, and *equal* in that they regard one another not just as formally equal in that each is recognized as having equal standing in the political process but also as

---

[52] See, e.g., Kymlicka 1995; Okin 1999; Nussbaum 2000; Barry 2001.

[53] As Nancy Rosenblum puts it, liberalism's central political thesis is "the need to defend individuals and groups against the oppressive demands and intrusions of authority" (1989: 5). See also Ian Shapiro, who defines democracy centrally as "a means for limiting domination" (2003: 51).

[54] Shklar 1989: 37.   [55] Barber 1989: 55.

[56] As David Held puts it, "If one chooses democracy, one must choose to operationalize a radical system of rights and obligations – obligations which follow from the necessity to respect the equal rights of others and to ensure that they enjoy a common structure of political activity" (1996: 318–19).

substantively equal in that their chances to contribute to and influence deliberation are insulated from the existing distribution of power and resources.[57] To be sure, there is disagreement among democratic theorists over the precise content of liberties and guarantees necessary for deliberation, but the disagreement seems to have more to do with *which* substantive constraints there should be rather than *whether* there should be any. Given the inequalities of power and resources that characterize contemporary societies, it is hard to deny that some substantive conditions are necessary for there to be genuinely free and reasonable public deliberation.

The foregoing discussion suggests that rather than being in conflict, the core commitments of liberals and democrats are mutually dependent. Liberalism requires democratic procedures for the realization of its aims, and democracy presupposes substantive commitments that make democratic procedures possible. As a provisional starting point, we might say that the substantive conditions necessary for deliberation include the basic rights of citizenship that I discussed above: not just political liberties but also freedoms of conscience, expression, and association.[58] In addition, measures to ensure that individuals have equal opportunity to contribute to and influence collective decision-making are also necessary, and this requires attention to the resources people have, as well as their capacities for deliberation.[59] Attention to capacities for participation is especially important in culturally diverse societies in which minorities may face linguistic barriers or a lack of familiarity with the needs and ideas that are necessary to formulate reasons accessible to others in intercultural dialogue. Here it is important to think about how individuals might develop deliberative capacities through democratic institutions, including schools, the media, and associations, as well as what sort of influence disadvantaged groups actually have on deliberation. The precise content of guarantees necessary for deliberation can be revisited and revised through deliberation; my point here is that without some minimal conditions ensuring the free and equal standing of participants, the legitimacy of deliberative outcomes is jeopardized.[60]

---

[57] Cohen 1989: 21; Benhabib 1996: 68.

[58] Dahl sees procedural rights, such as rights to voting equality and equal opportunities for effective participation in collective decision-making, as the only rights integral to democracy (1989: 170). Other democratic theorists have gone further, arguing that democracy requires a wider range of substantive guarantees. See, e.g., Cohen 1997 and 1998.

[59] See Cohen 1989: 23; Bohman 1996: 36; Knight and Johnson 1997: 280–81.

[60] Even more minimal models of deliberation explicitly or implicitly rely on rather demanding substantive normative principles that are seen as prerequisites for deliberation. See, e.g., Deveaux who defends a "more minimal" deliberative model centered on "negotiation, bargaining, and compromise" (2003: 791–92). Yet, she notes, "My argument does

In societies characterized by religious and cultural diversity, if individuals are to respect one another as free and equal, they must also offer certain kinds of reasons in criticizing institutions and policies, namely *mutually acceptable reasons*. My aim here is not to provide a generalizable account of what counts as mutually acceptable reasons. This will depend on context. In particular, we should think about what considerations count as reasons against the background of liberal democratic institutions. If individuals recognize one another as free and equal and also accept that there is reasonable disagreement over religious and cultural commitments, then they must offer reasons that go beyond appeals to their own particular interests, commitments, and identities in defending particular outcomes. Instead, they must state how the outcome they favor is in the best interest of all participants in the dialogue. Examples of mutually acceptable reasons in the context of debates on education might include ensuring that students master a certain set of skills, providing a common educational experience for students of diverse backgrounds, or assisting students who are performing least well.[61] To say that participants must offer mutually acceptable reasons is not to place any particular content-based restrictions on reasoning in advance of actual dialogue, nor to say how different reasons should be prioritized by participants. We cannot know in advance of deliberation what claims and perspectives will count as reasons. Adherents of different comprehensive views will have different interpretations of acceptable reasons and how those different reasons are to be prioritized. What is important is that participants appeal to considerations that are recognized by others as having considerable weight, not that they prioritize the reasons in exactly the same way or accept a particular political proposal for the same reason.[62] The view of reasoning

---

presuppose that deliberation about contested cultural practices takes place against the background of a liberal democratic state that protects fundamental rights and freedoms and that prohibits harm or other cruel treatment through criminal laws" (806, n. 55).

[61] Cohen and Rogers 2003: 242.

[62] This model of mutually acceptable reasons is intended to contrast with strong interpretations of the Rawlsian model of public reasoning in which citizens must not only endorse certain political values but also agree on the *weight* or *priority* to be given to those values. For example, in deliberating about whether abortion is permissible, citizens cannot place great weight on the political value of respect for human life while assigning no or little weight to other relevant political values, such as women's freedom and equality. As Rawls puts it, if two people give different weight to different principles, "then their conceptions of justice are different. The assignment of weights is an essential and not a minor part of a conception of justice" (Rawls 1971: 36–37). For an interpretation of Rawls's model of public reasoning as imposing strong constraints, see Freeman 2000: 403–404. For more weakly constrained models of public reasoning of the sort I am defending here, in which citizens appeal to reasons and principles that can be shared by fellow citizens but that don't require citizens to prioritize the reasons in the same way or to accept a particular outcome for the same reasons, see Gutmann and Thompson 1996 and Cohen 1998.

defended here is pluralistic in the sense that participants need not fully share a set of public reasons they regard as authoritative for them as citizens, nor must they aim at consensus.

This model of reasoning faces several important objections, many of which revolve around the concern that it would exclude people's deepest convictions and identities from the realm of public deliberation. This is especially problematic in the context of culturally diverse societies since members of minority groups may be prevented from adequately making claims of justice. Iris Marion Young has charged that the deliberative model of communication tends to privilege stereotypically Western and masculine speaking styles that are "assertive and confrontational" and "dispassionate and disembodied" at the expense of "the speech culture of women and minorities."[63] But the idea of mutually acceptable reasons does not preclude the expression of impassioned modes of discourse of the sort Young discusses, such as rhetoric, storytelling, and greeting. Young is right that such alternative modes may be crucial to allowing members of marginalized groups to elaborate their claims and, in the process, foster better understanding of their needs, interests, and identities. Before justifications for particular outcomes can be given, participants need to know what interests and identities are at stake. But these alternative modes of communication cannot entirely substitute for reasoned argument since they, too, may mirror and reinforce rather than challenge social hierarchies.[64] The powerless do not have a monopoly on rhetoric and storytelling; these alternative communicative modes can also be used by the powerful to ignore or distort the interests of the most vulnerable. These alternative modes of communication should be subject to critical evaluation, just as reasoned arguments are.

Another related worry about establishing any prior constraints on the conduct of public debate has been expressed by James Tully: that there is no way to know in advance what reasons will be acceptable to citizens generally or in what terms such reasons can be presented. In the context of intercultural dialogue, attempting to establish in advance of deliberation certain prior constraints on reasoning could lead toward excluding the perspectives of historically marginalized groups. Tully suggests that in the context of societies characterized by deep diversity, such as Canada and the United States, what he calls the "language of modern constitutionalism" excludes aboriginal voices from deliberation by denying them the opportunity to express the importance of their customs in their own languages and frameworks.[65] The concern seems to be that prior constraints on the deliberative process, however benign their intent, will have

---

[63] Young 1996: 123–24.   [64] Dryzek 2000: 67.   [65] Tully 1995: 71–78.

the effect of preventing some people from making their claims of justice. For instance, aboriginal groups may not be able to make tribal land claims since they must appeal to a distinctive conception of the relation of individuals to land, which may be excluded by prior constraints on reasoning.

The model of reasoning defended here does not attempt to specify in advance of deliberation the content of reasons that will be acceptable to participants. As I said above, it is not my aim to suggest a general account of what counts as mutually acceptable reasons – this will depend on the give and take of actual dialogue. Asking participants to offer mutually acceptable reasons does not preclude appeals to particular identities and traditions by members of aboriginal groups in their efforts to demonstrate the role these attachments play in their lives. The point of endorsing something like the condition of mutually acceptable reasons in the first place is to ensure deliberation that is as inclusive as possible. Asking participants – members of the majority culture, as well as members of minority cultures – to limit themselves to reasons that may be acceptable to others may actually help us overcome what Tully calls "diversity blindness," the failure to see that our own point of view is just one among many reasonable perspectives.[66] If I am not able to rely solely on appeals to my own interests and identities in supporting a particular policy, I must attempt to formulate reasons that can engage others who don't share my interests and identities, and such effort compels me to try to see the issue from other points of view.

To return to the example of the aboriginal land claim, on the model of reasoning defended here, members of aboriginal groups can appeal to their particular attachments and identities to present their claim. I think the Canadian Supreme Court case involving an aboriginal land claim of two related aboriginal groups, the Gitksan and the Wet'suwet'en nations of the northwest coast of Great Turtle Island, suggests that what constitutes mutually acceptable reasons in intercultural dialogue can be more inclusive than critics suggest.[67] Both aboriginal groups in this case insisted on the use of oral histories, totems, and other narrative discourses to explain their understanding of property and provide evidence for their land claims. More radical than the inclusion of oral histories as proof of occupancy was the expansion of the legal definition of property rights to include aboriginal perspectives – systems of property as not simply private and instrumental but also communal and spiritual. By pluralizing the modes of discourse and evidence deemed mutually acceptable, Canada's Supreme Court allowed for more inclusive deliberation. The court

[66] Tully 1994.   [67] *Delgamuukw* v. *the Crown*, 3 SCR 1010 (1997).

recognized the group's claims as being in the best interests of all Canadian citizens, thereby enhancing the legitimacy of its decision. It is not just dialogue itself but a certain kind of dialogue, in which participants attempt to engage others by offering mutually acceptable reasons, which may enable us to overcome "diversity blindness" and attain more legitimate outcomes and greater cross-cultural understanding.

In addition to fostering greater inclusion of cultural minorities, there are also several practical advantages to a deliberative approach. First, deliberation can help clarify the nature of cultural conflicts – both the nature of the interests at stake and the complex sources of conflicts. Cultural conflicts involve both struggles *within* minority cultural communities and struggles *between* cultural communities. Some cultural disputes over family law, land, and group membership laws have more to do, as Monique Deveaux has suggested in the context of discussing South African customary law, "with the concrete interests of members and the distribution of power in communities than they have with differences in moral value" between communities.[68] Or as Jacob Levy puts it, "Catalonia and Castilian Spain, Scotland and England, and the Swiss language and religion groups are all divided over much more ordinary problems than the incommensurability of values they might embody."[69]

Deveaux and Levy are right to suggest that cultural conflicts do not always involve disagreements over moral values, but rather are power struggles over concrete material interests and/or governance structures between different factions within and between communities. And as Deveaux suggests, some cultural conflicts are indeed internal to minority cultural groups, and deliberation can reveal this. We need to be careful here not to overstate the extent to which cultural conflicts are purely internal, or purely about struggles over material interests and not struggles over values. To be sure, politics is about interests and power; more often than not, about people abusing power to advance their interests, which in turn shores up their power. This applies to struggles over traditions and practices within minority communities. But as we'll see in examining the cases in later chapters, many cultural conflicts, including conflicts over gender norms and practices, are also about values and norms, as well as about interests, and such conflicts are not straightforwardly intracultural but often emerge out of intercultural interactions and struggles. The actions of minority group leaders to enforce group loyalty or uniformity in communal norms must be understood in the broader context of external pressures from the mainstream media, schools, or other institutions toward assimilation into mainstream values and beliefs.

[68] Deveaux 2003: 788.   [69] Levy 2000: 104.

Deliberation can clarify both the substance and the source of cultural conflicts.

A second advantage of addressing cultural conflicts through deliberation is that it can expose instances of cross-cultural hypocrisy and foster greater cross-cultural understanding. Deliberation affords members of minority groups the opportunity to challenge the dominant culture's stereotypes about minority groups, as well as point out double standards that the dominant culture or the state may deploy across different groups. Members of the majority culture may oppose minority cultural practices simply because they are unfamiliar to the majority or out of prejudice against particular groups. Deliberation can also provide members of the dominant culture the opportunity to learn the extent to which minority group identities and practices are contested, as well as to be reminded that their own political struggles toward greater equality, including gender equality, are incomplete and ongoing.

Deliberation over cultural conflicts is a two-way street. While the state or employer (or other institution involved in the conflict) bears the burden of justifying the burden imposed on the group, the minority group bears the burden of explaining how a particular law or policy imposes a burden on them. A deliberative approach would require the state or employer to offer justification only if a group makes a reasonable case that such a justification must be made. The group must demonstrate the nature of the interests at stake. To demonstrate the nature of what is at stake, the group may emphasize the religious or cultural significance of the practice in question and argue that the rule in question unfairly burdens their members in ways that it does not burden members of other religious or cultural groups. What counts as sufficiently burdensome such that the group should be accommodated in some way cannot be determined in advance of deliberative inquiry. It will depend on what else is at stake. If the group is able to demonstrate that a tradition or practice is of fundamental importance, then the state or employer must justify the burden by showing that a compelling interest is served by upholding the law. If the state or employer cannot demonstrate a compelling interest, then we need to ask how the burden might be more equitably distributed through some form of accommodation.

This presentation and weighing of reasons from both sides, what some have called balancing, is necessary to determine the extent of a law's burden on religious or cultural exercise.[70] The more important the

---

[70] The centrality test is one way of making such balancing judgments explicit, but inquiry into the centrality of traditions or practices suffers from several difficulties. The centrality test requires having a high degree of confidence in the competence of legislatures or

practice is to the group, the greater the burden imposed by the law or policy. As Laurence Tribe has put it in the context of discussing religion cases, "Clearly a conflict which threatens the very survival of the religion or the core values of a faith poses more serious free exercise problems than does a conflict which merely inconveniences the faithful."[71] American courts already apply heightened scrutiny analysis to laws that burden the free exercise of religion, and in doing so, they implicitly make judgments about the extent of the burden imposed upon religion. Similarly, courts already engage in assessing the validity and importance of identity-related claims in cases involving Native American groups seeking recognition as tribes or making land claims.

The hard cases involve those where a minority group tradition of fundamental importance is burdened by a law that serves a compelling interest. As I have stressed, demonstrating burdensomeness will not by itself suffice to decide a case in the group's favor. The nature of the burden imposed on the group has to be weighed against the compelling interest served by the law. On the egalitarian approach developed here, that certain cultural protections lead to the denial of basic rights of individual members counts as a reason against granting such protections. Even where the group's claim is overridden by a compelling reason, the two-part deliberative inquiry demonstrates respect for minority groups in a way that approaches which disregard the burdensomeness of generally applicable laws and policies do not – in particular, by creating a space for the expression of claims about burdensomeness in terms of appeals to particular attachments and identities.

Something like the two-part deliberative inquiry, focused on both the purpose and the impact of law on different groups, has already been developed in the context of First Amendment free exercise cases in the United States. Examining some of these cases illustrates how rights-respecting accommodationism might be applied to more purely cultural

judiciaries to make this inquiry and engage in fair balancing. In the context of religion cases, courts have refrained from making judgments about centrality out of fear that such judgments would alter religious groups' self-definition or worse, undermine their very survival, as well as out of a concern that courts are ill-equipped to determine what counts as central (Rosenblum 1998: 89–90; Jacobsohn 2003: 272–74). There is also the concern that courts making such inquiries may be biased toward viewing minority religions through the lens of mainstream practices and hence threaten the liberty of religious minorities (Sullivan and Gunther 2004: 1544). Centrality claims in the context of cultural identity are also controversial: they require analysis of historical records, anthropological analysis, and other social scientific means, and such evidence used in legal cases can be partial and misleading (Asch 1992). So the centrality test is limited, but some way of weighing reasons from different sides is still necessary to address free exercise claims (see Laycock 1990: 31; Jacobsohn 2003: 276).

[71] Tribe 1988: 862.

claims, which I take up in Part II. By highlighting legal cases, I do not mean to suggest that deliberation of the claims of religious and cultural minorities is best conducted within the courts. Addressing cultural conflicts in the courts may be second-best to addressing them in legislatures or through informal deliberations within civil society. Indeed, some legal cases have generated or fueled deliberation over minority religious and cultural practices within legislatures and in civil society, so we should not think of legal and deliberative solutions as opposed or mutually exclusive. I focus in the rest of this chapter on court cases in the US context in order to explore how deliberation over minority group claims might be conducted, although a deliberative process in which multiple governing institutions, including a variety of civic and other associations, are included is most desirable.

In the 1963 case, *Sherbert v. Verner*, the Supreme Court held that individuals acting on the basis of religious obligations were entitled to exemptions from otherwise applicable laws, unless the government could demonstrate a "compelling interest" against such exemptions.[72] Sherbert was a Seventh Day Adventist whose beliefs prevented her from working on Saturday, and she was discharged for refusing to work Saturdays. When she applied for unemployment compensation, the state of South Carolina denied her claim on the ground that she was voluntarily unemployed. On appeal, the Supreme Court found in Sherbert's favor, stating that the state's disqualification of Sherbert forced her to choose between religious observance and forfeiting benefits, on the one hand, and abandoning her religion in order to work, on the other. The Court argued that government imposition of such a choice burdened the free exercise of religion in the same way that a fine imposed against her for her Saturday worship would. On the rights-respecting accommodationist approach, this case was rightly decided not only because the burden imposed on Sherbert arose out of a clash between the law and her religious convictions rather than her religious beliefs alone, but also because her basic rights, including her freedom of conscience and economic livelihood, were at stake.

The Court also granted accommodation in the 1972 case, *Wisconsin v. Yoder*. Amish parents who refused to send their children to school after the eighth grade were prosecuted under a Wisconsin law that required school attendance until the age of sixteen. The Amish expressed concern about the "worldly influence" of public schools, arguing that "the values the public schools teach are in marked variance with Amish values and the

---

[72] *Sherbert* v. *Verner*, 374 US 398 (1963).

Amish way of life." Wisconsin countered by stressing the distinction between belief and action: while the state could not burden religious belief, it could regulate religious conduct. The Court found that "in this context belief and action cannot be neatly confined in logic-tight compartments." It asked Wisconsin to provide a compelling reason to justify the burden imposed on the Amish, and finding no such reason, it ruled in favor of accommodation.[73] Critics have argued that there was a compelling justification for the burden imposed by the Wisconsin law: the law aimed to protect the basic rights and opportunities of children – in particular, to foster their critical faculties and ensure their equal access to employment opportunities. Insofar as the accommodation threatens the basic rights of children, it should not be granted.[74]

Since *Yoder*, courts have limited religious accommodation and have moved away from considerations of disparate impact. In 1986, the Supreme Court upheld an Air Force uniform regulation against Goldman's claim, as I discussed above.[75] The Court viewed Goldman's interest in wearing his *yarmulke* as a matter of "desire" and "personal preference," and found the military's interest in uniformity as a reasonable burden on his "desire." But the Court failed to take seriously that what was at stake for Goldman was a matter of religious duty, not a mere preference.

Similarly, in a 1990 case, *Employment Division* v. *Smith*, the Court viewed religious practice as a mere preference in upholding a denial of unemployment benefits to two members of a Native American church who smoked peyote as part of a religious ritual. They were denied unemployment compensation on the grounds that they had lost their jobs as a result of misconduct. Writing for the majority, Justice Antonin Scalia

---

[73] *Wisconsin* v. *Yoder*, 406 US 205 (1972) at 210–11, 220.

[74] Arneson and Shapiro (1996) argue against accommodation on the grounds that the withdrawal of Amish children from public schools before the state-mandated age undermines their basic interests. For the opposing argument that such withdrawal has modest impact in terms of constraining children's liberties and opportunities, see Burtt 1996 and Rosenblum 1998: 101–102. Another point worth emphasizing here is that the Court's reasoning in support of accommodation in this case rested in part on what it saw as congruence between Amish values and American values. As Justice Burger put it, "The Amish communities singularly parallel and reflect many of the virtues of Jefferson's ideal of the 'sturdy yeoman' who would form the basis of what he considered as the ideal of democratic society" (*Yoder* at 225–26). This case offers a striking contrast to the Court's decision on Mormon polygamy in which Mormonism and the American way of life were seen as incompatible and opposed. I discuss this case in ch. 6. My point here is that the fact of congruence itself, if it does exist, is not sufficient to support a case for accommodation; we need to inquire into the justice of the congruent values and norms in question.

[75] *Goldman* v. *Weinberger*, 475 US 503 (1986).

ruled that the free exercise clause does not create a right to exemptions from "neutral, generally applicable laws," such as a ban against peyote use. Instead, he argued, the clause only forbids the government from singling out religious practices and banning them simply because "they are engaged in for religious reasons, or only because of the religious belief that they display."[76] The *Smith* rule is solely concerned with the first part of the test outlined above: the purpose of the law and whether it intends to burden a particular group, not the impact of the law. Currently in the United States any facially neutral law that incidentally but substantially burdens religious practice is presumed to pass constitutional muster under the free exercise clause.

The *Smith* ruling set off a political firestorm, drawing Congress and concerned citizens into public deliberation about how best to balance religious free exercise against the general interests served by laws that burden free exercise. In direct response to the *Smith* ruling, Congress passed the Religious Freedom Restoration Act (hereafter RFRA), showing greater deference to free exercise than the Court and supporting something like the balancing test set forth in *Sherbert*. The law stated that a governmental entity "shall not substantially burden a person's exercise of religion even if the burden results from a rule of general applicability," unless the entity "demonstrates that application of the burden to the person (1) is in furtherance of a compelling governmental interest; and (2) is the least restrictive means of furthering that compelling governmental interest."[77] The act provides for judicial relief for people whose religious exercise has been burdened in violation of this provision.

The *Sherbert* test, echoed in RFRA, comes closer to treating members of minority religious groups as equals. The difficulty of applying such a standard lies in defining what constitutes a "religion," a "substantial burden," and a "compelling state interest." Courts applying this rule would pay a price in terms of efficiency, but Justice Scalia's claim that such a test would require courts to "weigh the social importance of *all* laws against the centrality of *all* religious beliefs" is an exaggeration.[78] Here Scalia is highlighting the hobgoblin of common law adjudication, the slippery slope. It would be a quick slide down the slope from accommodating Goldman's claim to wear a *yarmulke* and Smith's claim to smoke peyote as part of a religious ritual toward Sikhs, Muslims, Rastafarians, and potentially countless others seeking accommodation of their practices.

[76] *Employment Division* v. *Smith*, 494 US 872 (1990) at 881, 877.
[77] Religious Freedom Restoration Act of 1993, 107 Stat. 1488, 42 USC 2000bb *et seq.*
[78] *Smith* at 890 (emphasis mine).

This is a serious concern, but it does not justify denying fair hearing to free exercise claims. This is not to say that every religious minority should win his claim for accommodation, or that courts are always the best place to decide these claims. Rather, the point is that where religious or cultural minority groups demonstrate that something of fundamental importance is at stake, the state or employer must justify the burden imposed. The value of equality is at stake here. An approach that includes a compelling state interest requirement would come closer to treating religious minorities as equals by providing protection against marginalization. As Kathleen Sullivan has emphasized, *Smith's* "big flaw" is that "it entrenches patterns of de facto discrimination against minority religions."[79] Justice Sandra Day O'Connor's opinion in *Smith* seems to acknowledge this when she criticizes the majority for making "the price of an equal place in the civil community" contingent on abandoning one's religious commitments. In her view, "the First Amendment was enacted precisely to protect the rights of those whose religious practices are not shared by the majority and may be viewed with hostility."[80] She argues that only state interests "of the highest order" should override individuals' interest in living their lives in accordance with their religious convictions.[81]

In addition to protection against marginalization, asking the state or employer to justify burdens on religious practice with compelling reasons might also provide more efficacious terms of integration for religious minorities. Improving the status of religious minorities relative to the religious and cultural mainstream could foster a greater sense of inclusion among minorities and thereby facilitate a more integrated political community. For instance, protecting members of the Native American Church from Oregon's drug law might foster greater social and political inclusion of Native Americans by showing respect for their traditions and thereby strengthen the legitimacy of state authority in their eyes.

The balancing of reasons in such cases should be taken up through deliberation, which can help clarify what is at stake for different parties. In some cases, deliberation will reveal that the law is not justified by a

---

[79] Sullivan 1992: 216.   [80] *Smith* at 897, 902.

[81] The Supreme Court overturned RFRA in *City of Boerne* v. *Flores*, 521 US 507 (1997), on the grounds that it exceeded Congress's power. Several members of the Court have argued for reconsidering the rule established in *Smith*. In her dissenting opinion, Justice O'Connor argued that the free exercise clause is "not simply an antidiscrimination principle that protects only against those laws that single out religious practice for unfavorable treatment"; rather, the clause is "best understood as an affirmative guarantee of the right to participate in religious practices and conduct without impermissible governmental interference, even when such conduct conflicts with a neutral, generally applicable law" (*Boerne* at 546).

compelling reason, or was not well formulated in the first place.[82] In other cases, the religious or cultural practice in question may not be of fundamental importance to the group, or even when it is, it may be outweighed by a compelling governmental interest. The hard cases, as I mentioned above, will be those where a compelling state interest is matched by a claim, on the part of the group, that the law burdens a practice that is of great importance to the group. But we cannot know in advance of deliberative inquiry in particular cases what kinds of interests and burdens are at stake.

It is important to emphasize that even where accommodation claims involve religious or cultural practices that are of fundamental importance to the group, it may still be outweighed by a compelling state interest. As I argued above, that a cultural protection threatens the basic rights of some group members is a reason against granting it. This applies to religious associations whose actions undermine the basic rights of women. Currently in the United States religious associations are granted certain exemptions from Title VII of the Civil Rights Act, including the provision that bans sex discrimination. Where the group can show that sex is a "bona fide occupational qualification reasonably necessary to the normal operation of that particular business or enterprise," religious associations are permitted to engage in sex discrimination.[83] Legal skirmishes around this exemption abound: the Salvation Army discharged a female minister after she complained to her superiors and to the Equal Employment Opportunity Commission (EEOC) about receiving lower pay and fewer benefits than comparably situated male ministers; a Catholic university denied tenure to several female teachers in its canon law department because they were women; a Christian school decided not to renew a pregnant teacher's employment contract on the grounds that mothers should stay at home with their preschool-age children.[84]

Insofar as the actions of religious associations undermine the equal rights and opportunities of female members, they should not be accorded accommodations.[85] Eliminating sex discrimination is a compelling state interest, as compelling as some ordinary criminal and civil law from which

---

[82] See, e.g., the city of Hialeah's ban on animal sacrifice, which was publicly expressed to be about animal cruelty but in fact sought to put a stop to a principal form of religious devotion among adherents of the Santeria religion (*Church of the Lukumi Babalu Aye, Inc.* v. *City of Hialeah*, 508 US 520 [1993]).

[83] 42 USC §2000e-2(e) (I) (1994).

[84] *Billie B. McClure* v. *Salvation Army*, 460 F.2d 553 (1972), cert. denied, 409 US 896 (1972); *EEOC and Elizabeth McDonough* v. *Catholic University of America*, 856 F. Supp. 1 (1994), affirmed, 83 F.3d 455 (1996); *Ohio Civil Rights Commission et al.* v. *Dayton Christian Schools, Inc.* 477 US 619 (1986).

[85] See Song 2006.

religious institutions are not exempt.[86] Religious associations are not exempt from laws against race discrimination.[87] Why then should they be exempt from laws against sex discrimination? Both sets of anti-discrimination laws serve the compelling interest of ensuring equal citizenship rights. Where women's citizenship rights are threatened, deference to religious claims should not be granted. The hard cases for those committed to both justice for religious and cultural minorities and justice for women will involve sex-discriminatory religious practices that are at the core of religion. The two-part deliberative inquiry can help clarify which cases are genuinely hard cases. I will examine more purely cultural cases where cultural accommodations conflict with the pursuit of gender equality in Part II. The aim there is to flesh out the rights-respecting accommodationist approach in the context of specific cultural dilemmas.

Before turning to the cases, I want to return to the concern about inequalities in opportunities and capacities for deliberation. This concern applies not just between groups but also within them. If we are to rely on a deliberative approach to addressing the problem of internal minorities, it is crucial that vulnerable members of minority groups have a real say in addressing cultural conflicts. Some members of minority groups, including women, may be denied opportunities to education and extra-familial social interaction necessary for developing capacities for participation, and this puts them at a disadvantage in contesting the prevailing rules or policies of their groups. The state can play a key role in ensuring that vulnerable members of minority groups have a voice in the resolution of cultural conflicts.[88]

One might object to any such role for the state on at least two grounds. First, one might argue that inviting government intervention to strengthen the position of the vulnerable threatens freedom of association, leaving groups vulnerable to domination at the hands of the majority.[89] But government intervention on behalf of a group's more vulnerable members is not straightforwardly a violation of a group's autonomy, for some group members might favor it if their voices could be heard. In any case, state intervention need not abrogate associational autonomy altogether; this is a matter of degree. The government's role

---

[86] For this line of argument, see Sunstein 2001: 217.
[87] See *Bob Jones University* v. *United States*, 461 US 574 (1983), which held that nonprofit private schools that prescribe and enforce racially discriminatory standards on the basis of religious doctrine do not qualify as tax-exempt organizations under the IRS Code, nor are contributions to such schools deductible as charitable contributions.
[88] I discuss some concrete measures for strengthening the position of vulnerable members within minority groups in examining the cases in Part II.
[89] See, e.g., Bader 2005: 335–37.

should be focused on strengthening the position of the vulnerable in decision-making procedures, leaving group members free to determine particular outcomes for themselves. That is, the state must ensure the conditions necessary for women to choose for themselves by protecting their basic rights and liberties, but it should refrain from determining the content of what is chosen. Where there is substantial disagreement over a cultural norm or practice, the state should be wary of granting group leaders the right of private censorship or control. Cultures are contested, and as we'll see in examining the cases, group leaders often have their own interests at stake in supporting particular narratives of culture over others. The state should lean toward an option that recognizes the contested nature of cultural practices. Ensuring that vulnerable internal minorities have a voice in internal decision-making does not mean externally imposing dissent, but rather in a great many cases, permitting already existing dissent to be heard.

A second objection to strengthening the position of internal minorities in deliberative processes has to do with what they would say if given the chance to speak. As Susan Okin asks, if the women of a group say "in large enough numbers and in clear enough terms that they support their group's illiberal norms and practices that seem oppressive to them, what should the state do?" Some liberal approaches would lean toward intervention, regardless of what these women say. As Okin puts it,

> [A] state that values liberalism above all would have no more need to consult with the women of such a group than it need consult with slaves before it insisted upon their emancipation or with workers before it insisted upon their protection from deadly workplace hazards . . . [T]he liberal would stress that basic rights . . . should not be granted or withheld depending on the outcome of democratic procedures.[90]

In contrast, on the deliberative approach I'm defending here, treating minority women at the center of these conflicts as equals requires that they have a voice in the governance of cultural conflicts. As I argued above, genuinely free and reasoned deliberation requires certain substantive conditions, including basic liberties and equal deliberative opportunities. Where such conditions are met, we are less likely to be concerned that women have been forced to endorse traditional group practices. Even in cases where such conditions ensuring fair deliberation are not met, cultural dissent is much more common than Okin suggests, as we'll see in examining the cases. In addition, as a prudential matter, minority women at the center of these conflicts possess the information and familiarity

---

[90] Okin 2005: 86.

with conditions on the ground that enable them to construct contextually appropriate solutions to the problems at hand. What constitutes gender subordination and how best to address it will not always be clear, and even when it is, intervention into minority cultural communities without drawing on the voices of minority women themselves may not best serve their interests. A deliberative approach to the problem of internal minorities requires ensuring that vulnerable internal minorities have real opportunities to participate.

If we take seriously this chapter's egalitarian argument for cultural accommodation, then the case studies examined in the following chapters present genuine dilemmas for those committed to both equality for cultural minorities and equality for women. The aim of these chapters is to flesh out the deliberative approach in the context of a number of specific gendered cultural dilemmas.

Part II

4　The "cultural defense" in American criminal law

In 1984, a 23-year-old Hmong man, Kong Pheng Moua, who had lived in the United States for six years, abducted a 19-year-old Hmong woman from the Fresno City College campus and forced her to have sex with him. The woman, Xeng Xiong, later called the police and accused the defendant of kidnapping and rape. In his defense, Moua claimed that he was performing the traditional Hmong practice of matrimony, "marriage by capture," in which even a woman who is willing to get married should resist in order to establish her virtue. He claimed he had not understood Xiong's resistance as expressing non-consent. The court dismissed the rape and kidnapping charges, and Moua was charged with false imprisonment and sentenced to 120 days in jail and a $1,000 fine.[1]

In another case, a Chinese immigrant, Dong Lu Chen, had resided in New York for one year before discovering that his wife was having an affair. A few weeks after this discovery, he beat and killed her. Drawing upon expert testimony from an anthropologist, Chen's defense stressed that in Chinese culture violent retaliation is an acceptable response to a wife's adultery. He was convicted of second-degree manslaughter and sentenced to five years' probation with no jail time, a much reduced punishment than that usually associated with a second-degree manslaughter conviction.[2]

These cases are examples of what scholars have called the "cultural defense." Although no jurisdiction has formally recognized culture as a defense, it has been raised in many areas of American law in both civil and criminal cases. In civil cases, individuals ask judges to consider cultural traditions in custody battles, in decisions over medical treatment for children, and in employment discrimination cases. In criminal cases, cultural evidence is presented in order to provide insight into the defendant's state of mind. In order to establish guilt under common law, the

---

[1] *Record of Court Proceedings, People v. Moua*, No. 315972-0 (Fresno County Super. Ct. Feb. 7, 1985).
[2] *People v. Chen*, No. 87–7774 (N.Y. Sup. Ct. Dec. 2, 1988).

defendant must be shown to have committed the act itself (*actus reus*) and to have possessed the requisite state of mind (*mens rea*). Cultural evidence in criminal cases has been introduced at various stages: before trial to determine whether to arrest and prosecute; during trial to negate an element of a crime or support an established defense, such as consent or provocation; during sentencing to mitigate punishment; or on appeal to overturn convictions on the grounds that the judge improperly excluded cultural evidence or failed to instruct juries properly on the consideration of cultural evidence.[3] If successful, cultural defenses can reduce or eliminate criminal charges, as well as mitigate punishment. In some cases, they have been used by immigrant men in defense against charges of violent crimes against women.

The two cases above, among others, have been at the center of recent feminist critiques of the cultural defense, as well as multiculturalism more generally. Both legal scholar Doriane Lambelet Coleman and political theorist Susan Okin have discussed these cases to illustrate tensions between cultural accommodation and gender equality, and to argue against the former.[4] While feminists have rightly criticized the use of cultural evidence that leads to differential punishment for immigrant and American defendants, they have neglected another and potentially greater problem: that mainstream legal doctrines themselves are formulated and applied in ways that support gender inequality across cultural communities. Immigrants' claims of cultural defense for actions that harm women seem to be most successful when they resonate with patriarchal norms in the wider society. The problem then is not only the troubling practices of cultural minorities but also mainstream gender norms and practices.

The cultural defense raises a dilemma for egalitarians. Those committed to the pursuit of equal justice for all cannot simply reject or accept it. One might object that such cases do not really illustrate tensions between group rights and gender equality since most theorists of group rights have not explicitly argued for the cultural defense, and many such cases involve immigrants, who are not granted a substantial set of accommodations by the most prominent theories of multiculturalism because they are seen to have chosen to relinquish their cultural ties.[5] It is true that most defenders of multiculturalism have not explicitly defended the cultural defense, but an equality-based case for cultural accommodation suggests a rationale for it. An outright ban would deny immigrant defendants equal access to existing criminal defenses. Many cultural defenses are not claims for

---

[3] For a range of cases, see Renteln 2004.   [4] Coleman 1996; Okin 1998 and 1999.
[5] Kymlicka 1995: 30–31, 113–15; Spinner-Halev 2001: 87.

complete exoneration or exemption from criminal laws but rather are requests for the consideration of cultural evidence in the application of existing criminal defenses, usually to shed light on a defendant's state of mind. For instance, to determine whether someone was honestly mistaken about the facts of a situation requires some understanding of the sorts of facts it is reasonable for people to be mistaken about, or to determine whether someone was reasonably provoked depends on some understanding of the sorts of things that reasonably provoke people. If the defendant's distinctive cultural traditions are deemed irrelevant, then his state of mind, shaped in part by his cultural traditions, is not being given the same weight as other defendants. In order to grant immigrants equal access to judicial defenses available to members of the majority culture, cultural evidence must be permitted.

On the other hand, insofar as that state of mind is shaped by patriarchal norms, allowing cultural evidence to be used to mitigate guilt not only gives legal recognition to patriarchal practices in minority cultures. It also writes deference to patriarchal values into American law more generally, setting precedents for these defenses to be used to mitigate guilt any time a defendant claims to view the world through patriarchal traditions, which remain powerful in American culture as well as minority cultures. If we are committed to both equality for cultural minorities and equality for women, what is the appropriate response?

"Marriage by capture" and the law of rape

In his defense, Kong Pheng Moua claimed that he was performing the traditional Hmong practice of matrimony translated as "marriage by capture" in which even a woman who is willing to get married should resist in order to establish her virtue.[6] He did not present cultural evidence to claim that he did not know that rape was illegal in the United States, nor did he argue that rape was not a category of offense in Hmong culture. Instead, he claimed that he did not understand Xiong's resistance as expressing non-consent. The confusion over whether her resistance was genuine was at the center of Moua's defense.

The prosecutor in the case spoke with members of Xiong's family about Hmong marriage customs and then decided not to charge Moua for kidnapping or rape. As the prosecutor put it, "I went to the victim's family and said, 'How would you resolve this in the old country?' ... The victim's aunt, who spoke English, told me $3,000 and no jail, $2,000 and

---

[6] In addition to California, incidents of "marriage by capture" have been reported in Colorado, Minnesota, and Wisconsin (Goldstein 1986: 135).

60 days, or $1,000 and 90 days, to restore the family honor and pride."[7] Moua's lawyer presented evidence of Hmong marriage customs, emphasizing that a Hmong woman's resistance is an important part of the Hmong courtship custom: "At the last minute the girl must say, 'No, no, I'm not ready,' and the boy must say, 'Baloney, you'll be mine tonight.' If those attitudes were not expressed, the girl would not appear virtuous enough to the man, and he would not appear strong enough to her."[8] Moua's lawyer presented a pamphlet on Hmong dating and marriage practices written by a Hmong man employed at the Laos Community Center in San Bernardino. It contains a brief description of a few types of marriage practices, but it does not use the phrase "marriage by capture," nor does it refer to abduction or rape.[9]

There is disagreement within existing scholarly work on Hmong customs over whether and to what degree Hmong women are able to choose their partners and how prevalent each of the variety of marriage practices is. One type of marriage is arranged by "go-betweens" selected by the families to act as negotiators. The engagement is a contract between the parents of young people.[10] According to two different studies of the Hmong in the United States, arranged marriages appear to be less prevalent than other forms of marriage.[11] The second type is an elopement, where the girl willingly accompanies the boy to his home. The boy sends representatives to inform the girl's parents of what has transpired and to make arrangements for the wedding that will take place three days later, when the couple returns to the bride's family. Elopement usually occurs in the face of parental disapproval of the marriage.[12] In an elopement, the bride's parents have some say in their daughter's choice of mate, but their wishes are less significant than the girl's preferences when these conflict.[13] The third type, called "marriage by capture" involves a boy kidnapping a girl with the help of his friends.[14] This may occur when the boy wants to marry a girl who has little or no interest in him, or if she does, she has not consented to run off with him. The girl is taken to the boy's sleeping area and held captive for three days, during which time "consummation" occurs.[15]

[7] Oliver 1988: 29.   [8] Sherman 1986: 36.
[9] Evans-Pritchard and Renteln 1995: 20–21.   [10] Vang 1982: 34; Thao 1986: 80.
[11] See Dana 1993: 31 and Donnelly 1989: 133.
[12] This type of marriage is called "going to the third day of the third moon" (Vang 1982: 35). See also Rice 2000: 38 and Meredith and Rowe 1986: 123.
[13] Donnelly 1989: 133.
[14] Donnelly translates this practice as "catch-hand marriage" (1989: 142). In Moua's case, this form of marriage was translated as "marriage by capture." Another source translates this practice as "marriage by abduction" (Tsawb 1986: 105).
[15] Tsawb 1986: 105–107.

Moua's defense stressed that in Hmong culture women are always expected to resist advances, blurring the line between "marriage by capture" and "marriage by elopement." Hmong girls "are instructed to be shy and avoid shame by not initiating and acting openly on their desires."[16] Even a willing Hmong bride should express reluctance to be married. Based on her eight-year study of the Hmong community in Seattle, Nancy Donnelly explains that marriage by capture "was generally arranged by the boy and girl beforehand, with the girl conventionally hanging back at the last moment to avoid implied disrespect to her own family. The youth would seize her, she would refuse to cooperate, and he would pull her away with whatever force was necessary. The girl's culturally prescribed prevarication was complemented by the boy's prescribed boldness."[17] During courtship, a Hmong girl is expected to resist, making it hard to discern when her protest is real. Donnelly observes that many first-generation Hmong in the United States were shocked by rape charges brought against Hmong men. If there is any misunderstanding in courtship, it is seen as the girl's responsibility since she is assumed to have invited a man's advances.[18]

Cultural evidence played a decisive role in the Moua case. Judge Gene M. Gomes of the Fresno County Superior Court accepted Moua's plea of guilty to a false imprisonment charge and dismissed the rape and kidnapping charges. Moua was sentenced to 120 days in jail and $1,000 fine, $900 of which was paid to the victim as a form of restitution. Consider the judge's reasoning:

If they do the act that the law declares to be a crime, then they are guilty. With general intent crimes, ignorance of the law is no excuse. Thus the principle of general intent blocks the use of a formal cultural defense, which rests on the argument that ignorance of the law is an excuse. Nonetheless, commission of a general intent crime by a refugee from another culture should not necessarily expose him to the same punishment that a convicted kidnapper and rapist from this culture would receive.[19]

The judge added that culture should be considered as a mitigating factor during sentencing rather than as a "pure defense" at the hearing or trial.[20] While Judge Gomes rejected a "formal" cultural defense, the use of cultural evidence led to a significant reduction in punishment. He took the cultural evidence as saying that Moua did not know what constituted rape under American law, and while the judge stated that ignorance of the

---

[16] Rice 2000: 34.   [17] Donnelly 1989: 142.   [18] Ibid. 141–42.   [19] Sherman 1986: 36.
[20] Ibid. 60.

law is in general no excuse for criminal behavior, he was willing to mitigate Moua's sentence because Moua was "from another culture."

Although the judge stressed cultural difference as the basis for special treatment, if we consider the "wife-capture" case in light of existing defenses in American rape law, we see a cross-cultural commonality in underlying gender norms. Not so long ago in the United States, unless there was obvious evidence of coercion, an American woman charging rape had to convince the court that she had resisted the defendant's advances "to the utmost." In the absence of such resistance, the defendant could claim that he made a "reasonable mistake" as to her consent. Many states have rewritten their laws minimizing the resistance requirement. Rape laws no longer require that women resist "to the utmost"; "reasonable" resistance is supposed to be sufficient. Yet, out of a concern that defendants would have fewer clues as to non-consent after the minimization of the resistance requirement, courts have been more willing than they have in the past to admit a mistake of fact defense. Rape traditionally has involved two elements: force on the part of the perpetrator and lack of consent on the part of the victim. In many states, a defendant charged with rape can raise a "mistake of fact" defense, which allows him to claim that his belief as to the other party's consent was honest and reasonable.[21] Most rape statutes still use some combination of "force," "threats," and "consent" to define the threshold of liability – the line between criminal sex and seduction.[22] In giving meaning to those terms at the threshold of liability, the law of rape continues to draw upon very powerful mainstream norms of male aggressiveness and female passivity.

In rape cases involving the Hmong, male defendants have formally or informally invoked the mistake of fact defense.[23] In Moua's case, the defense lawyer did not explicitly invoke the defense, but in response to the district attorney's assertion that he had "never heard of any other cultures

---

[21] Kadish and Schulhofer 1995: 326–27. See also Estrich 1986: 1094.

[22] Estrich 1986: 1184.

[23] In a 1989 case, a Hmong man invoked a mistake of fact defense and was acquitted of attempted rape. The defendant argued that Hmong women never really say yes to sex; instead they say no when they mean yes (*People* v. *Kue*, No. CR24956 (Ventura County, CA, Mun. Ct. filed July 11, 1989). In a 1991 Colorado case, the family of a 21-year-old man paid an $8,300 bride price for his unwilling 15-year-old cousin. While she was being held in their home, the man attempted to have sex with her. The defendant served no jail time, paid no fine, and performed no community service (McCullen 1991: 6; White 1991: 1). In a 1987 Minnesota case, in which a man abducted a 13-year-old Hmong girl, the prosecutor decided that cultural evidence of resistance by actually consenting women would make it too difficult to prove non-consent to a jury. The defendant's punishment was a $1,000 fine (Oliver 1988: 29).

getting a break because they thought [rape or kidnapping] was okay," Moua's lawyer replied that "in the California culture" defendants have been given some "credit" by the courts and cited a 1975 California case, *People* v. *Mayberry*.[24] This case involved a man who approached a woman at a local store, propositioned her for sex, and demanded that she go back with him to his home. When she refused, he struck her. The store personnel and other customers did not see them. Out of fear, she did not resist his demand to accompany him back to his home, and during the sexual assault at his home, she did not resist. The California Supreme Court reversed Mayberry's kidnapping and rape conviction on the grounds that in the absence of resistance, it was reasonable for him to believe she had consented to sex: "If a defendant entertains a reasonable and bona fide belief that a prosecutrix voluntarily consented to accompany him and to engage in sexual intercourse, it is apparent he does not possess the wrongful intent that is a prerequisite ... to a conviction of either kidnapping ... or rape by means of force or threat."[25]

This case is not an exception. In many states across the United States, intimidation short of physical threats, including pressure used by people in positions of authority over their subordinates, is treated as if it were mere persuasion. In one case, a high school principal who told a student that he would not allow her to graduate if she did not have sex with him was not held in violation of law.[26] In such cases, courts usually say the victim "consented." The vast majority of states have no law requiring courts to accept a verbal refusal at face value.[27] This is because the old idea – that women who say no to sexual advances don't really mean no – is still widely accepted in the majority culture. Some Hmong men may seek to perpetuate cultural practices that reinforce Hmong women's subordination, but the majority culture's own norms of male aggressiveness and female passivity, embodied in American legal doctrine and practice, have offered support for such practices.

"Wife murder" and the doctrine of provocation

In the case where the Chinese immigrant Dong Lu Chen killed his wife after discovering she was having an affair, the Brooklyn District Attorney, Elizabeth Holtzman, charged him with second-degree murder. Chen's

---

[24] *People* v. *Moua*, Record of Court Proceedings, 7, citing *People* v. *Mayberry*, 15 Cal. 3d 143, 542 P.2d 1337 (1975). Evans-Pritchard and Renteln argue that if Moua's lawyer had explicitly invoked a mistake of fact defense, Moua might have been acquitted altogether (1995: 25).
[25] *People* v. *Mayberry* at 1345.   [26] *State* v. *Thompson*, 792 P.2d 1103 (Mont. 1990).
[27] Schulhofer 1998: 11.

lawyer pursued two strategies to get the charge against Chen reduced from murder to manslaughter, and he marshaled cultural evidence in support of both. First, he drew upon the long-standing criminal defense of provocation under New York Penal Law to seek the lesser charge of first-degree or voluntary manslaughter (which carries a penalty of up to twenty-five years in prison), the defense that Chen had "acted under the influence of extreme emotional disturbance." Second, Chen's lawyer also sought to reduce the charge even further to second-degree or involuntary manslaughter (which carries with it a penalty of up to fifteen years in prison) by arguing that Chen had killed his wife involuntarily or unintentionally.[28] To make both arguments, Chen's lawyer used evidence of Chen's cultural background to explain his state of mind. He did not argue that the defendant was insane or irrational under the circumstances, but rather that Chen had acted under cultural forces after being provoked by the discovery of his wife's adultery.

To present the cultural evidence, Chen's attorney called on Hunter College anthropology professor, Burton Pasternak, who testified that in China women are severely punished for adultery. He explained that "in traditional Chinese culture, a wife's adultery is considered proof that a husband has a weak character, making him undesirable even after a divorce," and because of this stigma, a Chinese man could "reasonably be expected to become enraged" upon learning of his wife's infidelity. Pasternak stated that during his six-year stay in China he once saw a cuckold chasing his wife with a meat cleaver, and testified that Chen behaved reasonably for a man "from mainland China." Asked to compare Chen's reaction to his wife's adultery to that of a "reasonable" American husband, the anthropologist stated, "In general terms, I think that one could expect a Chinese to react in a much more volatile, violent way to those circumstances than someone from our own society."[29] He did not cite any cases from modern Chinese law where men had killed adulterous wives, nor did he present any evidence showing that such killings would go unpunished under modern Chinese law. The prosecution thought that the court would deny the use of cultural evidence, and as a result, neither challenged the expert about the cultural evidence nor raised competing cultural evidence.[30] The District Attorney believed the evidence was irrelevant on the ground that "[foreign] customs should not override American law." As the Assistant District Attorney put it, "In our wildest imaginations, we couldn't conjure up a scenario where the judge would believe that anthropological hocus-pocus."[31]

---

[28] Polman 1989: A1.   [29] Sherman 1989: 28; Yen 1989: A3.   [30] Renteln 1993: 480.
[31] Polman 1989: A1.

After considering the evidence, the court granted Chen a reduced charge and sentence on the basis of the cultural evidence. State Supreme Court Justice Edward Pincus noted that Chen's cultural background was integral to the reduction in criminal charges: "Were this crime committed by the defendant as someone who was born and raised in America, or born elsewhere but primarily raised in America, even in the Chinese American community, the Court would have been constrained to find the defendant guilty of manslaughter in the first degree."[32] But Chen was a recent immigrant from mainland China. In the court's view, he "was driven to violence by traditional Chinese values about adultery and loss of manhood" and these values made Chen more "susceptible to cracking under the circumstances."[33] Chen was convicted of second-degree manslaughter and was sentenced to five years' probation with no jail time.

Chen's reduced sentence set off a storm of criticism among Asian American groups and women's organizations. Brooklyn District Attorney Holtzman condemned the decision and filed a complaint with the State of New York Commission on Judicial Conduct asking for an investigation into the judge's decision. Holtzman criticized the sentence, stating, "There should be one standard of justice, not one that depends on the cultural background of the defendant. There may be barbaric customs in various parts of the world, but that cannot excuse criminal conduct here." Barbara Chang, coordinator at the Asian Women's Center in Chinatown, voiced concern about the effects of the decision on the Asian American community, "Our culture does not give a man possession to kill his wife regardless of what the situation was at home. It sends off a very powerful message to batterers in the Asian community: If you're Chinese and you batter or kill your wife, you can get off without any jail."[34]

A similar critique, however, could be made of the legal defense available to mainstream defendants charged with killing their partners. As in the *Moua* case, we find cross-cultural commonality when we consider the *Chen* case in light of the provocation defense for intimate homicide in American law. American men who kill their wives or girlfriends have recourse to a criminal defense that provides reduced charges and punishment. They are not called "cultural defenses," but they rely on deeply rooted cultural understandings about what constitutes reasonable behavior between intimate partners. The "heat of passion" defense in traditional common law or the "extreme emotional disturbance" defense in jurisdictions that have adopted the Model Penal Code is a partial excuse

[32] Volpp 1994: 73.   [33] Spatz 1991: 622.   [34] Trimarchi 1989: 29; Yen 1989: A3.

that mitigates murder to voluntary manslaughter. According to the common law formulation of the provocation defense, an intentional homicide committed in a "sudden rage of passion engendered by adequate provocation, and not the result of malice conceived before the provocation, is voluntary manslaughter."[35] In trying to develop an objective standard of provocation, common law jurisdictions have constructed specific common law categories of "adequate provocation," including aggravated assault or battery, commission of a serious crime against a close relative of the defendant, and the observation of a spouse committing adultery.[36] To deal with the variety of circumstances under which provocation could be raised, judges developed a "reasonable person" standard as an "objective" formula to assess whether certain circumstances were sufficient to have provoked a reasonable person. What distinguishes adultery from other traditional common law categories of provocative events is that it does not involve an actual or threatened physical assault.[37]

The provocation doctrine can be traced back to the seventeenth-century English conception of natural honor. Natural honor was "the good opinion of others founded in the assumption that the person honoured by the good opinion was morally worthy of such esteem and respect ... To treat a man with irreverence, disdain or contempt, to poke fun at him or to accuse him (even in jest) of failing in point of virtue, was, accordingly, to fail to treat him with respect."[38] In the face of a deliberate affront, a "man of honor" was expected to retaliate angrily to demonstrate that he was not a coward. The more serious the offense, the more violent the retaliation was expected to be. One of the most serious affronts to a man's honor was catching his wife in the act of adultery with another man. The cuckold was expected to retaliate violently to defend his honor. The law deemed such violent retaliation to be a rational response and excused the defendant by granting a reduction in charges from murder to manslaughter, which carries a much lighter penalty. The "sight of adultery" category of provocation was the first exception to the older rule requiring physical attack or mutual combat.[39] An early English case, *Regina* v. *Mawgridge* (1707), illustrates the courts' sympathy for the man who reacts violently to his wife's adultery:

[W]hen a man is taken in adultery with another man's wife, if the husband shall stab the adulterer, or knock out his brains, this is bare manslaughter; for jealousy is the rage of man, and adultery is the highest invasion of property ... If a thief comes to rob another, it is lawful to kill him. And if a man comes to rob a man's posterity

---

[35] Perkins and Boyce 1982: 84.   [36] Dressler 1995: 491.
[37] Kadish and Schulhofer 1995: 413.   [38] Horder 1992: 26.
[39] Kaplan, Weisberg, and Binder 1996: 427.

and his family, yet to kill him is manslaughter; so is the law, though it may seem hard, that the killing in the one case should not be as justifiable as the other.[40]

A wife was her husband's property; for another man to have her constituted an invasion of the husband's property and an insult to his honor.

Today, US law no longer treats wives as the property of their husbands, and current formulations of the provocation doctrine have jettisoned the language of honor in favor of "passion" and "extreme emotional disturbance." But the law still provides lenient treatment to cuckolds who kill their partners. The great majority of American jurisdictions follow more open-ended provocation tests than in the past. This has led to two important related changes in provocation law, both favoring defendants: judges are much more likely to give a manslaughter instruction to juries, and juries now consider a wider variety of provoking conduct. About half of American jurisdictions still instruct in terms of "heat of passion," whereas almost twenty states have adopted the Model Penal Code (MPC) standard of "extreme emotional disturbance."[41]

The MPC was written between 1952 and 1962 by an advisory committee of lawyers, judges, and legal scholars assembled by the American Law Institute (ALI). The ALI explicitly rejected the sexist legacy of property law and sought to reformulate voluntary manslaughter in a way that replaced the categorical sexism of the common law with an analysis of an individual's state of mind.[42] The ALI neither intended nor expected that the MPC would be adopted in total anywhere; rather, it hoped that the MPC would compel reevaluation of the penal law in many jurisdictions.[43] In her study of the development and use of the MPC's "extreme emotional disturbance" standard, legal scholar Victoria Nourse finds that the MPC reforms both broadened the range of relationships that might give rise to provocation claims (not just husband–wife but also boyfriend–girlfriend) and the types of conduct that might be classified as infidelity (not just having sexual relations with another but trying to leave a relationship). Many states that base their test on the MPC have amended it substantially such that the great bulk of

---

[40] *Regina* v. *Mawgridge* (1707) Kel. 1, 119, 137, cited in Horder 1992: 39.
[41] Lee 2003: 33, 285.
[42] By jettisoning the category of adultery and considering nontraditional relationships and focusing on defendants' state of mind, reformers thought they were staking out a progressive position on gender issues (Nourse 1997: 1386).
[43] By 1980, some thirty states had adopted revised criminal codes, and another nine had code revisions either underway or completed and awaiting enactment (Kaplan, Weisberg, and Binder 1996: 1157–60).

jurisdictions falls somewhere in between the traditional common law approach and the MPC approach.[44]

The provocation doctrine appears to be gendered in both its formulation and its impact. The substance of the legal rules concerning provocation that juries are asked to apply affects the behavior of all the decision-makers involved in a homicide case. The open-endedness of these rules influences judges in deciding whether to give a provocation instruction and prosecutors in deciding what to charge and what kind of plea bargain to accept. There is ongoing debate about whether current formulations of the provocation doctrine rely on what has been viewed as a masculine model of sudden and temporary loss of self-control: a one-time-only encounter between two men of roughly equal size and strength.[45] In jurisdictions where provocation is formulated in this way, it may be less available to women who are subjected to long-term physical or sexual abuse and who act against their abuser sometime after his last assault or while he is sleeping.

The question of explicit formulation of doctrine aside, what is harder to refute is the starkly disparate impact of the provocation defense along gender lines, which largely benefits men at the expense of women. Approximately 9 percent of homicides in the United States are committed by intimates, which the Department of Justice (DOJ) defines as current or former spouses, boyfriends, or girlfriends. A 1998 DOJ study found that it is increasingly the female rather than the male who are victims in intimate homicides. Men are arrested for more than 90 percent of all homicides, and almost three-fourths of all intimate homicide victims are female.[46] The DOJ data tell us only about the incidence of intimate homicides, not how many of these defendants claimed voluntary manslaughter or whether such claims were successful. But it also appears that men successfully utilize the provocation defense more often than women. As the authors of one criminal law casebook put it, "Indeed, it is hard to find cases where a woman has her charge of punishment mitigated on provocation grounds when she has killed her husband or her husband's lover."[47] Studies which compare women who killed their intimate partners with men who killed their partners have found differences in motives along gender lines: men were motivated by anger evoked by their

---

[44] Nourse 1997: 1331, 1342.
[45] For further discussion, see Crocker 1985; Schulhofer 1990; Maguigan 1991.
[46] Greenfeld et al. 1998: 1, 5, 33; Kaplan, Weisberg, and Binder 1996: 388–89; Rennison 2003: 1.
[47] Kaplan, Weisberg, and Binder 1996: 428. See also Kadish and Schulhofer 1995: 413.

partners' infidelity, whereas women were motivated by self-defense against the physical and psychological abuse of their partners.[48]

In her study of fifteen years of provocation cases, Nourse finds that courts have extended the provocation doctrine to include not just a wife's adultery but also the "infidelity of a fiancée who danced with another, of a girlfriend who decided to date someone else, and of the divorcée found pursuing a new relationship months after the final decree."[49] Juries have returned manslaughter verdicts in cases where the defendant kills his wife and claims "passion" because the victim left, moved the furniture out, planned a divorce, or sought a protective order.[50] According to Nourse, "one is as likely, if not more likely, to find a relationship that has ended, was ending, or in which the victim sought to leave, as one is to find an affair or sexual infidelity alone."[51] The majority of provocation cases analyzed in Nourse's study did not involve sexual infidelity at all; instead, they involved cases in which women attempted to leave the relationships they were in. In many states, current provocation law treats defendants who kill their intimate partners for trying to leave a relationship more favorably than in the past.

The provocation defense continues to operate in a way that reinforces the possessive norms rooted in a code of male honor: a woman's infidelity, which in some jurisdictions includes her attempts to leave a relationship, betrays a loyalty expected of her. American courts have deemed such betrayal to be worthy of compassion and accommodation by the law. This was precisely the logic at the heart of the *Chen* case. Although the defense stressed the cultural differences in the way that an American and Chinese man might respond to adultery, there is a striking cross-cultural similarity in the gender norms at work: a man's violent retaliation against

---

[48] Researchers have found that the most common motivation for men killing their partners is the perception that their partners were rejecting them or their dominance (Barnard *et al.* 1982: 271, 274 and Rasche 1993: 82, 88).

[49] See Nourse 1997: 1333, where she discusses the following cases: *Dixon* v. *State*, 597 S.W. 2d 77 (Ark. 1980) (defendant became enraged when his fiancée danced with another man); *Rodebaugh* v. *State*, 586 A.2d 1203 (Del. 1990) (defendant killed a man who was dating the woman that the defendant had earlier dated); and *State* v. *Wood*, 545 A.2d 1026 (Conn. 1988) (defendant discovered his ex-wife and her new boyfriend after their divorce had become final).

[50] See *State* v. *Little*, 462 A.2d 117 (NH 1983) (defendant was upset because his wife "didn't love [him] anymore" and had rejected his attempts at reconciliation); *State* v. *Reams*, 616 P.2d 498 (Or. Ct. App. 1980), aff'd, 636 P.2d 913 (Or. 1981) (defendant was upset because he had come home to find that his wife had moved out); *People* v. *Guevara*, 521 N.Y.S.2d 292 (NY App. Div. 1987) (defendant was enraged because his wife had filed divorce papers); *Perry* v. *Commonwealth*, 839 S.W.2d 268 (Ky. 1992) (defendant became enraged when a sheriff sought to execute a protective order).

[51] Nourse 1997: 1343.

his female partner's infidelity is deemed a reasonable response, whether committed out of honor, passion, or emotional disturbance.

A qualified defense of the "cultural defense"

How then should we respond to the problems raised by the cultural defense? One response would be to ban cultural defenses altogether. Both Coleman and Okin have called for jettisoning culture from the courtroom on the grounds that such defenses, when successful, have had the effect of denying equal protection of the laws to minority women and children since their assailants receive less punishment or none at all. Barry would most likely agree, in light of his argument that multiculturalist policies "are not in general well designed to advance the values of liberty and equality, and that the implementation of such policies tends to mark a retreat from both."[52] While he does not examine the cultural defense in either the American or English context, he makes a passing comment on the cultural defense: "[I]f I am right in claiming that justice does not require exemptions to accommodate cultural norms, it must follow that it does not require the acquittal of those who break the law, on condition that there are sound reasons for having the law in the first place (a condition that I take to be met by the law prohibiting murder)."[53] These critics have identified part of the problem: simple acceptance of cultural defenses would tolerate oppressive practices within minority cultures. But their conclusion, outright rejection of the cultural defense, is problematic for at least two reasons.

First, jettisoning culture from the courtroom would deny equal treatment to minority defendants by denying them access to existing criminal defenses. What does equality for members of minority cultural groups in such cases require? As I discussed in chapter 3, on one understanding of equality, the law should treat all under its authority similarly. This suggests that minority claims for exemptions or special treatment ought to be denied. As Barry puts it, "Usually ... either the case for the law (or some version of it) is strong enough to rule out exemptions, or the case that can be made for exemptions is strong enough to suggest that there should be no law anyway."[54] Barry suggests that equal treatment requires a ban on the cultural defense. But many cultural claims in criminal defenses, such as the cases considered above, are not claims for complete exoneration or exemptions from criminal laws, but rather requests for the consideration of cultural evidence in the application of existing criminal defenses, such

---

[52] Barry 2001: 12.   [53] Ibid. 334, n. 57.   [54] Ibid. 39.

as "mistake of fact" and "provocation." Minority defendants want to be judged in light of considerations about what, for example, it would be reasonable to be provoked by or to take as constituting consent. Because what it is reasonable to be provoked by or to take as constituting consent varies across cultural contexts, cultural evidence is needed to raise these legal defenses. As Alison Dundes Renteln has argued in defending the cultural defense, the "reasonable man" standard assumes the persona of the dominant culture and is thus "grossly unfair because it means that the provocation defense, which is supposed to be available to all, is a defense only for those who belong to the dominant culture."[55] Simply jettisoning cultural evidence from the courtroom would deny minority defendants equal access to existing criminal defenses and may, therefore, jeopardize their rights to due process and equality before the law. To permit the use of cultural evidence, however, is not to say that it should succeed in every case. I'll say more about this below.

One case that demonstrates the limits of a ban on the cultural defense involves an Afghani refugee living in Maine who was seen by a babysitter kissing the penis of his eighteen-month old son. Mr. Kargar was arrested and prosecuted on the grounds that his conduct fit Maine's statutory definition of "sexual contact," which includes "any act between two persons involving direct physical contact between the genitals of one and the mouth ... of the other."[56] A number of Afghani witnesses testified that kissing an infant son's penis is common in Afghanistan in order to show love for the child and that the kisser's intentions are not sexual. In spite of these testimonies, the court of first instance convicted Kargar. Maine's Supreme Judicial Court ruled that the lower court should have dismissed the prosecution under the state's statutory *de minimus* provision. The use of cultural evidence was crucial to Kargar's defense; without it, he would have lost custody of his child. In a similar sort of case, an Albanian Muslim father was prosecuted for touching his four-year-old daughter in a public gymnasium. An expert witness on Albanian culture testified that the touching was intended to express affection, and Mr. Krasniqi was acquitted. Unfortunately, however, prior to this criminal case, a family court had terminated his parental rights.[57]

A second reason that simple rejection of the cultural defense is problematic is that it would leave unchallenged the majority culture's own patriarchal norms embodied in legal doctrine and practice. As we saw,

---

[55] Renteln 2004: 32.
[56] *State* v. *Kargar*, 679 A.2d 81 (Me. 1996). See Wanderer and Connors 1999: 829.
[57] Renteln 2005: 50–51.

the trouble with the cultural defense has not just to do with minority practices but also with mainstream norms. One might argue for eliminating the extra reduction of charges and punishment that derive from the use of cultural evidence and leave it at that. But this only addresses part of the problem. While cultural defenses have explicitly appealed to cultural *differences*, there is a striking intercultural *congruence* between the gender norms of the majority culture and those of minority cultures. Minority practices such as "marriage by capture" and "wife-murder" resonate with and have found support in the gender norms that pervade the legal doctrines of the dominant culture: that a woman who says no does not really mean no, or that a man's violent retaliation against his partner's infidelity is a "reasonable" response. Thus, even if the extra reduction in punishment based on cultural evidence were eliminated, as Coleman and Okin advocate, the majority culture's own gendered understandings of agency and responsibility would remain. As Anne Phillips has argued in her analysis of the "cultural defense" in English courts, the larger problem with the use of cultural evidence is that they have proved to be the most effective when they resonate with mainstream norms.[58] So long as patriarchal mainstream norms pervade legal doctrine and practice, minority defendants will continue to find support for patriarchal practices from these doctrines. Those committed to the pursuit of gender equality then must not only scrutinize minority practices but also be attentive to such dynamics of intercultural congruence.

The neglect of the problem of congruence stems in part from the assumptions about culture underlying these critics' arguments: that cultures are self-contained wholes and that minority cultures are on the whole more patriarchal than the majority culture. But as we saw in examining the mistake of fact and provocation defenses in American law, patriarchy is a matter of degree, not an either/or, and interactions between majority and minority cultures can reinforce patriarchal norms and practices across cultural communities. Rather than accept the majority culture's gender norms as the baseline standard by which to judge minority cultures, we need to investigate the ways in which the gender norms of majority cultures and those of minority cultures are patriarchal and the ways in which they may be mutually reinforcing.

Another response to the problems raised by the case studies would be to ban the mainstream criminal defenses of provocation and mistake of fact. If such defenses reflect and reinforce patriarchal norms, then they should not be permitted at all, for mainstream or minority defendants.

---

[58] Phillips 2003: 510–31.

For instance, some legal scholars have called for abolishing the provocation defense on the grounds that mitigating charges and punishment in the name of provocation condones male violence against women, treating men as "natural aggressors."[59] In the same spirit, some states have jettisoned the mistake of fact defense in the context of rape law in favor of a strict liability standard. Juries are not asked to consider a defendant's state of mind at all; rather, prosecution turns on proving that the victim did not consent. The state of Massachusetts applies such a standard, holding individuals strictly accountable for obtaining consent from their sexual partners. For example, in *Commonwealth* v. *Ascolillo*, the defendant requested a jury instruction that a reasonable mistake as to consent could be a defense.[60] The victim was an acquaintance, and the defendant claimed to have had consensual sexual relations with her numerous times in the past. The trial judge denied the request to instruct a mistake of fact defense, and the Supreme Judicial Court affirmed the rape conviction, holding that an honest and reasonable mistake as to consent was not a defense against the charge of rape in Massachusetts. Under such a standard, the legal definition of rape could include cases where a person says no but does not physically resist, or where she submits in response to lies or threats. A few states have joined Massachusetts in choosing a strict liability standard on the consent issue, but the majority of states have not.[61]

I think a general ban on the provocation defense in murder cases would be misguided, but a ban on the mistake of fact defense in favor of a strict liability standard in rape cases may be appropriate under certain conditions. Existing defenses to murder and rape need to be reformulated and their application limited so that they are not used to mitigate guilt any time a defendant claims to view the world through patriarchal traditions. Consider first the mistake of fact defense. It is not just the Hmong but also members of the dominant culture who are biased toward thinking that when a woman says no she really means yes. As the legal scholar Susan Estrich has argued, every statute still uses some combination of "force," "threats," and "consent" to define the line between criminal sex and seduction.[62] But in practice, the law of rape reflects and reinforces the still pervasive norms of male aggressiveness and female passivity in the dominant culture of the United States. In light of this, those committed to the pursuit of gender equality might consider something like the following rule in evaluating permissible legal defenses for the charge of rape: the

---

[59] See Horder 1992: 192–94.
[60] *Commonwealth* v. *Ascolillo*, 541 N.E.2d 570 (Mass. 1989).
[61] Kadish and Schulhofer 1995: 326.   [62] Estrich 1986: 1184.

stronger the tendency toward male aggressiveness and female passivity in society, the more the burden of obtaining consent should fall to the more powerful party in the encounter – that is, the party who is better able to avoid the unwanted outcome of a rape charge and conviction.

At the very least, this means that the legal definition of rape, whether phrased in terms of "consent," "force," or "coercion" (or some combination of the three), would include at least those nontraditional rapes where the woman says no but does not physically resist, or where she submits in response to lies or threats, as opposed to physical coercion. In other words, a ban on the mistake of fact defense in favor of a strict liability standard is neither nonsensical nor undesirable. As in the state of Massachusetts, one way to challenge the powerful norms of male aggressiveness and female passivity in heterosexual encounters is for the substantive law to send the message that the more powerful party in the encounter will be held strictly liable for his actions. One common justification for strict liability is that it *ex ante* encourages individuals to exercise caution; the law can play a culture-transforming role by applying the strict liability standard in the context of rape law. This does not mean that rape, nontraditional or otherwise, will or should be easy to prove; the constitutional requirement of proof "beyond a reasonable doubt" may well be difficult to meet in cases where guilt turns on whose account is credited as to what was said and done. But in the absence of a mistake of fact defense, a defendant accused of rape would need to marshal evidence to show the victim consented. He could not appeal to his belief as to the other party's consent, whether based on his cultural understandings, the victim's appearance, or her sexual history.

As for the provocation defense, I think reformulation, not a complete ban, is the appropriate response. As the legal scholar Joshua Dressler has put it, the provocation defense "is about human imperfection, and more specifically, impaired capacity for self-control." The defense recognizes that anger and other emotions, such as fear, can sometimes undermine the self-control of agents. The provocation is understood as giving rise to violent inclinations and undermining the self-control that would otherwise have held those inclinations in check. Dressler concedes that the use of the provocation defense will result in "female-unfriendly outcomes" so long as males, more often than females, externalize their anger when provoked, but he argues that the defense "does not exist to justify or condone male violence or female victimization."[63] We might agree with

---

[63] Dressler 2002: 977, 979.

Dressler that the provocation defense is not intended to condone male violence against women, but it undeniably has the effect of doing so.

The provocation defense can be reformulated in ways that guard against this. The provocation defense consists of two tests: a "subjective" test that asks whether the defendant was provoked to lose his self-control and whether he committed the killing as a result of that loss, and an "objective" test that asks whether the provocation was sufficient to make the reasonable person act as the defendant did. So it is not sufficient that defendants show that they lost self-control and killed as a result of that loss; we need to distinguish cases in which killing as a result of loss of self-control in the face of provocation is reasonable from cases in which it is not.

Victoria Nourse suggests one way of making this distinction in intimate homicide cases.[64] To be granted mitigation of punishment on provocation grounds, the defendant must point to a criminal law (and not simply a widely shared social norm) that shows compassion for his emotion in the face of the provocative act and would justify punishing the decedent for the provocative action. In contrast to the current common law and MPC formulations of provocation, Nourse's test does not focus on the *intensity* of emotion in the face of a provocative act but rather on the *reason* for the emotion, that is, whether the emotion reflects a wrong that the law would independently punish. For example, provocation would not apply to a husband who catches his wife committing adultery since society is no longer willing to punish adultery. On this approach, we would be able to distinguish between a man who kills his wife for trying to leave the relationship and a woman who kills her husband for battering her. In the first case, the provocative act is leaving a relationship: since the law seeks to protect individuals' right to enter and exit relationships and because the man's outrage at his partner's departure does not reflect a wrong that the law would independently punish, the defendant would find no compassion from the law and would be denied the use of the provocation defense. In the second case, the provocative act is physical abuse: since the law condemns domestic violence and because the woman's outrage reflects a wrong that the law would independently punish, the defendant would find compassion from the law and could use the provocation defense.

The law should distinguish between a woman who kills her batterer from a man who kills his partner for trying to leave the relationship. In the case of the woman who kills her batterer, her act expresses outrage at the

---

[64] Nourse 1997: 1390–1406.

wrong of domestic violence, a judgment which the law already recognizes. In this case, we cannot distinguish the defendant's sense of being wronged from the law's own sense of appropriate retribution. But we cannot make the same claim in the case of the man who kills his wife for leaving him. His appeal is based on the idea that leaving deserves outrage, but the law tells us the opposite: leaving a relationship – unlike rape, battery, or robbery – deserves protection rather than punishment. In denying a provocation defense in such cases, the law would rightly say that reasonable men should not kill in these circumstances.

Nourse's reform proposal is worth considering since it takes seriously that the current formulation of the provocation defense reinforces male violence against women. But there are problems with applying the provocation defense based on the *legality* of the provocative act. On the one hand, there are some illegal acts for which we may not want to permit provocation claims. For example, some states still prohibit adultery, but it is not clear that Nourse would want to permit provocation claims to be brought in those states while denying provocation in other states.[65] On the other hand, there are some legal acts for which we may want to permit provocation claims because they are motivated by particular emotions and moral judgments for which the law currently does not but should show compassion. Legal and moral judgments may not always coincide; just because an act is illegal does not always mean that the act in question is morally repugnant. The provocation defense can and should be reformulated in such a way that condemns male violence against women while showing compassion for some emotions. Without protecting some emotions, criminal law contradicts itself. It punishes the very emotions implicit in the law's own judgments that killing and raping are wrong and deserve retribution. The question then becomes: which emotions should the law show sympathy for? This is a complicated issue that must be taken up in public deliberation among citizens and legislators. What I have tried to argue here is that reformulation of the provocation doctrine is both possible and desirable.

If these mainstream legal doctrines were reformulated and applied in ways that challenge rather than reinforce patriarchal norms, then minority defendants should be able to invoke cultural evidence in raising these more general criminal defenses. As I argued above, cultural defenses are required to ensure equal treatment for members of minority cultures. Under current practice, judges often exclude cultural evidence as irrelevant without any consideration. The process by which cultural evidence

---

[65] For example, Arizona criminalizes adultery as a Class 3 misdemeanor (Ariz. Rev. Stat. 13-1408 (2001)).

gets heard and evaluated could be made more systematic. Renteln makes the very sensible suggestion that courts ask three basic questions of defendants who invoke cultural evidence: whether the litigant is actually a member of the ethnic group, whether the group does have such a tradition, and whether the litigant was influenced by the tradition when he acted.[66] To aid this inquiry, state legislatures might devise an evidence rule that instructed prosecutors to include a range of perspectives from within affected communities about the practice in question. Courts might also seek the aid of academics or professionals with knowledge of the cultural groups in question. It is dangerous to rely on any one expert (recall anthropologist Burton Pasternak), but devising a code of ethics for expert witnesses and establishing a community of peer review and accountability on such matters could help counter distortions or abuse of cultural evidence.[67]

In addition to carrying out such factual inquiries, there is a role for deliberation both within the affected communities and among the wider citizenry about whether certain cultural traditions should be permitted to mitigate charges and punishment. While cultural defense cases take place within the courts, the normative questions raised by these cases have sparked public debate among immigrant communities and concerned citizens in local communities, as well as in the media. These cases compel citizens and newcomers toward having conversations about the place of cultural considerations in criminal law. Deliberation can reveal the contested nature of the traditions at the heart of cultural defense cases and also give cultural minorities the opportunity to counter racial and ethnic stereotypes based on uninformed views about their traditions.

Consider the *Moua* case. The prosecutor sought out cultural evidence in a haphazard manner. Drawing primarily on Moua's and Hmong elders' version of courtship customs, the prosecutor decided not to pursue kidnapping or rape charges and decided on the lesser charge of false imprisonment. Moua raised cultural evidence to show that he took Xiong's resistance as part of the courtship ritual and not as expressing genuine non-consent, and some elders of the Hmong community vouched for his position. Moua maintained that "marriage by capture" was indeed a Hmong custom and that he was influenced by the tradition. But even in terms of Hmong understandings of courtship customs, Moua did not act reasonably. On his account of "marriage by capture," no word or act on Xiong's part could have been understood as expressing non-consent.

---

[66] Renteln 2004: 207.
[67] Renteln suggests establishing a code of ethics for expert witnesses to minimize the possibility of the chance they are "hired guns" (2005: 65).

That some members of the Hmong community, including Xiong herself, did not think so, suggests that even on a "reasonable Hmong person" standard (a perspective that understands the meaning and value of the courtship custom), Moua's claim that he was reasonably mistaken as to Xiong's consent would have been questionable at best. He should have known that *some* members of the Hmong community did not approve of or wish to participate in the courtship custom, as it is not the only or primary mode of courtship and marriage. As Xiong's dissent shows, the meaning and importance of "marriage by capture" is contested in the Hmong community. Had the court conducted a more thorough examination of the role that the practice plays in Hmong culture, it may well have found that the importance of the practice to Hmong culture was questionable at best. What if a reasonably wide range of perspectives from the Hmong community were to affirm the importance of the practice, suggesting that Moua's actions were within the bounds of a "reasonable Hmong person" standard? Such consensus is doubtful, but even if it had existed, cultural accommodations should be limited by the protection of the basic rights of individual members of minority groups.

In the *Chen* case, the court failed to ask what if anything "wife murder" had to do with Chinese culture. As Stan Mark, the program director at the Asian American Legal Defense and Education Fund, emphasized at the time of the case, "[Chen's act] has nothing to do with his being Chinese or having a Chinese background. In modern China, under socialist law, it is not acceptable conduct."[68] Had the court assessed the testimony of the lone expert with testimony from other scholars of modern Chinese law and culture, it would have found mixed support at best for the claim that Chinese law and culture show sympathy for someone who kills in response to infidelity. As Wei Luo, a lecturer at the Washington University School of Law, puts it, "There are many contemporary Chinese cases in which husbands killed their wives after discovering their wives committed adultery. If you run a search of '*tonjian shaqi*' (adultery killing wife) on Google or Baidu.com, you will find plenty of such cases. In some of these cases, the husbands were sentenced to life in prison or death with two years' suspension of execution."[69] Contrary to Chen's expert witness, it seems that Chinese courts treat crimes of passion more harshly than American courts do, suggesting that what the *Chen* court called "traditional Chinese values about adultery and loss of manhood" was more a reflection of American stereotypes about

[68] Yen 1989: A3.   [69] Wei Luo, email correspondence, January 31, 2006.

Chinese culture than anything else. This suggests another reason to be worried about the use of cultural evidence: it may jeopardize equal respect for minority cultural groups by creating incentives for particular aggressors to rehearse and reinforce stereotypes about their culture that the majority may already hold. This would especially be true if judges and juries were simply to accept the defendant's interpretation of the minority culture in question, as in the *Chen* case.

This case sparked vocal dissent from members of the Chinese American community. Monona Yin of the Committee against Anti-Asian Violence objected, "Culture informs everything each person does. We are acutely aware of the pressures on an immigrant. But is adultery justification for extreme violence? I would say no."[70] The public dissent of Asian American and women's groups in the aftermath of the case challenges the contention that "wife murder" is a Chinese "tradition." More public discussion like those that followed the *Chen* verdict in the Chinese American community and among public officials and concerned citizens in New York City can help counter monolithic views of Chinese culture and expose the complex interconnections between dominant and minority gender norms.

Potential boomerang effects

Majority norms have influenced the gender norms of minority cultures, but influence can also run in the other direction. The legal accommodation of sexist practices within minority cultures, as in the cultural defense cases, may boomerang back to threaten the struggle toward gender equality within the wider society. This is the interactive dynamic that Okin and Coleman stress in their critique of multiculturalism. In practice, boomerang effects have been limited. Cultural defenses appear to have had mixed success in criminal cases across federal and state jurisdictions, and none, to my knowledge, has been cited in cases involving defendants of the dominant culture. But when courts rule in ways that tolerate sexist practices among immigrants, as some courts have, those cases may well feed back into the majority culture. Such "cultural" cases become potential precedents, and this fact alone means that mainstream law has been reshaped. In seeking a jury instruction of provocation, a mainstream defendant could point to such cases and argue that if immigrants can have access to the provocation defense, then he should, too. It is also important to be attentive to potential boomerang effects for the following reasons.

[70] Yen 1989: A3.

First, although several recent federal cases suggest that the boomerang effect is limited, judges have left the door open to the use of culture in the courts. For instance, in a 2001 case involving a Mexican woman convicted of a drug charge, Judge Richard Posner reversed a reduction in punishment granted by a sentencing judge on the basis of the defendant's "cultural heritage." Maira Bernice Guzman sought a reduced sentence for a drug charge for which she and her boyfriend had been convicted; she sought a reduced sentence on the grounds that "Mexican cultural norms dictated submission to her boyfriend's will."[71] Judge Posner argued that to mitigate punishment on the basis of cultural evidence would be an "abuse of discretion" because the US Sentencing Guidelines prohibit consideration of race, sex, national origin, creed, religion, and socio-economic status in determining sentences. Although "culture" or "ethnicity" is not specified in the guidelines, he suggests that the drafters thought that the stated exclusions encompassed culture and ethnicity. Giving judges leeway to consider "cultural heritage" in sentencing decisions, Judge Posner argued, "would inject enormous subjectivity and variance into a sentencing scheme designed to achieve reasonable objectivity and uniformity." But he leaves the door open to the use of cultural evidence in future sentencing cases, arguing that prohibition would "exclude all possibility of consideration of cultural factors in cases that we cannot yet foresee."[72]

Second, the cultural defense has not been limited to cases where the parties involved are from the same culture. For instance, in *Gonzales* v. *State*, the defendant was convicted of murder for fatally shooting his wife after a heated argument and sought a jury instruction that the situation be assessed from his own perspective, that of "a Hispanic farm worker who was living with a Caucasian woman on a low income."[73] The trial judge rejected the defendant's proposed jury instruction, but this case is, nonetheless, troubling since judges exercise considerable discretion on whether and how cultural evidence gets considered and also because the proposed jury instruction reflects the idea, increasingly made by minority defendants, that equal access to mainstream legal defenses requires consideration of cultural factors, including patriarchal traditions, in explaining a minority defendant's state of mind. This is precisely what a second-generation Japanese American man argued in a recent unpublished California case. Kobayashi sought to overturn his conviction for murdering Sheila Ann Randle, an African American woman with

---

[71] *United States* v. *Guzman*, 236 F.3d 830 (2001). See also *United States* v. *Contreras*, 180 F.3d 1204 (1999); *United States* v. *Natal-Rivera*, 879 F.2d 391 (1989).
[72] *Guzman* at 833–34.   [73] *Gonzales* v. *State*, 689 S.W.2d 900 (Tex. 1985).

whom he had had a relationship. On appeal, he argued that the jury should have been instructed "to evaluate the sufficiency of provocation from the standpoint of a reasonable person in terms of the defendant's position as a Japanese American." The expert psychologist in the case linked the defendant's state of mind with his cultural background: "[I]n Japanese culture, intense shame attaches to males who lack emotional control, who are unable to meet the expectations of others, and who violate their personal standards." Kobayashi argued that "equal treatment of ethnic minority defendants requires that if certain provocative acts are sufficiently offensive in mainstream American culture to reduce murder to manslaughter, then certain acts that are equally provocative in appellant's culture should be treated as equally mitigating." The state appellate court upheld the conviction, sidestepping the question of whether there is an equal protection and due process right to a culturally specific evaluation of the element of provocation, on the grounds that it had not been raised during trial.[74]

Third, while no cultural defense cases have been cited as precedents in cases involving defendants of the dominant culture, one published case has been cited as a precedent in another case, suggesting that "cultural" cases are not always a one-off matter and that boomerang effects can occur across minority groups. A federal appellate court held that cultural evidence may be admitted where it is relevant to the defendant's culpability for the crimes alleged. In this case, a Sikh man, Bains, was convicted as a co-conspirator in the murder of his sister's ex-husband Shergill. Cultural evidence was offered by the prosecution to make the case that Bains was motivated to kill Shergill in part because of his Sikh religion. Several witnesses testified that Sikh families "feel very strongly that a husband must comply with his half of the marriage contract, especially since if a husband leaves his wife, his wife is considered to be 'damaged goods' and an 'unmarketable commodity,' thereby causing the families of both spouses great hardship."[75] The *Bains* court permitted the use of cultural evidence in order to elucidate a possible motive for Bains to have Shergill killed. This case was then cited in a case involving an Indian immigrant, Hundal, who had been convicted of rape and spousal abuse. His wife had used cultural evidence to explain why she had been willing to agree to an arranged marriage and to stay with him despite a history of physical and sexual abuse. Hundal sought to overturn his conviction on the grounds that the prosecutor's stereotypical characterization of "Indian culture" – that "men control women" and "have a higher status

---

[74] *People* v. *Kobayashi*, No. B157685 (Cal. App. 2 Dist. 2003) at 9–11.
[75] *Bains* v. *Cambra*, 204 F. 3d 964 (2000) at 970.

than women" – had denied him a fair trial. The court upheld the conviction on the grounds that the prosecutor's improper questioning had not affected the jury's verdict and that the use of cultural evidence had been entirely proper because the prosecutor's questions about "whether appellant himself thought of the victim as an item of property were relevant to the charges at hand."[76]

In *Bains*, a man sought the admittance of cultural evidence to overturn his conviction for avenging what he understood to be his sister's dishonored status; in *Hundal*, a woman invoked cultural evidence to explain why she did not leave an abusive relationship in bringing a rape charge against her husband. But in both cases, courts permitted juries to consider patriarchal traditions to explain and partially excuse people's behavior. In both cases, juries chose to convict. But prosecutors and judges exercise considerable discretion in whether and how culture gets used in the courtroom, and federal and state jurisdictions have increasingly permitted juries to consider cultural defenses, including evidence of patriarchal cultural traditions, to explain defendants' behavior. In some locales, juries have allowed such defenses to serve as partial excuses for patriarchal behavior among immigrants, and mainstream or other minority defendants can point to these "cultural" cases in raising their own criminal defense claims. Given the increasingly diverse immigrant presence in the United States and the increasing use of cultural defenses, it is important to be attentive to potential boomerang effects, as well as congruence effects.

Conclusion

We saw that the problem raised by some cultural defense cases is not only a problem with minority practices but also with majority norms that offer support for those practices. Immigrants' uses of the cultural defense for actions that harm women seem to be most successful when they resonate with the norms of the wider society. The problem cannot be addressed by a simple ban on the cultural defense since that would deny immigrant defendants equal access to existing legal defenses. Moreover, even if the extra reduction in punishment based on cultural evidence were eliminated, the majority culture's own gendered understandings of agency and responsibility would remain. So long as patriarchal norms pervade legal doctrine and practice, minority defendants will continue to find support for patriarchal practices within mainstream law, and such support may

---

[76] *People* v. *Hundal*, No. F037541 (Cal. App. 5 Dist. 2002) at 6.

have boomerang effects in the wider society. Adequately capturing and responding to the problems raised by the cultural defense then requires reevaluating the majority culture's own norms and policies, alongside minority practices.

The challenges raised by the cultural defense can and do pertain more generally to other contexts beyond criminal law and beyond the United States. So long as the struggle toward equality, including gender equality, in liberal democratic societies is incomplete and ongoing, patriarchal norms will continue to shape the legal and normative frameworks within which minority claims are evaluated. In the next chapter, I continue to explore dynamics of intercultural congruence by examining how majority institutions and norms have shaped aboriginal communities.

5   Tribal sovereignty and the Santa Clara Pueblo case

In 1941, Julia Martinez, a member of the Santa Clara Pueblo, married a Navajo man. The couple and their eight children lived on the Santa Clara Reservation in northern New Mexico, speaking Tewa, the traditional language of the tribe, and practicing Pueblo religion and customs. In 1939, the Santa Clara Pueblo had changed its membership rules in an ordinance. It declared that the children of Santa Clara women who married outside the tribe could not be members, while children of Santa Clara men who married out would be granted membership. The Tribal Council reaffirmed this ordinance in a resolution passed in 1944. In the 1970s, Julia Martinez and her daughter Audrey tried to persuade the tribe to change its membership rules, and when their efforts met without success, they filed a lawsuit under the Indian Civil Rights Act (ICRA).[1] What was at stake for the Martinez family was not only symbolic affirmation as tribal members but also the rights and benefits of tribal membership, including voting rights, land assignments, and housing, education, and healthcare benefits. This case raises questions about the proper basis and limits of tribal sovereignty.

Prominent multiculturalists have endorsed the US Supreme Court's decision to defer to tribal sovereignty over the appeals of some members for intervention. For instance, on Kymlicka's argument for group rights, there is relatively little scope for legitimate coercive interference by democratic states into minority nations, including Native American tribes. As he puts it, "In cases where the national minority is illiberal, this means that the majority will be unable to prevent the violation of individual rights within the minority community. Liberals in the majority group have to learn to live with this, just as they must live with illiberal laws in other countries."[2] As we saw in chapter 3, Kymlicka's theory grants

---

[1] Indian Civil Rights Act of 1968, 25 USC §§1301–41 (1982).
[2] Kymlicka 1995: 167–68. He gives the Santa Clara Pueblo case as an example of a non-liberal minority and suggests that intervention by the state would be illegitimate (165, 233, n. 14).

virtually unlimited sovereignty to aboriginal groups. But as I'll argue, tribal authority, like any legitimate political authority, should not be absolute; ensuring equal protection for individual members is one important limit on tribal sovereignty.

This chapter also examines a related problem that has not received much attention in discussion of this case. Arguments in favor of deferring to tribal sovereignty, including arguments made in federal court decisions and by defenders of multiculturalism, tend to assume that indigenous cultures are distinct, self-contained wholes. Such a view ignores the constructed nature of indigenous cultures, how they have evolved through internal contestation and interactions with the US majority culture. The federal government has played a strong role in shaping Native American identity and membership practices, sometimes in patriarchal ways. In some cases, cultural accommodation in the form of deference to tribal sovereignty has been driven not so much by respect for indigenous difference but by congruence of patriarchal norms across cultures. Such intercultural congruence complicates the demand for sovereignty based on respect for indigenous difference or deep-rooted tribal traditions since indigenous ways of life are a hybrid product of intercultural interactions. The struggles over the Santa Clara Pueblo membership rule flesh out this difficulty.

Tribal sovereignty and gendered rules of tribal membership

Tribal governments have used radically different standards of membership. At least one tribal government enrolls "those with 1/256 Indian blood heritage"; other tribal governments require "one-half quantum from the mother's heritage." Still others follow the US government's long-standing practice of classifying anyone with one-quarter indigenous ancestry as "Indian."[3] In the case of the Santa Clara Pueblo, tribal authorities have held to a patrilineal membership rule, which excludes the children of out-marrying women from tribal membership.

In filing their lawsuit, Julia Martinez was certified to represent the class of all women who are members of the Santa Clara Pueblo and who have intermarried, and her daughter Audrey Martinez was certified as representing the class of all children born to marriages between Santa Clara women and men who are not Santa Clara. They filed a lawsuit under the ICRA, which states that equal protection is a constitutional right of all

---

[3] Wilson 1992: 121.

members of Indian tribes: "[N]o Indian tribe in exercising powers of self-government shall ... deny to any person within its jurisdiction the equal protection of its laws."[4] This case raises the question of what the basis and limits of tribal sovereignty should be.

At least since Chief Justice John Marshall's Supreme Court rulings, the self-government rights of Native American tribes have held a prominent place in US law. As Chief Justice Marshall put it, "The Indian nations had always been considered as distinct, independent political communities ... The constitution, by declaring treaties already made, as well as those to be made, to be the supreme law of the land, has adopted and sanctioned the previous treaties with the Indian nations, and consequently admits their rank among those powers who are capable of making treaties." He went on to emphasize that Indian territory was separated from that of any state by a boundary line established by treaties, that within their boundary they "possessed rights with which no state could interfere," and that the whole power of regulating intercourse with them was vested in the federal government.[5] Although the federal government has gone through cycles of weakening and strengthening tribal authority, Indian tribes have always been recognized as having some measure of sovereignty.[6] Tribal governments enjoy jurisdiction over family law, land use law, and criminal law pertaining to its own members, and they may allow commercial gambling on the tribal reservation regardless of whether the surrounding state permits it.[7]

What justifies tribal sovereignty? Some defend tribal sovereignty on the basis of cultural differences: the claim is that indigenous culture is not only distinct but incommensurable with all other cultures in liberal democracies, and therefore indigenous people should rule themselves.[8] But this cultural difference argument for tribal sovereignty relies on an unrealistic notion of indigenous cultures as self-contained, traditional wholes. As I discussed in chapter 2, such an argument overlooks how indigenous cultures have evolved through internal contestation and intercultural interactions and risks reinforcing entrenched inequalities within aboriginal communities. Other defenders of tribal sovereignty appeal to

---

[4] Indian Civil Rights Act, 25 USC §1302(8) (1982).
[5] *Worcester* v. *State of Georgia*, 31 US 515 (1832) at 559–60.
[6] See O'Brien 1989: chs. 4–5.
[7] Tribal law is incorporated into US law in a manner similar to the incorporation of one state's law by another state. The two legal jurisdictions must grant one another's acts "full faith and credit" and cooperate on jurisdictional matters. Disputes between state and tribal authorities are adjudicated in federal courts, which are obliged to protect tribal authority against interference by the states (Levy 2000: 173).
[8] Ivison, Patton, and Sanders 2000: 9–10.

the notion of "inherent sovereignty." The claim here is that from the moment of first contact Europeans should have recognized indigenous peoples as sovereign nations under the terms of European international law. Native American tribes exercised historical sovereignty over their lands and communities, a sovereignty that was unjustly taken away by conquest and forcible incorporation. The problem with the inherent sovereignty argument is that while a case can be made for the right of self-determination of living members of minority groups, it cannot be based on the putative sovereignty of their ancestors without resting on implausible claims about the timelessness of some collective entity such as the nation or tribe. The notion of prior sovereignty might be more appropriate: tribes possessed their own forms of self-government prior to the arrival of European colonists. This suggests that arguments for sovereignty must address considerations of historical injustice.

As I argued in chapter 3, a more persuasive case for tribal self-government is an argument from historical injustice. On this argument, aboriginal groups are recognized as having had their own institutions of self-government prior to contact with European colonists. Not only did colonists deprive aboriginal peoples of their own governing institutions but they perpetrated numerous other injustices against them. These injustices must somehow be remedied. The backward-looking nature of this argument does not mean that the argument is only about the past; rather, it looks backward in order to understand the causes of and to remedy the systemic disadvantages that aboriginal peoples face today. One way to address present disadvantages stemming from historical injustice is through the restoration of collective self-government rights.[9] But from the perspective of egalitarian justice, tribal authority, as with any political authority, requires justification. The exercise of tribal authority must be consistent with protecting the basic rights of its members. From an egalitarian perspective, just as the authority of the American or European governments should be subject to constraints that protect the basic rights of individual members through domestic bills of rights and judicial review or supranational institutions, the authority of tribal governments should be similarly subject. In the case of tribal authority, the appropriate forum of appeal may be domestic courts, or it may be an international body.

In the case of the Santa Clara Pueblo, a subgroup of tribal members sought to challenge tribal authority in the federal courts. The United States District Court for the District of New Mexico ruled in favor of the tribal

---

[9] For historical injustice arguments for aboriginal self-government rights, see ch. 3. See also Kymlicka 1989: ch. 9 and 1995: ch. 6; Buchanan 2003: ch. 9; Moore 2005.

government, arguing that the Santa Clara membership rule reflected deep-seated patriarchal traditions of the tribe and that undermining tribal decisions over membership would destroy their culture. The District Court argued that the male–female distinction was "rooted in certain traditional values," the patrilineal and patrilocal traditions of the tribe. The court maintained that the equal protection guarantee of the ICRA "should not be construed in a manner which would require or authorize this Court to determine which traditional values will promote cultural survival and should therefore be preserved." Such a determination should be made by the people of Santa Clara "not only because they can best decide what values are important, but also because they must live with the decision every day." The District Court concluded, "To abrogate tribal decisions, particularly in the delicate area of membership, for whatever 'good' reasons, is to destroy cultural identity under the guise of saving it."[10] The court's argument for deferring to tribal sovereignty is based on a concern to preserve indigenous identity, and in making its argument, it assumes that Santa Clara culture is static, isolated, and generally patriarchal, and that extending equal protection to out-marrying Pueblo women would "destroy" Santa Clara identity. Tribal members do have an interest in the preservation of tribal identity, but it is by no means clear that its survival would have been threatened by recognizing the membership of the children of out-marrying women.

On appeal, the Court of Appeals for the Tenth Circuit overturned the District Court ruling, challenging the view of Santa Clara culture as static and patriarchal. The court acknowledged that the tribe had an interest in retaining its culture: "[W]here the tribal tradition is deep-seated and the individual injury is relatively insignificant, courts should be and have been reluctant to order the tribal authority to give way."[11] The court recognized that Congress, in enacting ICRA, did not intend to subject a tribe to identical compulsions as those imposed by the equal protection clause of the US Constitution. But rather than taking the cultural claim at face value, the appellate court examined the cultural traditions of the tribe, questioning to what extent the gender-biased membership rule was integral to Santa Clara culture. The court ruled that the tribal interest in upholding the membership rule was not substantial enough to justify its discriminatory effect for two reasons. First, the membership rule did not rationally identify those persons who were culturally Santa Clara. The Martinez children had grown up with the Santa Clara Pueblo, spoke the

---

[10] *Martinez* v. *Santa Clara Pueblo*, 402 F. Supp. 5 (1975) at 16, 18–19.

[11] *Martinez* v. *Santa Clara Pueblo*, 540 F.2d 1039 (1976) at 1046, quoting *Howlett* v. *Salish and Kootenai Tribes*, 529 F.2d 233 (9th Cir. 1976).

language, and practiced the religion and customs of the Pueblo. In the view of the majority of the court, these practices were sufficient grounds for establishing tribal identity. Second, the membership rule was not part of a long-standing Pueblo tradition but rather, was "of relatively recent origin" and was motivated by "economics and pragmatics." The Tribal Council had acted on the belief that the offspring of mixed marriages would swell the population of the Pueblo and diminish individual shares of tribal property. The court concluded that, insofar as the membership ordinance was motivated by economic considerations, it was "an arbitrary and expedient solution" to the problems that were then confronting the tribe. The gender-biased membership rule constituted "invidious discrimination" and could be sustained only if justified by a "compelling" tribal interest, which the tribe had failed to show.[12] The Santa Clara Pueblo appealed to the Supreme Court.

Writing for the majority, Justice Thurgood Marshall did not address the equal protection issue involving the charge of gender discrimination at all, limiting the Court's consideration to the question of federal authority over tribal policy. Although he acknowledged that Indian nations possess a separate sovereignty that pre-existed the US Constitution and thus falls beyond its constraints, Marshall reasoned that the traditional powers of Indian self-government could be modified or eliminated by Congress. Through its plenary power, Congress could lawfully pass ICRA, which limited the authority of tribal governments. However, ICRA imposed "certain restrictions upon tribal governments similar, but not identical, to those contained in the Bill of Rights and the Fourteenth Amendment." Because Congress sought to protect tribes from "undue interference" by the federal government, the Court argued, the only express appeal remedy that ICRA is seen to provide is the habeas corpus provision, and this did not help the Martinez women because their case did not involve detention by the tribe.[13] As Justice Byron White observed in his dissent, habeas corpus relief is unlikely to be able to address violations of a range of freedoms protected by the US Bill of Rights, including freedom of speech, free exercise of religion, or equal protection.[14]

Although the Court focused on the procedural question of federal review of tribal policy, it went beyond purely procedural considerations by linking the question of tribal jurisdiction with a substantive concern for the maintenance of tribal identity. It argued that if the federal courts were to intervene in tribal decisions, they "may substantially interfere with the

---

[12] *Martinez* v. *Santa Clara Pueblo*, 540 F.2d at 1047–48.
[13] *Santa Clara Pueblo* v. *Martinez*, 436 US 49 (1978) at 63.   [14] Ibid. at 75.

tribe's ability to maintain itself as a culturally and politically distinct entity."[15] Defining who is and is not a member is essential to the maintenance of a group's identity. As the District Court explained: "The importance of this [membership rule] to Santa Clara or to any other Indian tribe cannot be overstressed. In deciding who is and who is not a member, the Pueblo decides what it is that makes its members unique, what distinguishes a Santa Clara Indian from everyone else in the United States."[16] The implication here is that sole jurisdiction over membership rules is necessary to ensure cultural survival. As Justice Marshall wrote, they remain "a separate people, with the power of regulating their internal and social relations."[17] The Court concluded that no cause of action existed for the equal protection claim raised by the Martinezes, and therefore the federal courts could not hear the discrimination charge.

Members of the Martinez family considered themselves members of two political communities, and they appealed to the larger political community to have their equal civic status within the minority community recognized.[18] At stake was not just recognition as tribal members but the material benefits that stem from tribal membership. Tribal sovereignty, like any political authority, should have limits. One important limit is ensuring the basic rights of all citizens. In deferring to tribal sovereignty in this case, the Court failed to uphold the civic equality of a particular class of Santa Clara women and their children. It did so in part on the basis of an argument about the threat of extinction. As we will see below, it is highly debatable at best that inclusion of the children of out-marrying female members would undermine the ability of the Pueblo to maintain itself. In addition to the equal protection argument, another reason supports the case for reforming the tribal membership rule: the rule did not emerge solely from within Santa Clara traditions but out of interactions between tribal authorities and the federal government.

The state's role in the politics of tradition formation

Rather than taking cultural practices at face value, we need to inquire into what Uma Narayan has called the "politics of tradition formation."[19] We need to ask how and why a particular practice came to be regarded as a central tradition of the group. Aboriginal traditions, as with any group's

[15] Ibid. at 72.   [16] *Martinez v. Santa Clara Pueblo*, 402 F. Supp. at 15.
[17] *Santa Clara Pueblo v. Martinez*, 436 US at 56, quoting *United States v. Kagama*, 118 US 375 (1886) at 381–82.
[18] Congress extended citizenship to all Native Americans in 1924. See Act of June 2, 1924, ch. 233, 43 Stat. 253.
[19] Narayan 1997: 61.

traditions, are the product of complex social and political dynamics both among members of the tribe and between the tribe and the state. Rather than taking the status of a "tradition" for granted, we need to understand the historical and political processes that enabled it to acquire this status.

Throughout its history, the US government has played a role in redefining gender relations within Native American communities in both direct and indirect ways. From their very first interactions, Christian settlers, missionaries, and government officials disparaged Native men for their lack of manliness on the grounds that they did not command their wives and children as heads of households. Native American marriage customs were viewed as completely foreign. As one government official reported to the Office of Indian Affairs, "some of the Indians have several wives, who sometimes live in different towns, and at considerable distance from each other; they are allowed by the Indian to own property not subject to their husbands."[20] In an attempt to "civilize" Native Americans, the federal government, often collaborating with evangelical Protestant missionaries, urged or forced Christian-model monogamy on Native communities.[21] Political and religious officials contended that the first step in assimilating Native Americans was establishing monogamous marriage, from which the conventional sexual division of labor, property, and inheritance would follow.

At least since the Dawes Severalty Act of 1887, the federal government has linked citizenship to gender. The law authorized the dissolution of the collective ownership of most tribal lands and forced Native Americans to accept a system of private property in which land was allotted to male heads of households. The act also established procedures for conferring US citizenship upon the male heads of households who accepted the allotments.[22] As one senator put it, Congress enacted this policy on the principle that "a home of his own" for "each head of a family" was "the way to start a people in the direction of civilization." Against the cultural traditions of many Native communities, patronymic family surnames were assigned to keep identification and property succession clear.[23] In short, the government tried to prepare Native men for citizenship by making them follow in the footsteps of men of the majority culture: they were made heads of households, legal husbands, and property-owners. The act had the anticipated effect of weakening the communal way of life

---

[20] Quoted from southwestern state court cases in Johnston 1929: 25–26.
[21] Prucha 1984: 135–48, 151.
[22] *Congressional Record*, 49: 2, vol. 17, Feb. 19, 1886, 1630–33; vol. 18, Dec. 5, 1886, 189–90.
[23] Cott 2000: 123.

among Native Americans by securing individual property-ownership. It also subverted Native American women's roles in agricultural work by instituting Native American men as landowners and farmers.

In 1928, a group called the Institute for Government Research issued a report criticizing the allotment program.[24] This report contributed toward a growing debate about federal Indian policy. In 1934, Congress passed the Indian Reorganization Act (IRA).[25] This act halted allotment and required the Secretary of the Interior to restore "surplus" tribal lands acquired during allotment. In the act, Congress declared its support for Indian self-governance and provided for the creation of tribal constitutions and laws. The act allowed Native Americans to refuse to organize under its provisions, and some groups, including the Navajos and some other Pueblo communities, have not done so.[26] The IRA also allowed for the imposition of the majority culture's gender norms upon Native American communities. John Collier, an anthropologist who became head of the Bureau of Indian Affairs and the architect of the IRA, designated Native men as tribal leaders and virtually disenfranchised Native women. The matriarchal, matrilocal, and matrilineal character of some Native communities was neither acceptable nor comprehensible to members of the dominant culture.[27]

The Santa Clara Pueblo was among the first tribes that established a constitution under the provisions of the IRA. In 1935, the US Secretary of Interior approved the Santa Clara Pueblo's Constitution and Bylaws.[28] Under the 1935 constitution, membership in the Santa Clara Pueblo extended to four groups of people: those "of Indian blood" whose names appeared on the 1935 census roll; all "persons born of parents both of whom are members of the Santa Clara Pueblo"; all "children of mixed marriages between members of the Santa Clara Pueblo and non-members, provided such children have been recognized and adopted by the council"; and all "persons naturalized as members of the pueblo." The 1935 membership provision did not make any gender-based distinctions. The Santa Clara Pueblo Constitution provided for amendment, subject to approval by the Secretary of the Interior.

Four years after its constitution was established, the Santa Clara Tribal Council amended its membership rules. The 1939 membership

[24] Canby 1988: 21.
[25] Indian Reorganization Act (IRA), 48 Stat. 984 (1934), codified as amendment at 25 USC §461 et seq. (1982).
[26] Philp 1977: 163.   [27] Green 1980: 250, 253.
[28] Constitution and Bylaws of the Pueblo of Santa Clara, New Mexico, approved December 20, 1935, reprinted in Supreme Court Brief of the Petitioners, Santa Clara Pueblo v. Martinez, No. 76–682, Appendix (Oct. Term, 1976).

ordinance stated, "[C]hildren born of marriages between female members of the Santa Clara Pueblo and non-members shall not be members," and "[p]ersons shall not be naturalized as members of the Santa Clara Pueblo under any circumstances."[29] Only two groups were eligible for membership in the Santa Clara Pueblo: all children born of marriages between members of the Santa Clara Pueblo, and children born of marriages between male members of the Santa Clara Pueblo and non-members. In 1944, the Tribal Council affirmed the gender-biased membership ordinance with a resolution, declaring "[t]hat all children of mixed marriages between female members of Santa Clara and non-members be shown as not enrolled in the Santa Clara census rolls if they are listed on such rolls."[30]

In considering these gender-biased amendments to the Pueblo membership rule, it is important to ask about the history of the tribal rule in order to understand whether federal intervention would destroy cultural identity, as the federal district court ruling suggested it would. If the Santa Clara Pueblo membership rule did not arise solely from tribal traditions but out of the tribe's interactions with the dominant culture and the federal government, then it becomes more difficult to argue for deferring to the tribal rule in the name of respecting tribal tradition. In inquiring into the history of the Pueblo membership rules, the District Court found that, prior to the 1939 amendment, there had been no "hard and fast rule" about the treatment of mixed marriages but rather case-by-case decision-making.[31] The appellate court contended that the membership ordinance was "the product of economics and pragmatics" and "historically ... cannot be said to represent the Santa Clara tradition."[32] Some current Santa Clara members insist that prior to 1935 membership rules were ad hoc. As Paul Tafoya, who was governor of the Santa Clara Pueblo at the time of the Martinez trial, puts it, "Membership was wide open then. There were no rules and regulations written down. We really can't say that the rules were definitely patrilineal or not. Hispanics, including a lot of men, had migrated into the Pueblo. They married in and became members. In fact, the Governor and Lieutenant Governor who signed the 1939 membership restriction into law were both naturalized into the Pueblo."[33]

Anthropologists have presented conflicting information about the gendered nature of Pueblo traditions. One anthropologist testified in the

---

[29] "Ordinance," Dec. 15, 1939, on file with the author.
[30] "Resolution of the Santa Clara Pueblo," Feb. 27, 1944, on file with the author.
[31] *Martinez* v. *Romney*, 402 F. Supp. at 16.
[32] *Martinez* v. *Santa Clara Pueblo*, 540 F.2d at 1047.
[33] Paul Tafoya, Interview by author, Mar. 14, 2006.

Martinez case that the Santa Clara Pueblo was a patrilineal community, but she noted that sexual equality was a general trait of a variety of tribes in New Mexico.[34] Another anthropologist, Elsie Clew Parsons, contended, "Distinctions of sex are marked in the Pueblo culture, in dress, in occupations, and in ceremonial life. The distinctions are a matter of division of functions between the sexes rather than of subordination of one sex to another."[35] She detailed a less rigid sexual division of labor among the Pueblo in which men and women reversed roles on some occasions, leading her to conclude that sex-based role differentiation "appear[ed] to count very little if at all in their personal relations, but in their preoccupations it is all controlling."[36] In contrast, another scholar argued that "women were considered second-class citizens at Santa Clara Pueblo" and that the male Pueblo members wanted to discourage women from marrying men who are not Santa Clara.[37] Although the kinship systems of the Pueblos had traditionally been organized along matrilineal lines, by the turn of the twentieth century, the Eastern Pueblos, including the Santa Clara Pueblo, were no longer organized straightforwardly in matrilineal terms. Partly as a result of the efforts of Spanish colonists and Franciscan friars to break down the Pueblos' matrilineal kinship patterns, by the late nineteenth century, the Eastern Pueblos no longer organized matrilineally. Anthropologist and Santa Clara Pueblo member Edward Dozier maintains that the Santa Clara Pueblo no longer organized matrilineally at the time of the 1939 membership rule change; like many of the other Pueblos, it had a bilateral kinship system in which lineage was determined by both parents.[38]

It is important to note that there is no straightforward relationship between mother/father-based lineage systems and male/female power in society. Anthropological accounts of this relationship among the Pueblo may say more about the ideology and concepts of anthropologists than they do about Pueblo norms and practices. Although the revised patrilineal membership rule may not have reflected deeply rooted patriarchal traditions among the Pueblo, it has clearly disadvantaged female members who marry out of the tribe by excluding their children from the benefits of membership while not similarly excluding the children of

---

[34] The Supreme Court Brief of the Respondents, *Santa Clara Pueblo* v. *Martinez*, No. 76–682, 36–37. See Hawley 1948.

[35] Parsons 1932: 378.

[36] Quoted in Jacobs 1999: 6. Parson's account of the Pueblo must be read in light of her attempts to use her study of the Pueblo as a way to articulate an alternative ideal of gender relations for the dominant culture – one in which sex differentiation counted for very little and in which there was a healthy attitude toward sexuality (Jacobs 1999: 74, 78).

[37] Hill 1981: 169, 20–21.   [38] Jacobs 1999: 7.

male members who marry out. This is precisely why Julia Martinez, a female member of the Santa Clara Pueblo, sought federal intervention.

Should it matter whether a tribal membership rule is rooted in an old or new custom? The Supreme Court disregarded the history of the rule and focused instead on whether Congress had intended to allow federal court oversight of tribal membership rules. However, as legal scholar Judith Resnik has suggested, if the history of tribal traditions is not relevant to understanding whether federal norms constitute an intrusion into tribal affairs, how can we make sense of many other federal government actions involving Indian tribes? For example, the Department of Interior distinguishes between "historic" Indian tribes and "non-historic" tribes. "Historic" tribes are those which predated the formation of the United States and are seen to have retained their "internal" sovereignty. In contrast, non-historic tribes have only those powers delegated to them by Congress or permitted to them by the Secretary of the Interior.[39] Likewise, groups seeking recognition as a "tribe" by the federal government must provide proof of historical continuity. For example, in the federal court trial in which the Mashpee Indians tried to obtain possession of land on Cape Cod, the court tried to "determine whether the group calling itself the Mashpee Tribe was in fact an Indian tribe, and the same tribe that in the mid-nineteenth century had lost its land through a series of contested legislative acts."[40] A tribe's claim for recognition is in part a demand for recognition of its existence over time. This puts reemerging or newly constituted Native groups at a disadvantage relative to communities that already have established a degree of nationhood and can therefore more easily demonstrate their historical continuity.

Even if we accept that considerations about historical continuity of traditions have normative significance for a group's quest for accommodation, the Santa Clara Pueblo could not make this argument. The tribal amendment of its membership rules was not solely or even primarily rooted in tribal traditions. Rather, it was motivated by pragmatic considerations that emerged out of interactions with the dominant culture and the US government. The federal government has long provided guidance to tribal governments over many aspects of social and political life, including the writing and codification of tribal constitutions and membership rules. The Indian Reorganization Act of 1934 gave Indian tribes the opportunity to follow US models of lawfully chartered associations. The Department of Interior prepared model constitutions for tribes, and the Bureau of Indian Affairs assisted tribes in drafting constitutions.

---

[39] Resnik 1989: 710.
[40] *Mashpee Tribe* v. *New Seabury Corp*, 592 F.2d 575 (1979). See Clifford 1988: 277–346.

Tribal constitutions were not approved unless they delegated extensive veto powers to the Secretary of Interior.[41]

The Secretary of Interior approved the Santa Clara Pueblo's original constitution in 1935. While the US government did not directly mandate or suggest membership restrictions along gender lines, it did pressure the Pueblo and other tribes to adopt more restrictive membership rules. As Audra Simpson has observed in the context of studying narratives of membership among Kahnawake Mohawks, Native peoples "witness the forced cultural transformation of native culture through the bounding of people and bounding space."[42] State efforts at boundedness are represented in the creation of reservations and compulsion to restrict membership. The idea of "membership" was itself imposed by the US government in order to count Native peoples and regulate the resources it distributed to tribes.[43] Julia Martinez sought recognition of her children as members of the Pueblo partly to obtain such benefits.

The Santa Clara tribal authority moved to restrict its membership along gender lines in direct response to a federal government circular. On November 18, 1935, in a circular titled "Membership in Indian Tribes," the US Department of Interior made a "declaration" to all "engaged in Indian Reorganization Act" that "Congress [has] a definite policy to limit the application of Indian benefits." The Department planned "to urge and insist that any constitutional provision conferring automatic tribal membership upon children hereafter born should limit such membership to persons who reasonably can be expected to participate in tribal relations and affairs." The government suggested ways to restrict membership, which reflected its own views about the proper bases of political membership – in particular, that both parents be recognized as tribal members or that an individual possess a "certain degree of Indian blood." When those without blood or marriage ties sought adoption, "provision for the adoption of non-members should require approval by the Secretary of the Interior." The Department stated that the declaration was intended for the benefit "of the Indians themselves ... [who] shall appreciate its importance as it applies to their own welfare through preventing the admission to tribal membership of a large number of applicants of small degree of Indian blood."[44] In

---

[41] A typical example is the Constitution and Bylaws of the Oglala Sioux Tribe of the Pine Ridge Reservation, which provides in Article IV "that the tribal council shall exercise, subject to review or approval of the Secretary of the Interior, the following powers ..." A study of 198 tribal governments by Barsh and Henderson indicate that more than half of the specific powers granted in tribal constitutions are subject to approval (1980: 116–17).
[42] Simpson 2000: 118.   [43] Resnik 1989: 719–22.
[44] US Dept. of the Interior, Circular No. 3123 (Office of Indian Affairs, Nov. 18, 1935), cited in *Opinions of the Solicitor General* [of the Dept. of Interior] 1–2, 813 (Apr. 12, 1938).

response, the Santa Clara Tribal Council amended the membership rules set forth in the 1935 Pueblo Constitution, proposing restrictive membership rules that excluded children born to out-marrying Pueblo women. The Department of Interior has let the gender-biased membership rule stand.

Intercultural congruence and the accommodation of tribal practices

In practice, the extent of federal intervention into tribal affairs has varied over time and across different social domains. The federal government has intervened in tribal affairs when it perceives tribal decisions as jeopardizing federal policy goals. For instance, in the same year it decided the Santa Clara Pueblo case, the Supreme Court ruled that Indian tribes lack authority to punish non-Indians who commit crimes on reservations. In this case, the Court stressed that tribal sovereignty is limited and that the US government has "overriding sovereignty" over tribal powers.[45] The Department of Interior has also withheld its approval of tribal policies in other cases. For example, in the early 1980s, the Secretary of Interior "rescinded a tribal ordinance of the Moapa Band of Paiute Indians that would have permitted houses of prostitution on the Moapa Reservation in Clark County, Nevada." In Nevada, houses of prostitution are permitted under certain circumstances. Although regional offices of the Department of Interior approved the Moapa Constitution that included provisions for prostitution, the Secretary of Interior retracted that approval on the grounds that such practices would create political hostility toward Indians and that the underlying activity was "frowned upon by federal policy."[46] The federal courts upheld the Secretary's decision. Yet, the Santa Clara Pueblo membership ordinance, which treated women and men differently for the purposes of membership, was not similarly frowned upon.

Why has the federal government deferred to tribal sovereignty in certain affairs and not in others? One important reason, which I discussed in considering the "cultural defense" in chapter 4, is the fact of intercultural congruence. The sorts of practices that the federal government has been willing to tolerate in Native American communities are similar to the sorts of practices it has tolerated in the dominant culture. With respect to the Santa Clara Pueblo case, it is important to acknowledge that America's own tradition of gendered citizenship laws bears striking similarity to the gendered membership rules of the Pueblo. Into the 1930s, American

---

[45] *Oliphant* v. *Suquamish Indian Tribe*, 435 US 191 (1978) at 209–10.
[46] *Moapa Band of Paiute Indians* v. *US Dept. of Interior*, 747 F.2d 563 (1984) at 564.

women endangered their citizenship status by marrying foreign men, whereas American men who married foreign women automatically made their wives into US citizens.

From the American Revolution until 1855, an American woman's hold on her nationality appeared to be about the same as an American man's, that is, not directly dependent on marriage. This was a legacy of the British common law insistence on indelible nationality. In an 1830 case involving an American woman who had married a British man, the US Supreme Court held that marriage to a foreigner did not *ipso facto* contravene an American woman's national membership.[47] Marriage alone did not alter a woman's political membership. In 1855, however, Congress passed a statute that made married women's citizenship dependent on their husbands' citizenship. The 1855 Naturalization Act declared, "Any woman who is now or may hereafter be married to a citizen of the United States, and who might herself be lawfully naturalized shall be deemed a citizen."[48] Politicians and judges tended to interpret this act as a mandate to assign married women, whether foreign or American, the citizenship of their husbands. Foreign women who married American men automatically became American citizens, making such women the first and only group of adults to receive US citizenship derivatively. Congress approved of this decision on the grounds that it spared female immigrants from having to go through the process of naturalization.[49] The 1855 law also granted American citizenship to children born abroad to American fathers and foreign mothers, but not those children born to American mothers and foreign fathers. By making wives' and children's nationality dependent on the male citizen's, this law affirmed male headship of the

---

[47] Cott 1998: 1455–56.

[48] Act of February 10, 1855, 10 Stat. 604, as reenacted in Revised Statutes of the US (1878), Sect. 1994.

[49] Not every woman who married an American man became a naturalized citizen. The exceptions to the rule were based on race and a record of immoral sexual conduct. When the federal government first granted automatic citizenship to foreign wives of American men, only free white persons could become US citizens through naturalization. After the Thirteenth and Fourteenth Amendments were ratified, Congress expanded the category of naturalization candidates to include people of African descent or nativity, but all other racial restrictions to naturalized citizenship remained in place (Act of Mar. 26, 1790, I Stat. 103; Act of Jul. 14, 1870, 16 Stat. 255–56). This rule was extended to Native American women, except members of the "Five Civilized Tribes" (Cherokee, Creek, Seminole, Chickasaw, Choctaw) in Indian Territory, by the Act of Aug. 9, 1888, 25 Stat. 392. The federal government amended the 1855 law to deny derivative citizenship to alien women of "sexually immoral classes" (Act of Feb. 5, 1917, 39 Stat. 874 at 889). This rule was part of a larger government effort to curb the immigration of foreign prostitutes. See Bredbenner 1998: 15–17.

family as a political norm and enhanced the citizenship privileges of American men.[50]

In contrast, under the 1855 law, American women who married foreign men were largely seen as forfeiting their US citizenship; such out-marrying women were expected to take up the nationality of their husbands. Some federal judges, as well as the State Department, had generally agreed that a female citizen who married an alien resident did not endanger her American citizenship unless she moved permanently to her husband's country.[51] But other judges maintained that American women lost their citizenship simply by marrying foreign men. In 1883, a Michigan circuit court judge wrote that "legislation upon the subject of naturalization is constantly advancing towards the idea that the husband, as the head of the family, is to be considered its political representative, at least for the purposes of citizenship, and that the wife and minor children owe their allegiance to the same sovereign power."[52]

This ambiguity over whether an American woman forfeited her citizenship by marrying a foreigner was clarified by the Expatriation Act of 1907, which made this gender-biased policy official: "Any American woman who marries a foreigner shall take the nationality of her husband."[53] Both before and after the 1907 expatriation law, maintaining a foreign domicile was the most common reason for expatriation. After 1907, the major exception became the expatriation of resident female citizens for marrying foreigners. The 1907 law imposed new restrictions on the ability of all naturalized Americans to live abroad and preserve their citizenship; Section 2 of the 1907 law denaturalized citizens who lived in their native country for two years or in any other foreign nation for five years. In stark contrast to these residency-based restrictions, American women married to foreign men were expatriated, regardless of residency. An American woman who married an alien automatically assumed her husband's nationality even if she never left the United States. This law discouraged American women from marrying immigrants and prevented immigrant wives from being naturalized on their own. The law once again affirmed that a wife's political allegiance should follow her husband's. An American man's wife was welcomed into the American political community, whereas an American woman and her alien husband were excluded from national membership.

---

[50] Cott 1998: 1461–62.   [51] Bredbenner 1998: 58–59.

[52] *Pequignot* v. *City of Detroit*, 16 F.211 (1883) at 216. This 1883 case was singled out by a commission appointed by President Theodore Roosevelt to evaluate and suggest reforms for the country's nationality laws. The commission's report heavily influenced the design of the 1907 citizenship law (Bredbenner 1998: 57–60).

[53] Sect. 3, Act of Mar. 2, 1907 (34 Stat. 1228).

These gender asymmetries in naturalization and citizenship policy were only partially overturned by the Cable Act, or Married Women's Independent Nationality Act, of 1922. An American woman who married a foreigner and remained in the United States would now remain a US citizen, but she would lose her citizenship if she lived in her husband's country for two years or if she married a man "ineligible for citizenship" – an Asian, a polygamist, or an anarchist. In contrast, an American man did not suffer such consequences for similar actions. There was a similar asymmetry for married immigrant couples seeking naturalization in the United States: an immigrant woman's ability to pursue naturalization or maintain US citizenship continued to depend on her spouse's eligibility for naturalization. As historian Nancy Cott puts it, the Cable Act reflected "the reluctance of Congress to give up its long-term priority for the male citizen as family head."[54] Congress supported American men who married foreign women in their efforts to start a family in the United States by, for example, lowering the residency requirement for foreign brides seeking naturalization. In contrast, Congress did not consider offering similar support for American women's foreign-born husbands. American women's marriages to foreign men were seen to carry cultural and political liabilities. As one American woman who had lost her citizenship by marrying a foreigner put it, "If for men it is even a patriotic deed to extend by marriage the influence and partnership of their country in foreign lands, why should it not be the same when it is an American girl who marries a foreigner?"[55]

Women's citizenship continued to depend on their husbands' citizenship status until legislative reforms in the 1930s. By 1934, American women were no longer seen to forfeit their citizenship by marrying foreigners, both sexes gained the same naturalization benefits for their foreign-born spouses, and mothers gained the same right as fathers to pass down citizenship to their children born abroad.[56] But the "Equal Nationality Bill" of 1934, as the National Woman's Party called it, did not amount to the attainment of full citizenship for married women. By 1934, women had won suffrage and access to political parties and office-holding, but they had not attained full access to the rights of citizenship.[57]

---

[54] Cott 2000: 165.   [55] Bredbenner 1998: 105.

[56] The 1934 amendments made the latter two changes. The 1930 and 1931 amendments are assembled in "American Citizenship Rights of Women," and the 1934 amendments in H. R. Report No. 131 [from the Committee on Immigration and Naturalization], *House Reports on Public Bills* . . ., vol. 1, 73rd Cong., 1st sess. The most extensive debate on the 1934 change, called "The Equal Nationality Bill" by its proponents, can be found in *Congressional Record*, 73rd Cong., 2nd sess., pt. 7, 7329–59 (Apr. 25, 1934).

[57] For example, from the 1920s to 1975, a large number of states still resisted equal admission of women to juries (Cott 1998: 1471). Citizenship law continues to remain gendered in certain respects. In a recent case, the Supreme Court held that the federal law

Seen in this broader historical context – in light of the majority culture's own membership traditions – the Santa Clara Pueblo's 1939 gender-biased membership amendment appears not foreign but remarkably similar to the majority culture's own gendered traditions of membership. At the time of its passage, the gender-biased Pueblo membership rule, which the Department of Interior has permitted to stand, was congruent with the majority culture's long-standing expectation that married women should follow their men.

The limits of tribal sovereignty

What should be done in cases where respecting tribal sovereignty conflicts with ensuring the basic rights of female tribal members? As I argued in chapter 3, from the standpoint of equality, limited self-government rights of Native tribes are justifiable as a remedy for the systemic disadvantages caused by a long history of oppression. Yet, an important limit on tribal sovereignty is the protection of the basic rights and liberties of individual members. Native American women like Julia and Audrey Martinez are not just tribal citizens but also US citizens and persons residing under US jurisdiction entitled to equal protection. In bringing the suit, they contested the assumption that upholding the gender-biased membership rule was central to Santa Clara culture. In denying their claim, the US Supreme Court failed not only to treat them as civic equals but also overlooked the US government's role in sustaining the gender-biased rule.

The authority of tribal governments, like that of any legitimate government, is not absolute. From an egalitarian standpoint, tribal authority, as with any political authority, should be subject to the requirement that it protect the basic rights of its members. As Justice White argued in his dissent in *Martinez*, "The extension of constitutional rights to individual citizens is *intended* to intrude upon the authority of government. And once it has been decided that an individual does possess certain rights vis-à-vis his government, it necessarily follows that he has some way to enforce those rights." Justice White emphasized the limited nature of the federal district court's actions had it decided to invalidate the tribe's membership rule:

The federal district court's duty would be limited to determining whether the challenged tribal action violated one of the enumerated rights. If found to be in violation,

---

providing different citizenship rules for children born abroad and out of wedlock depending on whether the citizen parent is the mother or father is consistent with the equal protection guarantee in the Fifth Amendment's Due Process Clause. The ruling seems to reflect the notion that mothers must care for "illegitimate" children, whereas fathers may ignore them. See *Tuan Anh Nguyen* v. *I.N.S.*, 533 US 53 (2001).

the action would be invalidated; if not, it would be allowed to stand. In no event would the court be authorized, as in a *de novo* review proceeding, to substitute its judgment concerning the wisdom of the action taken for that of the tribal authorities.

He pointed to the legislative history of ICRA, which indicates that Congress was concerned "not only about the Indian's lack of substantive rights, but also about the lack of remedies to enforce whatever rights the Indian might have." During its consideration of this legislation, the Senate subcommittee pointed out that although "protected against abridgment of his rights by State or Federal action, the individual Indian is ... without redress against his tribal authorities."[58] By deferring to tribal sovereignty, the Court left a particular class of Pueblo women and their children without legal redress.

In addition to the civic equality argument is the federal government's involvement in sustaining the gender-biased tribal membership rules. The irony here is that the tribal authority defended, as an expression of their sovereignty, a definition of tribal identity and membership strongly influenced by the dominant culture. The federal government did not directly impose the gender-biased dimension of the Pueblo membership rule, but the rule found support in the dominant culture's traditions in which American women's political membership status was made to depend on their husbands', and the Secretary of Interior, who has the authority granted by the Santa Clara Constitution to abrogate the ordinance, has allowed the rule to stand. The state's role in sustaining the gender-biased tribal membership rule supports a case that it should play a role in its reform.

But what role should state involvement take? One proposal is Ayelet Shachar's legal-institutional solution of "transformative accommodation" that divides jurisdictional authority between groups and the state. Her innovative model is one form that legal pluralist arrangements might take. Legal pluralist arrangements work best for groups whose members see themselves as bound by religious law, as well as for groups that are territorially concentrated and already enjoy a measure of legal authority, but not for immigrants or ethnic minorities who do not adhere to a comprehensive doctrine or who do not possess separate legal jurisdictional authority. Shachar's primary case is Jewish family law, but her arguments are also intended to apply to aboriginal groups.[59] Drawing

---

[58] *Santa Clara Pueblo* v. *Martinez*, 436 US at 83, 76, 80.
[59] Aboriginal self-government rights are similar to the standing that the laws of religious minority groups are granted in countries such as Israel and India. In these countries, family law, among other domains of law, are handled within each religious community, just as authority over family law is granted to tribal governments. The key difference between the incorporation of religious law and incorporation of indigenous law through self-government rights is the recognition of territorial sovereignty in the latter case.

upon family law, Shachar divides jurisdictional authority such that neither the state nor the group has a monopoly of power over an entire
"social arena," such as education, criminal justice, or resource development. Instead, governance over each social arena is divided according to
different functions or "sub-matters." In the arena of family law, groups
have the authority to demarcate membership while states govern the
distribution of rights and duties among group members.[60] In theory,
this initial division of authority is not intended to be permanent; individuals can "opt in" or "opt out" of specific group positions by reversing
jurisdictional authority in relation to a particular sub-matter. This suggests that if an individual member of a group dissents from her group's
membership rules, she can "opt out" and invite state intervention in
defining group membership. This "opt out" provision allows individual
members to pose a credible threat of exit since groups want to avoid the
reversal of jurisdiction that would bring state intervention, and this cre-
ates incentives for the group to serve its members better.[61]

Yet, in applying her approach to the Santa Clara Pueblo case,
Shachar's "opt out" provision regarding group membership rules disap-
pears. On her model, Audrey Martinez and other children of out-marrying
women can appeal to the state to obtain the same health and other
material benefits associated with tribal membership, but the tribe's discriminatory membership rule remains in place.[62] Audrey Martinez
receives the benefits associated with tribal membership, but she must
live with her outcast status. In effect, she must exit the tribe, albeit with
material benefits associated with tribal membership in hand. This outcome suggests the arbitrariness of the initial division of jurisdictional
authority that Shachar proposes. Who is to decide what this initial allo-
cation should look like, and whether it is justifiable? Instead of committing to a division of jurisdictional authority along "sub-matter" lines, as
Shachar's model does, from the standpoint of egalitarian justice tribes
should have primary jurisdictional authority over a wide range of social
arenas, including education and family law, but on the condition that
tribal governments respect the basic rights of its members. This would
mean that tribal authorities govern both issues of membership and issues
of material benefits, but that individual members have a real opportunity
to seek federal intervention where their basic rights are threatened.

In thinking about the state's role in the Santa Clara case, it is important
to distinguish two key matters that were at stake for the Martinez family:
the issue of tribal membership and the issue of federal benefits associated

---

[60] Shachar 2001: 51–55, 119–22.   [61] Ibid. 122–26.   [62] Ibid. 18–20, 142, n. 51.

with tribal membership. The Supreme Court ruling left the Martinez family without legal redress on both counts. On Shachar's proposal, Audrey Martinez should have been entitled to the federal benefits associated with tribal membership, though not to tribal membership itself. Egalitarian justice requires that Audrey Martinez and similarly situated children should receive the federal benefits associated with tribal membership. Should the state also compel the tribe to admit them as members? I think the answer turns on whether the existing membership rule is consistent with respecting the basic rights of these children. Here a legal-institutional approach alone cannot provide the answer; it requires a deliberative approach.

As I have stressed, deliberation can illuminate the nature of the interests at stake in cultural conflicts: What is the importance of tribal membership for Audrey Martinez and other similarly situated children beyond receiving the federal benefits associated with it? What are the costs of exit? If they receive federal benefits associated with membership, is exit a realistic option, or are the intrinsic and associative costs of exit so high as to render exit impossible? On the other side, it is important to ask whether the gender-biased rule is central to what it means to be Santa Clara, so central that to admit Audrey Martinez and other children of out-marrying women would threaten the survival of Pueblo culture and identity. Such questions must be taken up in political debate within Native communities. The state should play a role in this process – not by directly mandating a change in the membership rule but rather by strengthening the voice of vulnerable group members.

Skeptics of a deliberative democratic approach might argue that most Santa Clarans would, if given a real voice in the decision-making, endorse the gender-biased membership rule. Not only tribal authorities but also many female members themselves might insist that treaty-based sovereignty supersedes any other federal mandate, including anti-discrimination law. If a substantial majority of Santa Clarans were to endorse the gender-biased membership rule, on the one hand, and the costs of exit were insurmountable for out-marrying women and their children, on the other, this would make for a hard case in which a practice deemed central to most members of a historically oppressed group conflicts with the basic rights of a subgroup of members. The costs of exiting Native communities are great if not insurmountable, even for those who have the material means to leave, since there are great associative costs of leaving the tribal community in which one has grown up. Against the skeptics of a deliberative approach, it should be said that we have reason to doubt the claim that most Santa Clarans see the gender-biased membership rule as integral to tribal identity or traditions. The efforts of the Martinez family offer evidence of dissent over membership rules within the Pueblo community. A recent movement among the Pueblo to change the tribal rule from within provides further evidence that Pueblo membership traditions are contested.

Leading this recent movement is Paul Tafoya, who was the governor of the Santa Clara Pueblo at the time of the *Martinez* case and who at that time supported the gender-biased membership rule. His family has been directly involved in the membership issue since the 1930s: his father-in-law, Joseph F. Tafoya, was the governor who signed into tribal law the 1939 ordinance that excluded the children of out-marrying women, and his father, Cleto Tafoya, signed the 1944 resolution affirming the 1939 ordinance. Since the early 1990s, Tafoya has been working against his original position and has sought to change the membership rule to include the children of out-marrying Santa Clara women. As he put it, "Since 1977, after the US Supreme Court ruling in the *Martinez* case, the people of Santa Clara Pueblo have become more aware and concerned about its membership issues and how it discriminates against its own tribal people. More and more families are finding themselves being discriminated against by its own tribal government." At the time of the *Martinez* case, he said he had been concerned above all with protecting tribal sovereignty and had not thought seriously about the extent of the discriminatory effect the ordinance would have.[63] His initial strategy for reforming the rule was to seek an administrative solution by asking officials of the US Bureau of Indian Affairs to declare the 1939 and 1944 membership ordinances void and to restore the more inclusive membership rules established in the 1935 Constitution, but the Bureau of Indian Affairs has declined to get involved.[64] Tafoya now seeks a democratic solution to the membership issue.

At a meeting held at the Pueblo's community center in October 2005, Tafoya announced that he would circulate a petition among Pueblo members to amend the tribal law because it "violates individual civil rights of all children of mixed marriages whose mothers are tribal members of Santa Clara Pueblo and their fathers who are non-members, regardless of race."[65] One female member, Janice Vicente, who moved to the Pueblo with her young son after the death of her husband, a member of the Acoma Pueblo, expressed worry that her son would be left without any rights as a Santa Claran after she dies: "This is his home, and he needs to have a place

---

[63] Paul Tafoya, Interview by author, Mar. 14, 2006, Santa Fe, New Mexico.
[64] Letter from Gayle E. Manges, Field Solicitor, Southwest Region, Office of the Solicitor, US Department of Interior, Mar. 5, 1993; letter from Cameron Martinez, Superintendent, Northern Pueblos Agency, Bureau of Indian Affairs, May 13, 1997 (on file with the author).
[65] Shaw 2005: C1.

to go where he is accepted." Tafoya's daughter, Patricia Chavez, is married to a Hispanic man with whom she has four children. They have grown up on the tribal reservation. As she puts it, "It hurts me to know that I'm Santa Clara, but my kids aren't Santa Clara."[66] Chavez points out that her children are not entitled to federal scholarship funds administered through the tribe, nor to inherit individual rights of possession over her family's land or use common tribal land in the same way as members are: "Members are allowed to bring their spouses or girlfriends or boyfriends into the beautiful canyon here on the reservation, to hunt or just enjoy the scenery, but my kids aren't allowed to bring their fiancés or girlfriends." According to Chavez, her children suffer more than the denial of material benefits that flow from membership pertaining to education, housing, or land. They are also made to feel like second-class citizens in everyday interactions on the reservation. She said that she sent her children to public school off the reservation rather than the day school on the reservation "so they wouldn't get made fun of for being half-Indian or mixed." She speaks of her kids having an "identity crisis" since neither side, Pueblo or Hispanic, fully accepts them.[67]

Paul Tafoya estimates that amending the rule would increase membership by 40 percent. The population of the Santa Clara Pueblo is said to be between 3,000 and 4,000 members at present.[68] Tafoya said that once he gets the signature of 60 percent of the Pueblo membership he intends to send it to the US Bureau of Indian Affairs, which can then authorize a tribal election to change the law. To defend this procedure, Tafoya points to Article VIII of the Santa Clara Pueblo Constitution, which states, "No amendments or changes shall be made in the constitution or bylaws of the pueblo except by a decision of the *general pueblo*. At the request of the council the Secretary of the Interior shall submit any proposed amendment to the said constitution or bylaws to a vote of the people." He also points to the Code of Federal Regulation (CFR) 25, Parts 81 and 82, which authorize the Secretary of Interior or some authorized representative to call for an election to adopt tribal amendments upon receipt of a petition bearing signatures of at least 60 percent of the tribe's eligible voters.[69]

[66] "Ex-Santa Clara Governor Attempting to Change Tribal Law," *Associated Press*, Oct. 17, 2005.
[67] Patricia Chavez, Interview by author, Mar. 15, 2006, Santa Fe, New Mexico.
[68] Simon 2005: B5.
[69] Based on an estimate on the most recent elections of Tribal Council officials, the highest voter turnout among the Santa Clara Pueblo was 480. Sixty percent of 480 voters amounts to 288 voters required to sign the petition. Paul Tafoya, "A Brief Analysis in Response to 'An Open Letter to the People of the Pueblo of Santa Clara from the Santa Clara Pueblo Tribal Council,'" Oct. 13, 2005, on file with the author.

While Paul Tafoya is hopeful that his petition will get the support it needs, it met with immediate resistance from the Tribal Council. The 2005 Governor, Joseph Bruce Tafoya, who is Paul Tafoya's cousin, said he welcomed proposals on the "controversial and complex matter," but added that the Tribal Council "does not believe that it is productive for one person, or a small group, to try to circumvent our constitutionally established procedures by stirring up public controversy with a proposal that has not had the benefit of consideration by the Pueblo's elected leaders." He agreed that the Constitution may be amended by a vote of the Pueblo members called by the Secretary of Interior, but he emphasized that the role of the Secretary of Interior and the vote of the people must be made "at the request of the council." He stressed that there is no provision for initiating a vote by petition.[70]

Paul Tafoya insists that the petition drive is motivated not just by one person or a small group but reflects a broader sentiment among the Pueblo membership for amending the discriminatory membership rule. He maintains that the Tribal Council are misinformed about the procedures for amending the tribal constitution, emphasizing that the CFR applies to the Santa Clara Pueblo since it is a federally recognized tribe organized under the federal statute. In his view, Article VIII of the tribal constitution does not grant the Tribal Council *sole* authorization to submit any proposed amendment to the Secretary of Interior. He insists that the "Tribal Council cannot initiate any amendments on their own or without the *Pueblo people*'s participation." His aim is to take up the issue directly with members rather than going through the Tribal Council since the latter seems unwilling to listen. As he puts it,

In the last thirty years, the Santa Clara Tribal Council was made aware by the people of Santa Clara Pueblo regarding abolishing the 1939 Membership Ordinance and 1944 Membership Resolution for these reasons [i.e. because it excludes children of out-marrying women from tribal membership]. Although the Tribal Council became increasingly aware of these concerns, they made no effort to remedy or rectify the situation. Instead they chose to disregard and gave the membership issue low to no priority.[71]

There are reasons to doubt that the Tribal Council's position on the membership issue reflects the will of the Pueblo membership.[72] The

---

[70] Joseph Bruce Tafoya, Governor, "An Open Letter to the People of the Pueblo of Santa Clara from the Santa Clara Pueblo Tribal Council," Oct. 13, 2005, on file with the author.

[71] Paul Tafoya, "A Brief Analysis."

[72] The 2006 Governor and Lieutenant Governor of the Santa Clara Pueblo declined my requests for interviews.

extent to which governing structures within the Santa Clara Pueblo are democratic is unclear. While six of the fourteen positions on the Tribal Council are elected by secret ballot for one-year terms by the entire Pueblo membership, the remaining eight positions are reserved for "Representatives" who are appointed to the Council by each of the four recognized parties or factions within the Pueblo.[73] The four-party system was formed after disputes within the Santa Clara Pueblo arose in the 1930s, further evidence that Pueblo culture is not homogenous or tightly unified. The Santa Clara Pueblo was divided along two units of social organization called moieties, the Summer and Winter moieties, which serve as governmental divisions for the management of practical tasks and ceremonial activities. Throughout the nineteenth and early twentieth century, a number of Santa Clara families who opposed the dictates of the Pueblo authorities formed a group within the more progressive moiety, the Winter moiety.[74] They advocated a separation of religious and secular activities and argued that families, not officials, should determine planting and harvesting dates and that ceremonial participation should be voluntary rather than compulsory. A serious schism began in 1894 and lasted thirty years. New disputes arose, which split each of the moieties along progressive and conservative lines, resulting in four factions. All sides requested arbitration by the Indian Service in Santa Fe, which proposed an elective form of government under terms of the Indian Reorganization Act. A tribal constitution was drawn up by members of all four factions and Indian Bureau lawyers and advisors, and it was ratified by the Pueblo in 1935. The constitution clearly did not end all disputes, but it did separate religious and secular affairs and made ceremonial participation voluntary. The constitution grants the entire governing power of the Pueblo to this council, which has both legislative and judicial powers.[75]

A small number of families is said to dominate the party system. Paul Tafoya suggests that one reason for the Tribal Council's cool reaction to the movement for changing the membership rule may have to do with the issue of land inheritance. While the title to all Pueblo lands "shall forever remain in the pueblo itself and not in the individual members thereof," all

---

[73] Constitution and Bylaws of the Pueblo of Santa Clara, New Mexico, Article III.

[74] As the anthropologist and Santa Clara member Edward P. Dozier suggests: "It is opposition to the compulsory dictates of the Pueblo authorities which has brought about dissatisfaction and discord in the past as well as at present. Forced participation in all communal activities and the prohibition of all deviant behavior, though designed to discourage the rise of dissident groups, have often had the opposite effect and have resulted in frequent factional disputes" (quoted Arnon and Hill 1979: 302).

[75] Arnon and Hill 1979: 302.

individual members enjoy the right of possession and the right to make beneficial use of the land.[76] By excluding children of out-marrying women from the rights of membership, including the right to inherit land, the land of these women, upon their death, would fall under the control of the Tribal Council. This may allow powerful families who dominate the eight seats on the Council reserved for "Representatives" to acquire more land for themselves.[77] Patricia Chavez suggested another reason for the resistance of the fourteen-member Tribal Council to changing the rule: "The issue of membership is really about control. The male is seen as the provider. The husbands of women who marry out have businesses and homes elsewhere, so the women are expected to follow their husbands. Santa Clara men, on the other hand, can marry out and bring in wives with as little as 1/64 Santa Clara blood."[78]

The extent of support for the movement to amend the membership rule appears strong, but it is unclear how decisive such support will be given the Tribal Council's resistance and the federal government's refusal to get involved. Tafoya said he had already gathered 190 signatures out of the 288 needed to take the issue to the federal government. What is clear is that there is no settled consensus among the Pueblo community one way or the other. What Tafoya and his supporters aim to do is educate the general tribal population about the contested history of the membership rules. Patricia Chavez said that some Tribal Council members have tried to make people fearful of making any change in the membership rule by insisting that including the children of out-marrying female members as members would "open up the floodgates," taking land away from current members and giving it to non-members, and that such a move would destroy Pueblo culture. "Actually," Chavez says, "it would allow people who already live at Santa Clara and whose families already have land on the reservation to inherit it."[79] When asked about his motivations for wanting to change the membership rule, Tafoya says, "The future of our Pueblo, our existence, is our kids. I want to see their families grow."[80]

If the struggles of Native women in Canada are any guide, then those Santa Clarans seeking to change their tribe's membership rule will continue to face opposition from tribal authorities in the name of protecting tribal sovereignty. The Canadian government played a much more direct role than the US government in shaping aboriginal membership rules along gender lines. In 1869, the Canadian government passed the

---

[76] Constitution and Bylaws of the Pueblo of Santa Clara, New Mexico, Article VII.
[77] Paul Tafoya, Interview by author, Mar. 14, 2006, Santa Fe, New Mexico.
[78] Patricia Chavez, Interview by author, Mar. 15, 2006, Santa Fe, New Mexico.
[79] Ibid.   [80] Paul Tafoya, Interview by author, Mar. 14, 2006, Santa Fe, New Mexico.

Gradual Enfranchisement Act, which created the concepts of "status Indian" and "non-status Indian" and stipulated that any Native women who married persons without Indian status (including non-status Canadian Indians and American Indians, as well as white men) would lose their Indian status and any right to band membership. As in the Santa Clara rule, these women's children were denied membership and were expected to become members of their husbands' bands in contradiction to the matrilineal rules of some Native communities. In contrast, white women who married "status Indian" men were granted Indian status. This patrilineal descent rule was in effect until 1985. The act also denied women the right to vote in band council elections until 1951.[81]

Native women's groups mobilized over several decades in support of amending the act, whereas many Native band councils opposed these efforts. The sometimes violent opposition of band councils was not simply a function of sexism within Native communities, but rather resistance to continuing federal government infringement on their sovereignty. It was not until Sandra Lovelace, a Maliseet woman from Tobique, New Brunswick, took her case to the United Nations Human Rights Committee that the Indian Act was found to be in violation of the International Covenant on Political and Civil Rights. After consultation and proposed changes, the Canadian government passed Bill C-31, An Act to Amend the Indian Act, in 1985. Approximately 100,000 Native women and their children have received Indian status as a result of the bill.

The reactions of many First Nations to Bill C-31 have been negative, and some bands have raised legal challenges to the bill. Their concern is with tribal sovereignty, but what is puzzling is that Bill C-31 (which reinstates women and their children as members), not the original provisions of the Indian Act created and imposed by the Canadian government (which disenfranchised out-marrying women), is the target of criticism. The gender-biased provision of the Indian Act seems to have become a normalized aspect of Native life in many communities.[82] Some Native bands view the gender-biased provision as an expression of tribal sovereignty while viewing the gender egalitarian reform, Bill C-31, as something that threatens tribal sovereignty. In 1997, over thirty members of Cold Lake First Nation protested their band's refusal to reinstate those eligible for reinstatement under Bill C-31, as well as the band's discrimination against women who married non-status Indians or non-Natives *after* 1985. The Cold Lake band's defiance of Bill C-31 in the name of tribal sovereignty continues to make outcasts of women who marry

[81] Lawrence 2003.   [82] Lawrence 2003: 13–15.

non-Native individuals.[83] As in the Santa Clara case, what is ironic is that Native authorities embrace as an expression of their sovereignty gender-biased rules that were imposed (in the case of First Nations in Canada) or sustained (in the case of the Santa Clara Pueblo in the United States) by the federal government. In both of these cases, the state's involvement in creating or supporting inequality within tribal communities supports a case for its playing a role in addressing it. This role need not take the form of federal imposition of a different set of rules, but rather measures that support democratic processes within the tribe.

[83] Dumont and De Ryk 1997: 15.

6   Polygamy in America

The two preceding chapters illustrate an intercultural dynamic that discussions of multiculturalism must acknowledge: patriarchal practices in minority groups are sometimes accommodated because they are shaped by and congruent with the patriarchal norms of the majority culture. This chapter aims to highlight a different and more subtle intercultural dynamic: how critique of minority norms and practices, even by well-intentioned reformers, can divert attention from the majority culture's own inequalities, shielding them from criticism and perhaps even fueling discourses of cultural superiority within the dominant culture. Such a diversionary effect can be seen in the controversy over Mormon polygamy in nineteenth-century America, as well as in contemporary debates over minority cultural practices, including arranged marriage and female circumcision within immigrant communities.[1]

The movement against Mormon polygamy provides an early example of a minority group's demand for accommodation – in this case, a demand for immunity from prosecution, an exemption – and the dominant culture's overwhelmingly negative response. As one legal historian put it, the federal government pursued the campaign against polygamy with "a zeal and concentration" that was "unequalled in the annals of federal law enforcement."[2] Opponents of polygamy called for federal intervention to dismantle what was widely considered a deeply patriarchal practice. Some might look approvingly at the outcome of this case, pointing to it as a model for how liberal democratic states might deal with illiberal and

---

[1] The term "polygyny" refers to a form of marriage in which one man has more than one wife at the same time, whereas polygamy refers to marriage in which a person has more than one spouse at the same time and includes not just polygyny but also polyandry in which one woman has more than one husband. Mormons practiced polygyny, but discourse about the Mormon practice, in the nineteenth century and today, commonly refer to the practice as polygamy. I use the term polygamy, though it should be noted that it refers in the Mormon case, as well as in much contemporary usage to cases beyond the Mormons, to marriage between one man and several wives.

[2] Linford 1964: 312, 585.

nondemocratic groups. What they would miss, however, is not only how such intervention failed to improve the status of Mormon women but also how condemnation of polygamy helped divert attention from the majority culture's own patriarchal norms. The focus on polygamy helped shield Christian monogamy and the traditional gender roles associated with it from criticism. It also served as a useful tool in the government's assault on what was probably its bigger concern, the political power of the Mormon Church.

In this chapter, I examine the politics of the American antipolygamy movement to explore the intercultural dynamic of diversion. Antipolygamy activists gave two main arguments against polygamy: that it violated Christian public morals and that it subordinated women. Turning to examine the contemporary practice of polygamy, I consider whether the concern for equal protection of women supports a case for qualified recognition of polygamy with an emphasis on ensuring a realistic right of exit, as well as discuss other contemporary cases in which the diversionary effect is at work.

The rise and fall of Mormon polygamy

In 1830, Joseph Smith, a New York farmer, founded the Church of Jesus Christ of Latter-day Saints. The Book of Mormon, as translated by Smith, described the Hebrew origins of Native Americans and established America as God's chosen land. In 1843 in Nauvoo, Illinois, Smith had a revelation mandating "plural marriage," but the revelation was not made public until 1852 after the Mormons had settled in Utah.[3] While Mormon leaders began practicing plural marriage in Illinois, it was on the western frontier that the practice grew, offering a systematic alternative to Christian monogamy. Responding to what they perceived to be the increasing secularization of marriage in the dominant culture, Mormon leaders solemnized marriages without state involvement.[4] Public outrage against the practice grew. The Republican Party condemned the "twin relics of barbarism – polygamy and slavery" in its

---

[3] The revelation, as dictated by Smith, endorsed polygyny and implies a restriction on polyandry: "If any man espouse a virgin, and desire to espouse another, and the first give her consent, and if he espouse the second, and they are virgins, and have vowed to no other man, then he is justified: he cannot commit adultery . . . [I]f one or either of the ten virgins, after she is espoused, shall be with another man, she has committed adultery, and shall be destroyed; for they are given unto him to multiply and replenish the earth" (Van Wagoner 1989: 56).

[4] Foster 1981: 135–36 and Hardy 1992: 6.

party platform of 1856 and asserted the sovereign power of Congress over the territories.[5]

Efforts by American citizens and government officials to dismantle Mormon polygamy spanned from 1862 to 1890. In 1862, Congress criminalized bigamy in the territories.[6] The law proved unenforceable since Utah did not register marriages and Mormon juries would not convict polygamists. In 1874, Congress followed up with the Poland Act, which transferred jurisdiction of criminal and civil cases from probate courts in the Utah Territory, whose judges were often Mormon bishops, to federal territorial courts and gave federal judges considerable power over selection of jurors.[7] In 1879, the US Supreme Court upheld a bigamy conviction in *Reynolds* v. *US*, but the decision did not eliminate the practice since prosecutors could not easily prove plural marriage.[8] Congress followed up in 1882 by renaming the offense described as "bigamy" to "polygamy" and made it easier to procure polygamy convictions by criminalizing "unlawful cohabitation." It also denied polygamists the right to vote and hold public office and required a man to swear he was not a polygamist and a woman to swear that she was not married to one.[9] Some Mormons who were denied the vote in the 1882 election because they refused to take the oath sued the registrar of ballots. Two years later, the US Supreme Court held that it was appropriate for Congress to make marital status "a condition of the elective franchise," adding that a sovereign power could legitimately "declare that no one but a married person shall be entitled to vote."[10]

In 1887, Congress stepped up the assault by repealing the incorporation of the Mormon Church and directing the US Attorney General to expropriate its property holdings over $50,000.[11] The act also disenfranchised Mormon women, who had had the vote for seventeen years before that point. The Mormons resisted and continued to practice polygamy, but in 1889, the Supreme Court upheld Congress's power to dissolve and expropriate the church's property against the church's claim that it was a protected religious body.[12] Finally, in 1890, Mormon President Wilson Woodruff issued a manifesto accepting the federal prohibition of polygamy and encouraged members to refrain from contracting any further polygamous marriages.

---

[5] Linford 1964: 312.   [6] Morrill Anti-Bigamy Act, 12 Stat. 501 (1862).
[7] Poland Act, 18 Stat. 253 (1874).   [8] *Reynolds* v. *United States*, 98 US 145 (1879).
[9] Edmunds Act, 22 Stat. 30 (1882).   [10] *Murphy* v. *Ramsey*, 114 US 15 (1884) at 43.
[11] Edmunds–Tucker Act, 24 Stat. 635 (1887).
[12] *Late Corporation of the Church of Jesus Christ of Latter-day Saints* v. *United States*, 136 US 1 (1890). For further discussion of these statutes and court cases, see Linford 1964 and Gordon 2002.

The antipolygamy movement and the diversionary effect

Why did American citizens, legislators, and judges in the nineteenth century deem polygamy to be intolerable? The leading arguments against polygamy were that it offended Protestant public morals and that it was deeply patriarchal. While patriarchal power was not unique to the polygamous form of marriage, citizens and government officials targeted it because it was seen to embody an extreme form of patriarchy inconsistent with democracy. If we examine the broader social and political context in which antipolygamy activism arose, however, we see that while motivated by a concern to improve the status of Mormon women, the antipolygamy movement was also fueled by a concern to protect traditional monogamous marriage and dismantle the political power of the Mormon Church. The focus on polygamy served these latter goals well by shielding monogamy from feminist criticism and gathering support for the federal attack on the political power of the Mormon Church.

The context in which antipolygamy arose was a period of increasing anxiety over sexual values, family structure, and the proper role of women. Social changes in the majority culture – the spread of prostitution, the rising incidence of divorce, and lax morality of growing cities – stirred anxieties about the preservation of Christian-model monogamy. By the time the issue of polygamy arose on the national political stage, nineteenth-century women's rights activists had already been unsettling prevailing gender norms. By the 1840s, family reformers, fearful of utopian experiments and the demands of women's rights activists, diagnosed a "crisis of the family" and expressed "moral panic" around the issue of marriage reform.[13] The antipolygamy movement's persistent focus on the theme of sexual perversion allowed members of the majority culture to displace its anxieties about these social changes onto subversive minorities. In addition to subversive sexual practices, Mormonism's association with lenient divorce laws and female enfranchisement fueled fears that all three were part of a plot to undermine the traditional American family and Christian civilization itself.[14]

Polygamy challenged the Christian concept of marital unity and the related common law concept of coverture. In the eyes of the law, the husband and wife were one legal person represented by the husband with the legal existence of the wife "covered" by his authority. According to the preeminent expert on common law William Blackstone, a woman's legal

---

[13] Grossberg 1985: 10, 83.
[14] Davis 1960: 214, 216; Smith 1997: 388; and Gordon 2002: 52–54.

identity was subsumed by her husband's upon marriage.[15] What helped soften the image of the patriarchal nature of monogamy, in contrast to polygamy, was the rising ideology of romantic conjugal love, premised on consent and focused on one person. The metaphor of "one flesh" was recast as the spiritual union of the couple based on mutual love and consent, offering a gentler version of coverture.[16]

The patriarchal nature of polygamy was the focus of the *Reynolds* case. The Court held that the establishment and free exercise clauses did not protect local difference in domestic relations. Writing for the majority, Chief Justice Morrison Waite recognized polygamy as a religious doctrine, but he argued that the First Amendment protection of religious freedom extended to belief, not action.[17] In justifying government restrictions on religious action, he did not address Mormon arguments that highlighted questions of jurisdiction and the powers of Congress over the territories, focusing instead on questions of sexual behavior and the connection between marriage structure and political structure.[18] Chief Justice Waite expressed concern for the "pure-minded women" who were the "innocent victims of this delusion," and argued for upholding Congress's proscription on polygamy on the grounds that it "leads to the patriarchal principle ... which, when applied to large communities, fetters the people in stationary despotism, while that principle cannot long exist in connection with monogamy."[19] Such condemnation of patriarchy seems disingenuous insofar as nineteenth-century opponents of polygamy neither challenged patriarchal power within monogamy nor advocated the equality of women outside marriage. Yet, the Court was genuinely concerned with the patriarchal nature of polygamy: Mormon life was seen to embody patriarchy of a nature and degree unmatched by monogamy.[20] Such extreme patriarchy was seen to be inconsistent with democracy. Considered against notions of romantic conjugal love that (at least in theory) promised marital unions based on consent and mutual love, polygamy was truly a form of bondage.

The Court cast the conflict as between a secular state and religion and affirmed the state's civil interest in preserving monogamy. The case for

---

[15] Nineteenth-century American legal treatise writers, including James Kent and Joseph Story, sustained the importance of coverture (Basch 1982: 49, 62, 64–65).
[16] Gordon 2002: 67–68.   [17] *Reynolds* at 162.
[18] For a detailed account of the lawyers' arguments in the case, as well as how the *Reynolds* court drew on the jurisprudential lessons of the states in its decision, see Gordon 2002: ch. 4.
[19] *Reynolds* at 167–69.   [20] Rosenblum 1997: 77.

the civil interest in marriage was based on the widely accepted view that marriage structure was intimately connected with political order:

Marriage, while from its very nature a sacred obligation, is nevertheless, in most civilized nations, a civil contract, and usually regulated by law. Upon it society may be said to be built, and out of its fruits spring social relations and social obligations and duties, with which government is necessarily required to deal. In fact, according as monogamous or polygamous marriages are allowed, do we find the principles on which the government of the people, to a greater or less extent, rests.[21]

To buttress his claim about the state's civil interest in protecting monogamy, Chief Justice Waite drew on dominant ideas in the political thinking of his day – in particular, the claim that monogamy fostered democracy, whereas polygamy led ineluctably to despotism.

The association between monogamy and freedom, on the one hand, and polygamy and despotism, on the other, can be traced at least as far back as Montesquieu's idea that "domestic government" shaped "political government."[22] He also made the connection between family and political order in his 1728 epistolary novel, *Persian Letters*. Although Montesquieu's target had been the despotic elements of the French government and not non-Western cultures, his work initiated the Enlightenment association of polygamy with despotism. The harem signified coercion and despotism, whereas monogamy connoted consent and political liberty. The leading political and legal philosophers of the early American republic contrasted monogamy with polygamy in order to illustrate the superiority of Christian morality over "oriental despotism." For example, William Paley's *The Principles of Moral and Political Philosophy* (1785), which became the most widely read college text on the subject in the first half the nineteenth century, acclaimed the social benefits of monogamous marriage. In contrast, polygamy, he argued, produced the evils of political distrust, as well as the abasement of women. Such views linking monogamy with public order were accepted and developed by the jurist James Wilson in the 1790s and by the leading antebellum legal thinkers, Chancellor James Kent and Supreme Court Justice Joseph Story.[23]

Chief Justice Waite followed in this tradition of associating polygamy with patriarchy and despotism, buttressing this claim with widespread Christian revulsion against polygamy. He combined moral revulsion with racial revulsion by drawing upon the work of Francis Lieber, a German émigré who had become one of America's most influential political

[21] *Reynolds* at 165–66.   [22] Montesquieu 1989: 270, 316.   [23] Cott 2000: 22–23.

scientists.[24] Lieber hailed monogamy as the centerpiece of white, Christian civilization. While Chief Justice Waite did not go as far as Lieber in racializing polygamy, he did follow Lieber in mapping polygamy onto non-Christian and non-Western parts of the world: "Polygamy has always been odious among the northern and western nations of Europe, and, until the establishment of the Mormon Church, was almost exclusively a feature of the life of Asiatic and of African people."[25]

The *Reynolds* court reflected the antipolygamy discourse of the 1870s and 1880s, which associated polygamy with non-white and non-European peoples. Americans commonly linked polygamy to places deemed barbarous, including the "Incas of Peru," "Mohammedan countries," or "the Barbary states."[26] The linkage of monogamy with European culture and whiteness had begun earlier in the discourse of Christian missionaries. Upon their return from foreign missions, Protestant missionaries supplied America with descriptions of "heathen" societies, such as India and China. Women in these societies were depicted as slaves, degraded by practices such as seraglio, polygamy, and *sati*. In contrast, American women were portrayed as having been emancipated by Christianity.[27] Protestant women also organized home missions and benevolent societies to save degraded groups in America, including Native Americans, Roman Catholics, and Mormons.[28] Antipolygamists associated Mormon polygamy with Turkish harems, and anti-Mormon fiction borrowed from a popular book of the Victorian era, *The Lustful Turk* (1828).[29] In addition to missionary discourse, the experiences of European imperialism and theories of evolution also contributed to the discourse of "civilization" which suggested a linear path of progress from barbarism to civilization with white Europeans and Americans in the lead. The *Reynolds* court both drew upon and reinforced this discourse of racial and cultural superiority of

---

[24] *Reynolds* at 164–66. Chief Justice Waite found Lieber's statements on polygamy in Chancellor Kent's *Commentaries on American Law*, a treatise of the 1820s used by generations of American lawyers and judges. Lieber's major works, *Manual of Political Ethics, Designed Chiefly for the Use of Colleges and Students at Law* (1838–1839) and *On Civil Liberty and Self-Government* (1853) became popular college texts. Politicians and judges, including President Lincoln during the Civil War, drew on his advice, and his work was regarded as authoritative well into the 1870s and 1880s. See Weisbrod and Sheingorn 1978: 833 and Cott 2000: 114–15.

[25] *Reynolds* at 164. See Rosenblum 1997: 75 and Gordon 2002: 142.

[26] Cott 2000: 116–17.   [27] Brumberg 1982: 347–71.

[28] Iversen 1997: 104, 133–57. On antipolygamy discourse in the popular fiction of the day, see Gordon 1996a.

[29] Foster 1993: 115–32.

whites over others, casting the American-born Mormon religion as foreign and other.

By using rhetorical questions and analogizing polygamy with human
sacrifice and the Hindu "tradition" of *sati*, the Court implied that no
reasonable individual could contest the ban on polygamy. As Chief
Justice Waite put it,

> Suppose one believed that human sacrifices were a necessary part of religious
> worship, would it be seriously contended that the civil government under which
> he lived could not interfere to prevent a sacrifice? Or if a wife religiously believed it
> was her duty to burn herself upon the funeral pile [*sic*] of her dead husband, would
> it be beyond the power of the civil government to prevent her carrying her belief
> into practice? So here, as a law of the organization of society under the exclusive
> dominion of the United States, it is provided that plural marriages shall not be
> allowed.[30]

The Court saw the deeply patriarchal nature of polygamy – a monstrous
practice on a par with human sacrifice – as inconsistent with democratic
political life, whereas monogamy was indispensable for civilized society
and republican government.[31]

Yet, even as it recast a religious conflict between Christians and
Mormons as a conflict between a secular state and religious individuals,
the *Reynolds* court endorsed the marriage form of America's dominant
religious tradition. The Court's conception of marriage and its view of the
connection between marriage and public order were undeniably
Protestant. Chief Justice Waite drew on the theory and history of state
court rulings on religion, which deemed the Christian structure and
meaning of marriage as integral to the flourishing of democracy. As the
Chief Justice himself observed, the offense of polygamy was considered
an offense against Christianity. Civil courts assumed the authority for-
merly wielded by ecclesiastical courts, but this did not mean that religious
understandings of marriage were then supplanted with secular or more
ecumenical understandings. Rather, the Court integrated the protection
of Christian marriage into the First Amendment.[32] In subsequent cases
involving the Mormons, the Court's religious favoritism was more
explicit: polygamy was "a return to barbarism ... contrary to the spirit
of Christianity and of the civilization which Christianity has produced in

---

[30] *Reynolds* at 165–66.
[31] In *Murphy* v. *Ramsey*, 114 US 15 (1884) at 43, 45, the Court explicitly linked monogamy
with republican government. It argued that monogamy was "wholesome and necessary"
to a "free, self-governing commonwealth," and that on these grounds Congress could
take political power away from those who were hostile to monogamy.
[32] Gordon 2002: 135.

the Western world."[33] To call polygamy "a tenet of religion is to offend the common sense of mankind."[34]

The perceived threat of Mormon polygamy to Christian monogamy and civilization was heightened by Mormonism's association with easy divorce and woman's suffrage. On the divorce question, in 1852 the Utah territorial legislature enacted a divorce statute that simply required the petitioner to demonstrate that he or she was "a resident or wishes to become one." In addition to this lenient residency requirement, Utah's divorce law also included an omnibus clause allowing a divorce "when it shall be made to appear to the satisfaction and conviction of the court, that the parties cannot live in peace and union together, and that their welfare requires a separation." These provisions made Utah the most permissive of any jurisdiction in America on divorce. Some scholars contend that divorce was more prevalent among nineteenth-century Mormons in Utah than in any other jurisdiction in the United States, especially when divorces in polygamous marriages (granted by ecclesiastical courts after plural marriage was made illegal in 1862) are included in the total.[35] Historians Lawrence Foster and Louis Kern have argued that Mormon women had the primary initiative in determining when to end a relationship, while the husband could not so easily divorce if his wife was opposed. Kern finds that 73 percent of all divorce actions in Utah territory were taken by women and argues that divorce may have served as a means to redress the dissatisfactions of plural wives, suggesting that polygamy actually worked out as serial polyandry.[36] Residents of other jurisdictions also took advantage of the lenient divorce laws. Divorce rates rose in the 1870s after the transcontinental railroad was completed; Utah's lenient residency standard allowed Eastern lawyers to flood local courts with divorce petitions.[37]

Antipolygamy activists found common cause with advocates of stringent divorce laws: both polygamy and divorce treated marriage as a capricious thing and threatened to destroy it. Anti-divorce activists called divorce "the polygamic principle" or "polygamy on the installment plan."[38] The mobility of the population after the Civil War undercut

---

[33] *Late Corporation of the Church of Jesus Christ of Latter-day Saints* v. *United States*, 136 US 1 (1890) at 49.

[34] *Davis* v. *Beason*, 133 US 333 (1890). Martha Minow (1987: 962–67) has argued that the Supreme Court in the 1920s, 1960s, and 1970s used state regulation of the family as an arena for struggles between competing groups over religion, morality, and different ways of life. She points to *Reynolds* v. *United States* as a "foreshadowing" case.

[35] Campbell and Campbell 1978: 4–23; Mangrum 1988: 325–27; Daynes 2001: 141–59; Firmage and Gordon 2002: 176.

[36] Kern 1981: 168–69; see also Foster 1981: 218.   [37] Gordon 2002: 176.

[38] Ibid. 173.

the ability of state governments to control the law of marriage and divorce, and there was increasing anxiety over rising divorce rates and abandonment. Anti-divorce and antipolygamy reformers joined forces in calling for a "United States marriage law," which would establish uniform marriage and divorce laws. In 1886, Republican Senator George Edmunds, Congress's leading antipolygamy spokesman, attempted to get a bill through Congress that would authorize the government to collect divorce statistics as a first step toward restricting divorce.[39]

In addition to lenient divorce laws, the Mormon experiment with woman's suffrage heightened their image as cultural subversives. In 1870, the Mormon-controlled Utah territorial legislature had unanimously approved the enfranchisement of women, including all female citizens over twenty-one and all the wives, widows, or daughters of native-born or naturalized men. These women of Utah were among the first women to vote in America, and they had the vote for seventeen years before they were disenfranchised by the Edmunds–Tucker Act.[40] Mormon leaders seem to have endorsed woman's suffrage largely out of the desire to ensure their own political domination in Utah by "voting their wives," which doubled their constituency in the face of rapid settlement of "gentiles."[41] In the 1870s, suffragists outside Utah also defended the enfranchisement of Mormon women on the grounds that revoking woman's suffrage would aid polygamy. The expectation here was that once women in Utah had a political voice they would use it to unshackle themselves from polygamy. Indeed, in 1869, a congressman from Indiana had actually introduced a woman's suffrage bill to the Committee on Territories with the hope that female enfranchisement would lead to the abolition of polygamy.[42]

Instead, Mormon women voted the way their husbands did and mobilized in defense of polygamy, and this played into the hands of those who opposed Mormon women's suffrage on the grounds that they were too degraded to exercise an independent political voice. As one observer put it, "Mormon women hold mass-meetings in Salt Lake City that are

[39] Ibid. 129–30, 177; Iversen 1997: 106–107.
[40] Grimes 1967: 33–40. Both the New Jersey constitution written in 1776 and a New Jersey election law passed in 1790 granted the vote to all "inhabitants" who were otherwise qualified to vote, permitting property-owning women to vote. But in 1807 the state legislature restricted the vote to "free, white male citizen[s]," disenfranchising the women of New Jersey. After this retrenchment, women everywhere in the nation were barred from the polls (Smith 1997: 106, 110; Keyssar 2000: 54). Wyoming was the first among the territories and states to pass a bill granting woman suffrage in 1869, but women in Utah actually went to the polls first (Foster 1981: 214).
[41] Lerner 1971: 139; Flexner 1975: 165; Gordon 2002: 168–71.
[42] Kern 1981: 193.

engineered by the church and assert that they are perfectly satisfied with their condition. Before the abolition of slavery the world was assured that negroes were happy in their chains, and individual slaves may have said as much."[43] Even liberal Republicans sympathetic to woman's suffrage outside Utah distanced themselves from the issue. The *New York Times*, which had supported federal legislation to enfranchise the women of Utah, argued after the Female Suffrage Bill passed the Utah legislature that "the downfall of polygamy is too important to be imperiled by experiments in woman suffrage." A few prosuffrage Republicans and women's rights activists argued against revoking female enfranchisement in Utah; they asked why former polygamists should keep the right to vote while their wives lost it. A few Southern Democrats, all of whom opposed woman's suffrage as a matter of federal policy, argued that suffrage was better left to the states and territories.[44] But there was overwhelming support in favor of revocation. Moderate Republicans led the campaign, which met with little resistance in Congress. Republican Senator George Edmunds, the sponsor of the bill that disenfranchised the women of Utah, expressed a widely shared sentiment that likened Mormon women to slaves, stating that revocation would "relieve the Mormon women of Utah from the slavehood of being obliged to exercise a political function which is to keep her in a state of degradation."[45] The disenfranchisement bill had the support of middle-class evangelical women, who were concerned to protect Christian-model monogamy. In 1884, Angie Newman, founder of the Woman's Home Missionary Society and a leading antipolygamy spokeswoman, drafted a petition calling for Congress to abolish woman's suffrage in Utah and obtained 250,000 signatures from among the nation's organized Christian women's groups in support of the bill.[46]

Polygamy, easy divorce, and woman's suffrage were all linked in the minds of antipolygamy activists. To condemn these practices by the Mormon minority was to stand with Christian monogamy. But women's rights activists, including Elizabeth Cady Stanton and Susan B. Anthony, recognized that polygamy and these other "subversive" Mormon measures served as a handy foil that deflected criticism of monogamy and downplayed the limited but not inconsequential improvements in women's status brought about by Mormon-led reforms on divorce and suffrage. While the enfranchisement of women in Utah may not have been intended to advance women's rights, it had the consequence of

---

[43] Quoted in Gordon 1996b: 830.
[44] Congressional Record, 49th Cong., 1st Sess., v. 17, pt. 1, 406–407.
[45] Gordon 2002: 168–71.   [46] Iversen 1997: 103–107, 162–63.

encouraging women's political participation, especially as Congress's assault against polygamy gained momentum. Shortly after they were enfranchised, Mormon women began publishing the *Woman's Exponent*, which ran articles criticizing the inequitable treatment of women in all domains of life and defended polygamy in the name of women's rights. They also established contact with leading women's rights activists, and by 1872, Mormon women held office in the National Woman Suffrage Association (NWSA), the suffrage organization led by Stanton and Anthony. Emmeline B. Wells, the editor of the *Woman's Exponent*, printed news of suffrage activities, and Mormon women helped gather signatures for the NWSA in support of the woman suffrage amendment.[47]

Stanton and Anthony were invited by Mormon suffragists to speak in Salt Lake City in 1871. In her lecture from the pulpit of the Mormon Tabernacle, Stanton attacked patriarchal power and the subordination of women by organized religion and argued that there was just as good reason for polyandry as there was for polygyny. Accompanied by NWSA members, two prominent Mormon women, Emmeline B. Wells and Zina Young Williams, delivered a memorial to the House Judiciary Committee on behalf of all Mormon women, defending their practice of polygamy and asking Congress to repeal the Morrill Act of 1862. They maintained that Mormon women were contented wives and mothers and the effect of enforcing antipolygamy legislation would make fifty thousand women outcasts and their children illegitimate.[48] The alliance between the NWSA and Mormon women was possible in part because NWSA members questioned women's status within all forms of marriage and within all religious communities. Unlike many public officials and citizens of their day, they did not see the *form* of marriage as the key to women's emancipation, emphasizing that women were subordinated within all forms of marriage.

It is within this larger context of mainstream gender practices that Stanton and Anthony viewed the controversy over Mormon polygamy. Stanton herself distinguished among three kinds of "polygamy": Mormon polygamy, bigamy based on fraud, and polygamy involving one wife and many mistresses "everywhere practiced in the United

[47] Iversen 1997: 4–5, 28, 61. The *Woman's Exponent*, which was published between 1872 and 1914, was largely managed and produced by women; it was not officially sponsored by the Mormon Church. Its masthead slogan was "The Rights of the Women of Zion, The Rights of the Women of All Nations," and it criticized the unequal treatment of women in politics, education, and the professions while defending polygamy (Foster 1981: 214–15).
[48] Iversen 1997: 25–26, 29–30.

States."[49] Rather than condemn Mormon polygamy and defend
Christian monogamy, Stanton criticized all contracts of marriage as
oppressive for women: "In entering this contract, the man gives up
nothing that he before possessed – he is a man still; while the legal
existence of the woman is suspended during marriage, and henceforth
she is known but in and through the husband." She sought to improve
women's status within marriage by arguing for greater equality within
marriage and greater freedom to divorce.[50] Similarly, Anthony urged
suffragists to avoid "shouts of puritanic horror" against polygamy and
offer a "simple, loving, sisterly clasp of hands" in order to help abolish
"the whole system of woman's subjection to man in both polygamy and
monogamy."[51] As she would stress many years later, what was important
was women's independence, regardless of marriage form: "What we have
tried to do is to show ... that the principle of the subjection of woman to
man is the point of attack; and that woman's work in monogamy and
polygamy is one and the same – that of planting her feet on the ground of
self-support."[52] The NWSA were careful to separate support for
Mormon women from support for the Mormon religion and polygamy,
but they did not focus their efforts on attacking Mormon polygamy, as
many middle-class evangelical women did, in part because they saw all
forms of marriage as subordinating women and because Mormons had
enfranchised women and provided women with greater freedom to
divorce. When the federal government moved to disenfranchise the
women of Utah with the Edmunds–Tucker bill, NWSA activists argued
against the use of "federal power to disenfranchise the women of Utah,
who have had a more just and liberal spirit shown them by Mormon men
than Gentile women in the States have yet perceived in their rulers."[53]

Antipolygamists who sought to defend Christian monogamy in the face
of attacks by women's rights activists found a convenient diversion in
Mormon polygamy. As legal historian Sarah Barringer Gordon puts it,
"The popular appeal of antipolygamy gave legislators a convenient out –
here was a form of marriage that *truly* replicated 'slavery' for white
women. By enacting laws to prohibit the 'enslavement of women in
Utah,' congressmen could deflect attention from domestic relations in
their own states and direct it towards a rebellious territory. In this sense,
Utah became a handy foil."[54] Antipolygamists attacked what they believed

[49] Weisbrod and Sheingorn 1978: 841.
[50] Stanton, Anthony, and Gage, vol. I, 1848–61: 738–40. On Stanton's views on divorce,
see Clark 1990: 34–38.
[51] Iversen 1997: 35.   [52] Weisbrod and Sheingorn 1978: 842.
[53] Stanton, Anthony, and Gage, vol. III, 1876–85: 128.   [54] Gordon 2002: 54.

to be a deeply patriarchal practice, but the focus on polygamy served the cause of those who defended Christian-model monogamy and the patriarchal roles associated with it. Both Anthony and Stanton's remarks on Mormonism and their emphasis on women's subordination within all forms of marriage suggest that they saw past the diversionary rhetoric.

The focus on polygamy was not only a handy foil against critiques of monogamy, but also a diversion from the federal government's attack on what was probably its bigger concern: the political power of the Mormon Church. In contrast to other nineteenth-century American communal experiments, such as the Shakers and Oneida Perfectionists, the Mormon Church had grown too politically powerful to be ignored. As President Hayes recorded in his diary in 1880, "Laws must be enacted which will take from the Mormon Church its temporal power. Mormonism as a sectarian idea is nothing, but as a system of government it is our duty to deal with it as an enemy of our institutions, and its supporters and leaders as criminals."[55] Reverend Josiah Strong put it more colorfully: Mormonism was "an *imperium in imperio* ruled by a man who is prophet, priest, king and pope, all in one ... he out-popes the Roman by holding familiar conversations with the Almighty, and getting, to order, new revelations direct from heaven." The real danger of Mormonism was "ecclesiastical despotism"; polygamy is "not a root, but a graft."[56] The Mormons were not merely a small separatist community seeking a free exercise exemption from civil marriage laws; they challenged the political authority of the American state by claiming a right to self-government in the Utah Territory. In 1849, Mormons established an autonomous state of Deseret and envisioned a western empire in the Great Salt Lake basin of Utah that was to encompass all of Nevada and Utah and parts of California, Oregon, Arizona, New Mexico, Colorado, and Wyoming. Mormons petitioned for statehood for the Utah Territory in 1850, and when the federal government rejected it, Brigham Young, the first governor of the territory, continued to rule it as a theocracy. They had to accept federally appointed judges, but the Mormon-dominated legislature appointed probate judges in each county with jurisdiction over divorce, alimony, guardianship, and property cases. Children of polygamous wives were recognized and permitted to inherit property, and the courts upheld a variety of living and support arrangements for polygamous families.[57]

Supreme Court Justice Bradley summed up the political threat of Mormonism by pointing to "the past history of the sect, to their defiance

---

[55] Hansen 1981: 144.   [56] Strong 1891: 112–15.   [57] Foster 1981: 216–20.

of the government authorities, to their attempt to establish an independent community, to their efforts to drive from the territory all who were not
connected with them in communion and sympathy." Mormonism was
more than a deviant religious group; it was also an "immense power in the
Territory of Utah" which was "constantly attempting to oppose, thwart,
and subvert the legislation of Congress and the will of the government of
the United States."[58]

Polygamy proved an effective weapon for those whose real concern was
Mormon political power. As Senator Frederick T. Dubois of Idaho
explained,

> Those of us who understand the situation were not nearly so much opposed to
> polygamy as we were to the political domination of the Church. We realized,
> however, that we could not make those who did not come actually in contact with
> it understand what this political domination meant. We made use of polygamy in
> consequence as our great weapon of offence and to gain recruits to our standard.
> There was a universal detestation of polygamy, and inasmuch as the Mormons
> openly defended it, we were given a very effective weapon with which to attack.[59]

Scholars of Mormon history disagree about whether polygamy or
Mormon political power was the real issue behind federal intervention.[60]
What is clear is that the use of polygamy as the federal point of attack
proved politically effective, not only for dismantling Mormon power but
also for deflecting attention from monogamy and the patriarchal norms
associated with it.

Mormon polygamy today

Which arguments from the nineteenth-century debate on polygamy, if
any, are relevant for the contemporary practice of polygamy among
fundamentalist Mormons in America or any minority group engaging in
the practice in liberal democratic societies?

With regard to Mormon polygamy today, government officials have
largely taken a laissez-faire approach, a departure from their approach in
the earlier part of the twentieth century. In 1935, the Utah legislature
declared cohabitation with "more than one person of the opposite sex" a

---

[58] *Mormon Church* v. *United States*, 136 US 1 (1890) at 49, 63–64.
[59] Hansen 1981: 145.
[60] Hansen argues that the theocracy established by the Mormon Church was the primary
concern of anti-Mormon action, whereas Lyman argues that polygamy was at the heart of
the matter (Hansen 1967: xvii–xviii; see also Lyman 1986: 2–5). Gordon contends that
both these views are essentially correct since polygamy and church authority were seen to
be mutually dependent (Gordon 2002: 260–61, n. 6).

criminal felony.[61] Although the code is vaguely worded, this law was invoked in several polygamy cases in the 1930s and 1940s. Using the 1935 legislation on cohabitation, Utah and Arizona authorities took several actions against fundamentalists, including a raid on the Short Creek fundamentalist Mormon community in 1935 and a raid on various locales on charges of kidnapping, cohabitation, criminal conspiracy, and "white slavery" in 1944. The charges of kidnapping and conspiracy were not upheld, but on appeal, the US Supreme Court affirmed convictions based on the Mann or White Slave Traffic Act, which forbids the transportation of women across state lines for immoral purposes. The Court focused on the question of whether Mormon polygamy was a practice of debauchery and immorality within the reach of federal law. Drawing upon arguments from nineteenth-century decisions against Mormon polygamy discussed above, Justice William O. Douglas, writing for the majority, affirmed that it was. In his dissent, Justice Frank Murphy introduced an unprecedented pluralistic perspective into the nation's highest court. He called polygamy "one of the basic forms of marriage" and argued that it did not constitute sexual enslavement, nor was it "in the same genus" as prostitution or debauchery. Citing anthropological findings that monogamy, polygamy, polyandry, and group marriage were four different forms of marriage practiced by different cultures, Justice Murphy argued that Mormon polygamy was "a form of marriage built upon a set of social and moral principles" and ought to be recognized as such.[62]

State and federal authorities have not followed Murphy's lead and gone as far as recognizing polygamy as a legitimate form of marriage; polygamy is still illegal.[63] In practice, however, government officials have increasingly taken a "don't ask, don't tell" approach toward Mormon polygamy. The last major raid against Mormon polygamy took place in 1953 against the Short Creek community in Arizona. There was much public criticism in reaction to photographs of children being torn from their parents and taken to foster homes.[64] Since then, government officials have taken a

---

[61] The Utah penal code states: "If any person cohabits with more than one person of the opposite sex, such a person is guilty of a felony" (Chapter 112, Section 103-51-2).

[62] *Cleveland* v. *United States*, 329 US 14 (1946) at 24–29.

[63] The Utah Criminal Code states, "A person is guilty of bigamy when, knowing he has a husband or wife or knowing the other person has a husband or wife, the person purports to marry another person or cohabits with another person." Bigamy is a felony of the third degree (Utah Criminal Code, 76–7–101). The Utah Constitution also states, "Perfect toleration of religious sentiment is guaranteed. No inhabitant of this State shall ever be molested in person or property on account of his or her mode of religious worship; but polygamous or plural marriages are forever prohibited" (Article III, § 2).

[64] Altman and Ginat 1996: 46.

more tolerant stance. In 1991, the Utah Supreme Court ruled that polygamous families were eligible to adopt. A leader of the Fundamentalist Church of Jesus Christ of Latter-day Saints hailed the Canadian court decision that overturned the ban on polygamy on grounds of religious freedom as a sign that the United States would soon legalize polygamy.[65] This prediction was supported by then Republican Governor Michael O. Leavitt's public statement that polygamy might enjoy protection as a religious freedom. After protests from women who had left polygamous marriages, the governor quickly amended his stance, saying that "plural marriage is wrong, it should stay against the law, and there is no place for it in modern society."[66]

In such a laissez-faire legal climate, the number of individuals living in polygamous families in various communities in Utah and Arizona has increased steadily, and the total number of individuals living in polygamous families is estimated to be between 20,000 and 40,000.[67] In explaining why these communities are growing and few people exit, anthropologists Irwin Altman and Joseph Ginat suggest that the main reason appears to be religious devotion. Mormon fundamentalists are committed to the founding doctrines regarding plural marriage. In speculating about whether there are sexual motives, Altman and Ginat contend that for men "any sexual motives must surely pall after a while, as the day-to-day pressures of plural family life cumulate – the financial burdens, the needs of large families, family tensions and conflicts."[68] They add that the widespread occurrences in American society of serial marriages and divorces, cohabitation of unmarried couples, and affairs and mistresses appear much simpler and more "romantic."

For Mormon women today, as in the nineteenth century, there are strong economic motivations to enter and remain within polygamous relationships. While many women convert to fundamentalism on the grounds that they've discovered the true and underlying basis of Mormonism, many are also divorcées or widows in need of economic support. These women gain "the security of a community and family, the support and assistance of other women, someone to care for their children, and a highly structured set of roles with respect to their husband and children."[69] Women who enter polygamous marriages tend to be women seeking economic security; for them, conversion to the group is usually

---

[65] The Canadian case involved a small group in British Columbia affiliated with the fundamentalists of Hildale, Utah, and Colorado City, Arizona (*Salt Lake Tribune*, June 16, 1992).
[66] Brooke 1998: 12.
[67] Altman and Ginat estimate between 20,000 and 50,000 (1996: 51, 54).
[68] Ibid. 439.   [69] Ibid. 440.

followed by striking upward social and economic mobility. Janet Bennion notes that the Mormon fundamentalist group provides "lower-class female recruits" the chance to "ascend to a position of higher marriage (hypergamy)" and a higher level of economic satisfaction than male recruits to Mormon fundamentalism.[70] Compared to women from the mainstream LDS Church, Bennion finds that Mormon fundamentalist women participate more in social and religious work and also pursue paid work outside the home at higher rates. She argues that polygyny "develops independent women who bear much of the financial responsibility for their families." But her study also finds that men in these communities seek to counteract egalitarian values from the wider society with harsher rules and restrictions for women.[71]

If we listen to what Mormon women themselves are saying about polygamy, we find a contested practice. On one side is Tapestry of Polygamy, a group of former polygamous wives, who support the legal ban on polygamy and favor its strong enforcement. They argue that *de facto* accommodation of polygamy reinforces women's subordination within fundamentalist Mormon communities. On the other side are women living in polygamous relationships, such as members of Women's Religious Liberties Union, who favor decriminalization of polygamy in the name of religious freedom. They also argue that polygamous arrangements are good for women because they allow them to pursue both career and family by sharing childcare and household responsibilities. A website they maintain denounces forced marriage and incest, and echoing the sentiments of Stanton and Anthony, states that "[a]buse is not inherent in polygamy and can exist in any society."[72] Non-Mormons have also made secular arguments in favor of polygamy. In contrasting monogamy and polygamy, one advocate maintains that frequent divorce and remarriage, separation of children from parents, multiplication of step-relationships, and total breakdown of paternal responsibility suggest that the institution of serial monogamy is in serious trouble and may be no better than polygamy per se.[73]

---

[70] Bennion (1998: 64–65) finds that of the women who converted to the Allred fundamentalist Mormon group, 69 percent (706 women) had graduated from high school, and of that number, 12 percent (143) had earned a college degree. Overall most women who became plural wives and who worked for wages were low-skilled workers.

[71] At least 25 percent of women Bennion interviewed expressed desire to leave if they could do so without losing their children (Bennion 1998: 134, 136, 151–52).

[72] See Mary Batchelor, Marianne Watson, and Anne Wilde's *Voices in Harmony: Contemporary Women Celebrate Plural Marriage* (2000) and www.principlevoices.org.

[73] See Kilbride 1994.

A case for qualified recognition

What then is the appropriate response to the contemporary practice of polygamy? The charge that polygamous relationships are oppressive is contingent, and needs to be investigated by looking at individual relationships and their context, just as monogamous relationships should be. On a rights-respecting accommodationist approach, the importance of polygamy for Mormon fundamentalists must be weighed against protecting the basic rights of Mormon women and children. On the one hand, liberal democracies should respect people's religious liberty and the liberty to pursue the kinds of intimate relationships that accord with their convictions and desires.[74] Mormon fundamentalists maintain that polygamy is of great importance to their beliefs and way of life. If Mormon women maintain that they have freely chosen to remain in polygamous marriage in accordance with their religious convictions, the state should respect their choices but on the condition that they are free to exit. Determining whether women have realistic rights of exit is no easy matter; it requires consideration of the sorts of conditions necessary for genuine consent and exit, as well as contextual inquiry to see whether such conditions obtain in any given case.

Exit has recently received considerable attention as a solution to the problem of internal minorities. Some liberal political theorists defend toleration of illiberal religious and cultural groups, endorsing a principle of state nonintervention, when these groups meet certain minimal conditions necessary for exit.[75] The central claim here is that religious and cultural groups should be let alone so long as membership in these groups is voluntary. Not voluntary in the sense that a religious belief and cultural attachments are experienced as choices, but rather that individual members can, if they wish, exit groups. The appeal of exit as a solution to the problem of internal minorities has not only to do with its providing vulnerable members with a way to escape internal oppression but also with the transformative potential that the *threat* of exit can have. As Albert O. Hirschman famously argued, the threat of exit can enhance one's voice in decision-making.[76] In the context of minority groups, the idea is that if many members can credibly threaten to exit the group on account of their disagreement with particular aspects of group life, the group's leaders

---

[74] Laurence Tribe has long maintained on civil libertarian grounds that polygamy should be constitutionally protected and has predicted for the last two decades that *Reynolds* would be overruled (1988: 521–28).

[75] See Rosenblum 1998; Spinner-Halev 2000 and 2005; Shachar 2001; Galston 2002; Kukathas 2003.

[76] Hirschman 1970.

would be compelled to reform those aspects. In the Mormon polygamy case, if the threat of exit by women opposed to polygamous marriage was serious enough, it could compel group leaders to reform their marriage practices or to abolish polygamy altogether.

While exit is a real option for members of many religious and cultural minority groups in contemporary America, whether it really is in any particular case depends on the costs of exit and the nature of the group in question. Describing people's convictions and attachments as voluntary seems appropriate against, as Nancy Rosenblum puts it, "a background of fluid pluralism, where other religious homes are open to splitters and the formation of new associations is a real possibility." So long as members are free to exit, religious and cultural associations need not be congruent with public norms and institutions "all the way down."[77] But how far down state intervention will have to go in order to ensure realistic rights of exit for vulnerable internal minorities is an open question. First, there is the issue of how isolated or open the group is to the wider society. Groups that are relatively isolated and which socialize their members into the inevitability of sex hierarchy, as may well be the case with Mormon fundamentalist communities, are especially worrisome. There is also the issue of the costs of exit, not just the material costs of leaving but also intrinsic and social costs. Leaving means losing not just the cultural or religious affiliations themselves and the intrinsic value they hold for members (intrinsic costs) but also the social relationships afforded by membership (associative costs). In addition, there may be extrinsic costs of educational and employment opportunities or other material benefits associated with membership.[78] There is not much the state or the wider society can do about intrinsic or associative costs, but it can assist those trying to leave their communities with the extrinsic costs of exit.

Okin's criticism of the strategy of exit highlights a different kind of obstacle having to do with the *capacity* for exit, conditions of knowledge and psychology, which require a different sort of response than providing material resources. In many minority groups, there may be strong countervailing pressures that undermine the capacity for exit for women and girls in particular. Okin highlights three such pressures: girls are much more likely to be shortchanged than boys in education; they are more likely to be socialized in ways that undermine their self-esteem and that encourage them to defer to existing hierarchies; and they are likely to be forced into early marriages from which they lack the power to exit.[79]

---

[77] Rosenblum 1998: 85, 4.

[78] For an excellent discussion of different types of exit costs, see Barry 2001: 150–51.

[79] Okin 1999: 128; 2002: 216–22.

Under such conditions, women and girls within religious groups can hardly be said to enjoy a realistic right of exit.

These concerns suggest the need to think carefully about the sorts of conditions under which women can genuinely make free choices to stay or leave and what the state can do to foster those conditions. Minimal standards necessary to ensure the worth of a right of exit include members' freedom from abuse and coercion; access to decent health care, nutrition, and education; and the existence of genuine alternatives among which to make choices, including real access to a mainstream society to exit to.[80] To address the concerns about capacity raised by Okin, education must play a key role. Children should be taught about their basic constitutional and civic rights so they know that liberty of conscience exists in their society and that apostasy is not a legal crime.

Some argue that even these minimal standards are too robust, and that the existence of a surrounding market society is all that is required for exit to be a meaningful option.[81] But such an approach overlooks the serious obstacles to exit that the state can help ameliorate and assumes that any state action to address these obstacles would be worse in terms of violating basic individual freedoms (especially freedom of association) than leaving vulnerable members to cope on their own. This minimalist position is right to stress that states have oppressed minority groups. As I argued in chapter 3, this fact supports some minority group claims for accommodation. But the fact of past oppression of minority groups should not rule out state involvement in contemporary problems. For some individual members of minority groups, group authorities may be experienced as more oppressive than the state. Here the state can play a role in protecting the basic rights of individuals. Giving a role to the state does not mean any form of intervention goes; rather, the state's role should be limited to meeting the minimal conditions necessary for exit.

What do these considerations about exit suggest for the contemporary case of Mormon polygamy? A legal regime of qualified recognition of polygamy can, I think, more effectively ensure Mormon women's rights to exit their communities than outright proscription. The current ban on polygamy leaves polygamous wives and their children even more vulnerable to domination by driving polygamous communities into hiding. In May 2001, Tom Green, a husband of five and father of twenty-nine, was

---

[80] Other specific proposals include an exit fund to which group members must contribute to enable members to meet the economic costs of exit should they decide to leave (Spinner-Halev 2000: 77–79) and state regulation of the economic aspects of divorce in the context of legal pluralistic arrangements (Shachar 2001: 124–25, 134–35).

[81] See, e.g., Kukathas 1992, 2003.

convicted on four counts of bigamy, the first prosecution of polygamy since 1953. Green's conviction has caused anxiety among some members of polygamous communities. They fear that prosecution of polygamy will discourage the group's most vulnerable members from reporting abuse of women and children. As Anne Wilde, who has been in a polygamous marriage for thirty-two years, put it, "This has pushed people a little further underground." She adds that the *Green* case had done a major disservice to the estimated 30,000 polygamists who live in Utah and neighboring states by presenting a false image of their chosen way of life. She contends that Green is an anomaly among polygamists for having wives and children in far greater numbers than average polygamist husbands. A more common family includes two to three wives and eight to ten children. Even worse, she says, the separate charge of child rape against Green for having one wife who was thirteen at the time of their marriage may leave the impression that all polygamist husbands marry under-age girls and abuse children when in fact most do not. Sidney Anderson, director of Women's Religious Liberties Union, also argues that fear of prosecution for polygamy almost assures that when child abuse does happen it is more likely to go unreported: "The state is forcing them into an abusive situation, and some men are using it to convince women that they have to live in isolation for the unit to be safe. So women who need help can't get it out of fear." Ms. Anderson argues that the best way to help vulnerable members within polygamous communities is to decriminalize bigamy altogether, which would make it easier for members of plural families to seek help when they need it.[82]

A strategy of qualified recognition of polygamy was pursued in reforming the customary marriage laws in South Africa, and this case is instructive for the case of Mormon polygamy. Drawing on provisions in the South African constitution, reformers sought simultaneously to respect customary law and protect women's rights.[83] On the one hand, the constitution recognizes the rights of cultural and religious groups, including various systems of customary African law. On the other hand, it specifies equal individual rights and prohibits racial and sexual discrimination, among other forms of discrimination. In the discussions leading up to reform, many different groups were consulted, including the traditional leaders' Congress, women's groups, legal reform groups, and scholars of constitutional and customary law. The actual lived practices of customary marriage were at the center of discussion. The chiefs were

[82] Janofsky 2001: A14.   [83] Here I draw on Chambers 2000 and Deveaux 2003.

persuaded that reforming the customary marriage laws was less likely to erode their authority than retaining traditional customary marriage laws.

What emerged from the deliberations was the Recognition of Customary Marriages Act of 1998. It recognizes all past customary unions as "marriages" while also reforming customary marriage itself. The law declares women and men formal equals within marriage and grants the state a role in regulating customary marriage. The law requires all marriages to be registered with a government agency, and it requires that divorce and child custody proceedings be conducted by a family court judge, as opposed to a tribal court. Customary groups are permitted to retain *lobolo* (bride price) as a condition of valid marriage, and polygyny was preserved in a modified form. In order to take a second wife, a man must make a written contract with his existing wife fairly dividing the property accrued at that point and persuade a family court that the contract is fair for all involved.[84]

Qualified recognition of polygamy, as in the case of the modified customary marriage law in South Africa, can offer Mormon women the protection of the law while also respecting their religious commitments. If the law were to recognize polygamy, it could secure legal rights for polygamous wives and ex-wives by regulating the conditions of entry into and exit from such relations. As in the South African case, the state might require a man seeking an additional wife to obtain the consent of his existing wife and to draw up a contract that fairly divides the property they had accrued at that point. If she approved, the couple would then have to obtain the approval of a family court judge. A state that recognizes polygamy could also secure rights for ex-wives and the rights of inheritance for children of polygamous relationships by regulating the terms of property division after divorce. Currently, a polygamous husband may abandon any wife beyond his first without providing any assistance to her and her children. Securing Mormon wives' exit rights could help strengthen their voice within polygamous relationships.

Utah authorities have moved toward a *de facto* regime of qualified recognition. They have shifted away from prosecuting polygamy per se toward cracking down on abuses that occur within polygamous marriages. The Utah attorney general publicly advised prosecutors to avoid prosecuting cases of consensual adult bigamy. Instead, Utah authorities have reached a consensus to crack down on child abuse, statutory rape, and incest. In 1998, the Utah Legislature raised the age for statutory rape to seventeen from sixteen. In 1999, the Legislature raised the minimum

---

[84] Chambers 2000: 112–13.

marriage age from fourteen to sixteen.[85] The attorney general said he planned to ask the state legislature for money to hire additional investigators for matters relating to "closed societies" so that more traditional crimes do not go unpunished. He favors reducing the charge of bigamy from a felony to a misdemeanor in order to encourage people to provide information about serious crimes in polygamous families.[86] These reforms may stem more from the practical difficulties of prosecuting polygamy: as in the nineteenth century polygamous men generally obtain marriage licenses only for their first wives and subsequent marriages are performed secretly. But in addition to these prudential concerns, there are principled arguments in favor of decriminalization. The public morals argument pressed by nineteenth-century antipolygamy activists, that polygamy was offensive to Christian public morals, does not offer a compelling reason, but the other argument, the concern for equal protection, does. We have good reasons to think that qualified recognition of polygamy can better protect the basic rights of Mormon women and children in polygamous households than a ban on polygamy.

Conclusion

In this chapter, as in the previous two chapters, we have seen how the gender norms of the dominant culture have shaped its responses to the gender practices of minority cultures. In the case of nineteenth-century Mormon polygamy, the dominant culture's opposition to polygamy appears to have been motivated less by a concern to empower women and more by a desire to uphold the public morals of the dominant culture. Citizens and public officials opposing polygamy sought to protect Christian-model monogamy, and the focus on Mormon polygamy helped shield the dominant culture's own patriarchal practices from criticism.

The diversionary effect can be seen beyond the case of Mormon polygamy. Focusing on cases of domestic violence and forced marriage in immigrant communities can serve to reinforce a false dichotomy between oppressive minority cultures and egalitarian Western majority cultures, deflecting attention from the reality of domestic violence and underage marriage within the latter. Marriage practices within immigrant communities should be evaluated alongside practices that are common to

---

[85] Utah Statutes, §76, ch. 5, 401.2; §30, chs. 1, 9.

[86] Janofsky 2001. In contrast to the case of Tom Green, in the more recent case of Warren Jeffs, the leader of the Fundamentalist Church of Jesus Christ of Latter-day Saints, state authorities are not charging him with bigamy itself but with being an accessory to rape by arranging marriages between underage girls and older men (Newman 2006).

the majority culture: parental pressure over whom to marry and parent-arranged blind dates. Mainstream marriage practices should receive the same kind of scrutiny as the marriage practices of minority communities with the issue of a woman's consent to marriage and a minimum age for all marriages at the forefront of these considerations.

Similarly, while Western feminist criticism of female circumcision among immigrant communities is animated by a concern for gender justice, the focus on immigrant practices can simultaneously serve to divert attention from the variety of cosmetic surgeries and bodily alterations, such as breast enlargement, facelifts, and labiaplasty, commonly practiced in Western societies.[87] Charges of a double standard arose in the context of a debate over female circumcision among the Somali immigrant community in the Seattle area.

Somali immigrants residing in the West have generally handled female circumcision discreetly, but in 1996, some Somali mothers who gave birth to daughters in a Seattle hospital asked doctors to perform clitori-dectomies on their daughters. The doctors initially refused, but they reconsidered when Somali parents stated that they would either send their daughters back to Somalia or to Somali midwives in the Seattle area to perform what would most likely be a physically impairing form of circumcision. Somali parents offered both cultural and religious reasons for the practice. As a cultural matter, their daughters would be "shamed, dishonored, and unmarriageable if they were not cut, an act that shows their purity."[88] As a religious matter, although there is debate within the Muslim community about whether Islam requires female circumcision, some Muslim families from Somalia insist that "their faith requires it, much as the Jewish faith does male circumcision."[89] In response, doctors and medical ethicists formed a committee and met with Somali parents and daughters to devise an alternative to traditional circumcision that would meet both the cultural and religious demands of the Somali community and protect young Somali girls from physically impairing harm. The parties involved agreed to a compromise proposal: a modified form of circumcision which amounted to "a small cut ... with no tissue excised" and "conducted under local anesthetic for children old enough to understand the procedure and give consent in combination with informed consent of the parents."[90] The doctors defended this alternative surgery as a way to accommodate the cultural commitments of Somali immigrant parents and their daughters while avoiding physically impairing forms of female circumcision, such as infibulation and clitoridectomy.

---

[87] Navarro 2004.   [88] Brune 1996.   [89] Ostrom 1996.   [90] Brune 1996.

News of the hospital's compromise proposal quickly spread across the country, and some feminist groups criticized the proposal as legitimating a barbaric practice that subordinates women. Patricia Schroeder, who led the effort to enact federal legislation proscribing female circumcision, wrote to the Seattle hospital, stating that their proposal would violate federal law.[91] Under fire, the hospital abandoned the compromise proposal. Feminist critics were right to be concerned about the harm caused by female circumcision and to question its dangers. But their efforts to ban the compromise proposal altogether undermined their own professed goal of reforming the practice of female circumcision, and their interventions cut short further intercultural dialogue that had developed between Somali immigrants and the larger community of doctors and concerned local citizens. It was by engaging Somali parents in conversations about the practice of female circumcision that the Seattle doctors had been able to gain acceptance for the modified version of the practice.

The opponents of the compromise proposal were also vulnerable to the charge of imposing a double standard by seeking a ban on the modified version of female circumcision while permitting male circumcision. Somali parents had questioned the Seattle doctors about the basis of this distinction. It is not evident that the modified form of female circumcision harms girls in a way that male circumcision does not harm boys. Looking further for comparable practices in the dominant culture, we might point to young American girls who are permitted to get their bodies pierced or receive cosmetic surgeries with their parents' approval. Insofar as modified forms of circumcision are comparable to the dominant culture's practices of male circumcision, body piercing, and cosmetic surgery and are consistent with ensuring the basic rights of those undergoing these procedures, it is not clear why they should be banned.[92] This is not to say that the majority culture should encourage modified versions of female circumcision but rather that there may be good reasons for permitting them, namely to recognize that the practice is viewed as an important rite of passage for young women in the Somali community and to prevent physically impairing versions of the genital operation. There may well be a good case to be made that certain forms of female circumcision, especially when they involve young girls, should be limited in ways that other forms of bodily alterations commonly practiced in the West are not. The

[91] Because the symbolic cut proposed by the Seattle doctors did not involve excision or infibulation of any tissue, it seems unlikely that it would have violated state child abuse laws or the Federal Prohibition of Female Genital Mutilation Act of 1994. See Coleman 1998: 751–59.
[92] For this line of argument, see Carens and Williams 1998 and Shweder 2000.

point here is that such practices should be analyzed alongside comparable majority practices and in the broader context of Western reaction to such practices, lest we overlook the diversionary effects that can reinforce gender hierarchies across cultures. These cases also suggest the need for critics in the West to guard against reproducing colonial discourses of cultural and racial superiority while voicing feminist concerns. One way to do so is to examine the social contexts of both ritual practices and the national and international discourses surrounding them with special attention to long-standing power inequalities between East and West.

7   Epilogue

Liberal democracies can pursue both equal justice for cultural minorities and equal justice for women. I have argued that rights-respecting accommodationism is the best expression of these dual commitments. To counter egalitarian critics of multiculturalism, I explored circumstances in which liberal democracies must go beyond uniform treatment toward granting special accommodations for cultural minorities. At the same time, sharing the concern of many feminist critics of multiculturalism, I stressed that the protection of the basic rights of vulnerable members of minority groups is an important limit on accommodation.

In defending rights-respecting accommodationism, I have argued for acknowledgment of the constructed, polyvocal, and interactive character of cultures and the complex sources of the problem of internal minorities. We saw in the foregoing chapters that cultures are not as coherent and self-contained as prominent defenders and critics of multiculturalism have assumed. As the historical and contemporary struggles of the Santa Clara Pueblo suggest, the criteria and value of tribal membership have long been contested. Upholding the tribe's existing gender-biased membership rules in the name of respecting long-held traditions ignores not only such contestation but also the influence of intercultural interactions in shaping Pueblo membership practices. The state has played a key role in shaping the practices at the center of many gendered cultural dilemmas. In some cases, accommodation of minority practices has been driven not by considerations of justice centered on equal respect for cultural minorities but by the congruence of inegalitarian norms between majority and minority cultures. Like the Santa Clara Pueblo case, the "cultural defense" cases demonstrate the ways in which the dominant culture can offer support for the patriarchal practices of minority cultures. Even in cases where minority practices are not accommodated, intercultural dynamics are at work. Condemnation of minority practices can divert attention from the majority culture's own patriarchal practices, as in the case of nineteenth-century struggles over Mormon polygamy and

169

contemporary conflicts over arranged marriage and female circumcision in immigrant communities.

These findings have several important implications for how we understand and respond to the problem of internal minorities. First, they compel us to reformulate the problem. Once we recognize the interactive and interconnected nature of cultures, it no longer makes sense to frame the problem of internal minorities in ways that suggest that minority cultures are the sole problem. Rather, we need to be attentive to both inegalitarian practices within minority cultures and inegalitarian aspects of Western majority cultures and how they may interact. Formulating the problem in this way allows for consideration of the ongoing role that mainstream norms and institutions play in shaping minority practices, whether in ways that protect or undermine the rights of vulnerable group members. On this reformulation, then, "culture" is not the problem; oppressive practices are. This is a point emphasized by many minority women who are at the center of gendered cultural conflicts and who seek both equality for cultural minorities and equality for women.

A second implication has to do with devising solutions to gendered cultural dilemmas. If we conceive of these dilemmas as "multiculturalism v. equality" or "culture v. gender," we are faced with an either/or choice between siding with multiculturalism at the expense of equality and siding with equality at the expense of multiculturalism. This either/or strategy falls short. On the one hand, as feminist critics have stressed, simply saying yes to cultural accommodation fails to protect vulnerable members within minority communities. But simply saying no to accommodation and demanding assimilation or saying no until minorities liberalize up to the level of majority cultures also falls short since the majority culture is in certain respects not less patriarchal than minority cultures, just differently so, and because, as I argued in chapter 3, rejecting accommodation altogether fails to accord equal respect to members of minority cultural groups. An appropriate response to these dilemmas requires simultaneously addressing inequalities within both minority and majority cultures.

Taking the "cultural defense" cases examined in chapter 4 as an example, addressing the problems raised by such cases requires reevaluating the majority culture's own norms and policies, alongside minority practices. Simply asking whether to permit or ban the cultural defense is not enough. On the one hand, permitting the use of cultural defenses without the critical scrutiny I suggested would leave minority women at the center of these cases without equal protection of the law. But simply banning the cultural defense would deny immigrant defendants equal access to existing legal defenses and leave intact the majority culture's own gendered understandings of agency and responsibility. So long as patriarchal norms pervade mainstream legal doctrine and practice, minority defendants will continue to find support for patriarchal practices within mainstream law. An adequate response requires reformulating mainstream legal doctrines, such as provocation, as well as challenging minority practices that reinforce women's subordination.

The case studies also suggest the importance of giving those at the center of particular cultural conflicts a voice in the resolution of those conflicts. A central argument of this book has been that the specific policies and solutions addressing gendered dilemmas of culture are best determined through democratic deliberation in the context of specific cases. The aim of my rights-respecting accommodationist argument has been to offer an egalitarian normative framework by which to evaluate specific proposals, but it is through intercultural democratic dialogue that legitimate and contextually wise solutions must be negotiated and revised. Justice requires that multicultural accommodations be rights-respecting, and the best way to achieve rights-respecting results is through a deliberative process that includes the voices of all those affected by the rules or traditions in question. Such inclusion not only comes closer to treating members of minority cultural groups as equals; it also has practical advantages. In the case of gendered cultural conflicts, what constitutes gender subordination and how best to address it will not be self-evident. A deliberative approach is crucial for clarifying what is at stake and for whom, whether basic rights are threatened, and what the sources of the threat are.

Consider the issue of veiling among Muslim women and girls. Many Western observers may be inclined to view the Muslim headscarf as a symbol of women's oppression, fueled by the larger tendency in the West today to think in binary oppositions between an enlightened West and a backward East. Such a view echoes earlier colonial discourses on veiling. At least as far back as the nineteenth century, British imperialists viewed women's veiling as a key symbol of Eastern backwardness. As Leila Ahmed argues, in nineteenth-century Western discourse, "the veil and segregation epitomized [women's] oppression, and ... were the fundamental reasons for the general and comprehensive backwardness of Islamic societies. Only if these practices 'intrinsic' to Islam (and therefore Islam itself) were cast off could Muslim societies begin to move forward."[1] Not unlike some contemporary feminist criticism of multiculturalism, Western colonial discourse constructed an either/or choice

---

[1] Ahmed 1992: 152.

between embracing Islam and permitting women's oppression, on the one hand, and rejecting Islam and supporting women's empowerment, on the other. But such dichotomous thinking ignores the polyvocal character of Islam and of the practice of veiling in particular. The practice of veiling has been shaped through varied, conflicting discourses of religion, culture, nationhood, and gender, and there is vast disagreement about the meaning and importance of veiling among Muslims. In light of this, an approach that is sensitive to the particularities of context and which draws on the voices of those at the center of controversies over veiling is crucial.

Whether and how veiling is practiced varies greatly across different contexts. Veiling is compulsory in Iran, whereas it is prohibited in many public places in Turkey, although Muslim women in universities have demanded the right to wear headscarves while attending classes.[2] There are distinct styles of veiling. Many who defend veiling point to a well-known verse in the Qur'an that prescribes modesty for women and interpret it as requiring modest dress through covering certain parts of the body.[3] The *chador* refers to the long black robe that covers the hair and entire body and is most commonly associated with Iran; the *nikab* is a veil for the face that leaves the area around the eyes clear and is worn with an accompanying headscarf; the *hijab* refers to a scarf covering the head and neck. Those Muslim women who wear the *hijab* believe modesty requires that they cover their hair and necks while those who wear the *nikab* extend the idea to their faces. Those who do not wear headscarves or veils believe they can guard their modesty by other means, for instance, by covering their arms and legs and avoiding clothes such as bikinis, mini-skirts, and garments that are transparent or fit tightly to emphasize their figures.[4]

It is not just the practice of veiling that is varied, but also Muslim women's views of the practice. Some Muslim feminists see veiling as largely oppressive. As Fatima Mernissi argues, "[T]he veil can be interpreted as a symbol revealing a collective fantasy of the Muslim community; to make women disappear, to eliminate them from communal life, to relegate them to an easily controllable terrain, the home, to prevent them from moving about, and to highlight their illegal position on male territory by means of a mask."[5] Other Muslim feminists view veiling and other practices of the seclusion of women as empowering devices that shield them from the lustful gaze of men and which help them preserve their cultural traditions in the face of pressures to westernize.[6] Valentine Moghadam suggests that such seclusion "provides the opportunity for preserving one's identity and a certain stability in the face of external

---

[2] Göle 1997.   [3] See Engineer 2004.   [4] Afshar 1995.
[5] Mernissi 1982: 189.   [6] Abu-Odeh 1992: 1529–31.

pressures." Yet, she also argues that seclusion's value as a symbol of resistance has served more to "strengthen the men's will to resist" rather than women's. She suggests that the more covered women are required to be and the more extensive the segregation, the more oppressed they are.[7] Still others argue that veiling is a minor issue, which distracts from more urgent problems of women's health and education, economic dependence, violence against women, and divorce and child custody.[8] Some question the practice of veiling as intrinsic to Islam.[9] These conflicting views of veiling suggest that the question of whether it is an expression of women's agency or a sign of their subordination cannot but be pursued in light of the particularities of context.[10]

This applies to Western contexts in which controversies over the headscarf have arisen. As is well-known, it has been the subject of greatest controversy in France, where the headscarf has come to symbolize the dilemmas of French national identity in a postcolonial multicultural age. *L'affaire foulard* began in 1989 when three Muslim girls were expelled from their school in Creil for wearing headscarves.[11] The three girls had apparently decided to wear headscarves on the advice of Daniel Youssouf Leclerq, the head of an organization called Integrité and the former president of the National Federation of Muslims in France. The event generated a political storm, mobilizing many Muslim groups, but this mobilization did not generate unity among Muslim organizations in France since there are diverse views within Islam about the issue of veiling and more generally the public nature of Islam.[12] The Minister of National Education took the case to France's highest administrative court, the *Conseil d'État*. The court ruled that wearing religious signs or dress did not violate the French republican principle of *laïcité* but added that they could be forbidden if through "pressure, provocation, proselytism or propaganda" they interfered with the statutory mission of state education, which included fostering respect for individuals and guaranteeing equality of the sexes. The court's nuanced ruling left the decision of whether the wearing of headscarves was compatible with the principle of *laïcité* to be made by local school officials on a case-by-case basis. While many local schools reached compromise through dialogue with Muslim pupils and their families, some schools reacted by introducing restrictive

---

[7] Moghadam 1994: 82.   [8] Ahmed 1992: 166.   [9] al-Hibri 1982: 216.
[10] For an illuminating discussion of veiling in a variety of contexts, see Hirschmann 2003: ch. 6.
[11] See Laborde 2005 and Poulter 1997 for accounts of the controversy.
[12] Warner and Wenner 2006: 470.

measures banning religious dress, resulting in many expulsions of Muslim girls who wear the headscarf.[13]

The controversy continues. In 2003, President Jacques Chirac established an independent commission to study the implementation of the principle of *laïcité* in the French republic. The commission was led by Bernard Stasi and was composed of twenty experts, mostly academics and lawyers, including Patrick Weil, a prominent scholar of French politics and immigration. In writing about the experience, Weil explains that he began with the idea that a law was probably unnecessary for resolving the disputes.[14] Yet, after four months of public hearings involving representatives of religious groups, political parties, trades unions, and NGOs, as well as principals, teachers, parents, and students, he signed on to the commission's report recommending twenty-five different measures, including a national ban in public schools on "the wearing of signs or clothes through which pupils ostensibly express a religious allegiance." In 2004, the French National Assembly and the French Senate overwhelmingly voted in favor of a ban on religious signs or clothes in primary and secondary public schools, which includes Muslim headscarves, Jewish *yarmulkes*, and large Christian crosses. In explaining why he favored a national legal ban over local nonlegal solutions, Weil emphasizes matters of context: "[I]n the last two to three years, it has become clear that in schools where some Muslim girls do wear the headscarf and others do not, there is strong pressure on the latter to 'conform.' This daily pressure takes different forms, from insults to violence. In the view of the (mostly male) aggressors, these girls are 'bad Muslims,' 'whores,' who should follow the example of their sisters who respect Koranic prescriptions." In testimonies, a majority of girls who do not wear the headscarf asked the commission for legal protection through a ban on all public displays of religious belief. The public hearings made clear that the issue of veiling in France has become more than a matter of individual freedom to express religious belief or cultural identity; it has become, in Weil's words, "a France-wide strategy pursued by fundamentalist groups who use public schools as their battleground." If this is true, then a ban on headscarves may be the best way to protect the majority of Muslim girls who do not wish to veil from the pressures to do so.

The limits of the ban are clear: those Muslim girls who freely want to wear the headscarf in public schools for a variety of reasons, whether out of religious devotion, as a marker of cultural identity, or as a political statement, without pressuring anyone else are denied the freedom to do

---

[13] Poulter 1997: 60–62.   [14] My discussion here draws on Weil 2004.

so. It is possible that the girls themselves, brought out of patriarchal homes and into public schools, have felt empowered to reinterpret the meaning of wearing the headscarf, and the French ban curbs such opportunities for expression and empowerment.[15] Yet, it is also possible, as Weil argues, that the patriarchal norms of home and religion have found their way into public schools through the practice of veiling. If the aim is to protect the basic rights of Muslim girls and the conditions are such that a great many of them feel coerced into wearing the headscarf and actually seek legal protection from such coercion, then a ban on the headscarf in public schools seems appropriate. The legal ban is limited to minors attending public schools and does not preclude other forms of accommodation to Muslim minorities, which should be provided for the reasons I discussed in chapter 3. The ban on headscarves in public schools was only one of twenty-five proposals of the Stasi commission, which included measures to address discrimination against North African immigrants and their children, reform school history curriculum to acknowledge slavery and colonization as part of France's national history, and recognize the most important religious feasts of minority faiths as public holidays. The effects of the French ban remain to be seen. If the ban drives many Muslim families to withdraw their daughters from public schools and send them to private Muslim schools and if such withdrawal has the effect of jeopardizing the girls' access to adequate education and employment opportunities, then the ban should be reconsidered.

Controversies over the practice of veiling in other Western countries will require different responses depending on the particularities of context. Muslim women in the United States who wear the headscarf have reported incidents of discrimination, verbal abuse, and death threats, suggesting that the events of September 11 transformed the headscarf from an exotic symbol of difference to a threatening one in the eyes of many Westerners.[16] This has led some Muslim organizations, such as the Muslim Women's League, to urge Muslim American women not to veil in public for reasons of safety, stressing that the Qur'an is clear that the aim of Islamic dress is to avoid harassment.[17] In spite of these incidents, the issue of veiling has proved less divisive in the United States than in France and has not attracted widespread national attention. This may partly be due to the greater affluence and diversity of Muslim minorities in the United States and the greater percentage and geographic concentration of Muslim minorities in France whose relations with the dominant culture are shaped by the legacy of colonialism, but it may also be due to

---

[15] Benhabib 2002: 117–18.   [16] MacFarquhar 2006.
[17] www.mwlusa.org/publications/Sept11/hijab_dangerous_times.htm.

differences in civic ideals, especially public commitment to religious and cultural diversity. Disputes over veiling in the United States have been handled at the local level. In a 2003 case, a Florida state judge rejected a Muslim woman's request to have her face covered by a veil on her driver's license photograph.[18] The judge acknowledged the sincerity of Sultaana Freeman's belief and examined the burden of requiring her to be unveiled in the photograph. To justify the burden, the state stressed the security interest in having individuals be fully visible on the primary form of state identification, and the judge deemed the state's interest as sufficient justification of the burden imposed on Ms. Freeman's belief.

In other contexts in the United States, however, state authorities may not be able to provide compelling reasons justifying burdens on religious dress. In the fall of 2003, a fifth-grade Muslim student, Nashala Hearn, was suspended for wearing a headscarf in her Oklahoma public school. The school argued that the headscarf violated its dress code, which banned hats and other head coverings.[19] But a reason more compelling than uniforms for uniformity's sake must be provided to justify the weighty burden imposed on the girl's religious observance. The school must demonstrate that a ban on religious dress serves an important purpose or real need, rather than a mere convenience, and show that viable alternatives are not available to meet that purpose. As I argued in chapter 3 in the context of other religion cases, a compelling purpose might be established in cases where wearing the headscarf could put the health, safety, or basic rights and opportunities of vulnerable members of minority groups at risk. Determining whether wearing the headscarf has such effects requires the aid of deliberation, making sure to include the voices of those at the center of these controversies. In the absence of a compelling reason for a uniform dress policy and in the absence of evidence that accommodation would threaten the basic rights of the girls involved, accommodation should be granted. In Nashala Hearn's case, the school district and Justice Department, which intervened on her behalf, reached an agreement in which the dress code policy permits exemptions for religious reasons. As part of its efforts to address complaints of discrimination and hate crimes brought by Muslim and Arab Americans, the Justice Department's settlement with the school district also required the district to establish training programs for all teachers and administrators about the new dress code and to discuss the change with students. Where consistent with protecting the basic rights of vulnerable group members, accommodation not only expresses equal

[18] *Freeman* v. *State*, 2003 WL 21338619 (Fla. Cir. Ct. June 6, 2003).
[19] Anderson 2004.

respect for Muslim minorities but can help foster their social and political inclusion.

These controversies over the headscarf in Western contexts bring us to a third implication that follows from recognizing the intercultural dynamics examined in this book. Citizens of liberal democracies should approach intercultural democratic dialogue with a spirit of cross-cultural humility, especially in an age when we are encouraged to think in binary terms of "us v. them." Intercultural dialogue cannot but begin on a terrain of already overlapping intercultural relations and practices. If we look closely at this terrain, we see that cross-cultural interactions, far from straightforwardly improving women's status, have sometimes reinforced gender inequality across cultures. Cross-cultural humility requires acknowledging that the traditions of religious and cultural minority groups are contested and that struggles toward equality in Western societies are incomplete and ongoing. It also means recognizing the ways in which our own patriarchal or otherwise unjust norms and institutions are implicated in the injustices that we decry in the communities of others, whether through long histories of colonialism and domination or through more recent forms of indirect support. Justice between and within cultural communities may not ultimately be attainable, but if we are to pursue it, we should do so deliberatively and with a spirit of cross-cultural humility.

References

Abu-Odeh, Lama. 1992. "Post-Colonial Feminism and the Veil: Considering the Differences." *New England Law Review* 26: 1527–37.

Afshar, Haleh. 1995. "Islam Empowering or Repressive to Women?" In *God's Law versus State Law*. Michael King ed. London: Grey Seal Books.

Ahmed, Leila. 1992. *Women and Gender in Islam: Historical Roots of a Modern Debate*. New Haven: Yale University Press.

al-Hibri, Azizah. 1982. "A Study of Islamic Herstory: Or How Did We Ever Get into This Mess?" In *Women and Islam*. Azizah al-Hibri ed. New York: Pergamon Press.

Altman, Irwin, and Joseph Ginat. 1996. *Polygamous Families in Contemporary Society*. New York: Cambridge University Press.

Anderson, Benedict. [1983] 1991. *Imagined Communities: Reflections on the Origin and Spread of Nationalism*. 2nd edn. London: Verso.

Anderson, Curt. 2004. "Muslim Girl in Oklahoma Can Wear Head Scarf to School under Federal Settlement." *Associated Press*, May 19.

Anderson, Elizabeth. 1999. "What Is the Point of Equality?" *Ethics* 109 (2): 287–337.

Anthony, Susan B. 1871. "The Liberal Party at Salt Lake." In *The Papers of Elizabeth Cady Stanton and Susan B. Anthony*. Patricia H. Holland and Ann D. Gordon eds. Microform, 1831–1906.

Appiah, Kwame Anthony. 1994. "Identity, Authenticity, Survival: Multicultural Societies and Social Reproduction." In *Multiculturalism: Examining the Politics of Recognition*. Amy Gutmann ed. Princeton: Princeton University Press.

2004. *The Ethics of Identity*. Princeton: Princeton University Press.

Arneson, Richard, and Ian Shapiro. 1996. "Religious Liberty and Democratic Autonomy: A Critique of *Wisconsin v. Yoder*." In *Nomos XXXVIII: Political Order*. Ian Shapiro and Russell Hardin eds. New York: New York University Press.

Arnon, Nancy S., and W. W. Hill. 1979. "Santa Clara Pueblo." In *Handbook of North American Indians*, vol. IX: *Southwest*. William C. Sturtevant gen. ed. and Alfonso Ortiz vol. ed. Washington, DC: Smithsonian Institution.

Asch, Michael. 1992. "Errors in Delgamuukw: An Anthropological Perspective." In *Aboriginal Title in British Columbia: Delgamuukw v. the Queen*. Frank Cassidy ed. Vancouver and Montreal: Oolichan Books.

Bader, Veit. 2005. "Associational Democracy and Minorities within Minorities." In *Minorities within Minorities: Equality, Rights and Diversity*. Avigail Eisenberg and Jeff Spinner-Halev eds. Cambridge: Cambridge University Press.

Barber, Benjamin R. 1989. "Liberal Democracy and the Costs of Consent." In *Liberalism and the Moral Life*. Nancy L. Rosenblum ed. Cambridge, MA: Harvard University Press.

Barnard, G. W., H. Vera, M. I. Vera, and G. Newman. 1982. "Till Death Do Us Part: A Study of Spouse Murder." *Bulletin of the American Academy of Psychiatry and the Law* 10 (4): 271–80.

Barry, Brian. 2001. *Culture and Equality: An Egalitarian Critique of Multiculturalism*. Cambridge, MA: Harvard University Press.

Barsh, Russel Lawrence, and James Youngblood Henderson. 1980. *The Road: Indian Tribes and Political Liberty*. Berkeley: University of California Press.

Basch, Norma. 1982. *In the Eyes of the Law: Women, Marriage, and Property in Nineteenth-Century New York*. Ithaca: Cornell University Press.

Batchelor, Mary, Marianne Watson, and Anne Wilde. 2000. *Voices in Harmony: Contemporary Women Celebrate Plural Marriage*. Salt Lake City, UT: Principle Voices.

Benhabib, Seyla. 1996. "Toward a Deliberative Model of Democratic Legitimacy." In *Democracy and Difference: Contesting the Boundaries of the Political*. Seyla Benhabib ed. Princeton: Princeton University Press.

  2002. *The Claims of Culture: Equality and Diversity in the Global Era*. Princeton: Princeton University Press.

Bennion, Janet. 1998. *Women of Principle: Female Networking in Contemporary Mormon Polygyny*. Oxford: Oxford University Press.

Bohman, James. 1996. *Public Deliberation: Pluralism, Complexity, and Democracy*. Cambridge, MA: MIT Press.

Bredbenner, Candace. 1998. *A Nationality of Her Own: Women, Marriage, and the Law of Citizenship*. Berkeley: University of California Press.

Brooke, James. 1998. "Utah Struggles with a Revival of Polygamy." *New York Times*, Aug. 23: 12.

Brown, Michael F. 2003. *Who Owns Native Culture?* Cambridge, MA: Harvard University Press.

Brumberg, Joan. 1982. "Zenanas and Girlless Villages: The Ethnology of American Evangelical Women, 1870–1910." *Journal of American History* 69 (2): 347–71.

Brune, Tom. 1996. "Refugees' Beliefs Don't Travel Well: Compromise Plan on Circumcision of Girls Gets Little Support." *Chicago Tribune*, Oct. 28: 1.

Buchanan, Allen. 2003. *Justice, Legitimacy, and Self-Determination*. Oxford: Oxford University Press.

Burtt, Shelley. 1996. "In Defense of *Yoder*: Parental Authority and the Public Schools." In *NOMOS XXXVIII: Political Order*. Ian Shapiro and Russell Hardin eds. New York: New York University Press.

Campbell, Eugene E., and Bruce L. Campbell. 1978. "Divorce among Mormon Polygamists: Extent and Explanations." *Utah Historical Quarterly* 46: 4–23.

Canby, Jr., William C. 1988. *American Indian Law in a Nutshell*. 2nd edn. St. Paul, MN: West Publishing Co.

Carens, Joseph H. 2000. *Culture, Citizenship, and Community: A Contextual Exploration of Justice as Evenhandedness.* Oxford: Oxford University Press.

Carens, Joseph H., and Melissa S. Williams. 1998. "Islam, Immigration, and Group Recognition." *Citizenship Studies* 2 (3): 475–500.

Chambers, David L. 2000. "Civilizing the Natives: Marriage in Post-Apartheid South Africa." *Daedalus: Journal of the American Academy of Arts and Sciences* 129 (4): 101–24.

Choudhry, Sujit. 2002. "National Minorities and Ethnic Immigrants: Liberalism's Political Sociology." *Journal of Political Philosophy* 10 (1): 54–78.

Clark, Elizabeth B. 1990. "Matrimonial Bonds: Slavery and Divorce in Nineteenth-Century America." *Law and History Review* 8 (1): 25–52.

Clifford, James. 1988. "Identity at Mashpee." In *The Predicament of Culture: Twentieth-Century Ethnography, Literature and Art.* Cambridge, MA: Harvard University Press.

Cohen, G. A. 1999. "Expensive Tastes and Multiculturalism." In *Multiculturalism, Liberalism, and Democracy.* Rajeev Bhargava, Amiya Kumar Bagchi, and R. Sudarshan eds. Oxford: Oxford University Press.

Cohen, Joshua. 1989. "Deliberation and Democratic Legitimacy." In *The Good Polity.* Alan Hamlin and Philip Pettit eds. Oxford: Blackwell.

1997. "Procedure and Substance in Deliberative Democracy." In *Deliberative Democracy: Essays on Reason and Politics.* James Bohman and William Rehg eds. Cambridge, MA: MIT Press.

1998. "Democracy and Liberty." In *Deliberative Democracy.* Jon Elster ed. Cambridge: Cambridge University Press.

2003. "For a Democratic Society." In *The Cambridge Companion to Rawls.* Samuel Freeman ed. Cambridge: Cambridge University Press.

Cohen, Joshua, and Joel Rogers. 2003. "Power and Reason." In *Deepening Democracy: Institutional Innovations in Empowered Participatory Governance.* Archon Fung and Erik Olin Wright eds. London: Verso.

Coleman, Doriane Lambelet. 1996. "Individualizing Justice through Multiculturalism: The Liberals' Dilemma." *Columbia Law Review* 96 (5): 1093–167.

1998. "The Seattle Compromise: Multicultural Sensitivity and Americanization." *Duke Law Journal* 47: 717–82.

Cott, Nancy F. 1998. "Marriage and Women's Citizenship in the United States, 1830–1934." *American Historical Review* 103 (5): 1440–75.

2000. *Public Vows: A History of Marriage and the Nation.* Cambridge, MA: Harvard University Press.

Crenshaw, Kimberle. 1991. "Mapping the Margins: Intersectionality, Identity Politics, and Violence against Women of Color." *Stanford Law Review* 43: 1241–99.

Crocker, Phyllis L. 1985. "The Meaning of Equality for Battered Women Who Kill Men in Self-Defense." *Harvard Women's Law Journal* 8: 121–53.

Dahl, Robert A. 1989. *Democracy and Its Critics.* New Haven: Yale University Press.

Dana, Annette Frederico. 1993. "Courtship and Marriage Traditions of the Hmong." Unpublished MA thesis, California State University, Fresno.

Davis, David Brion. 1960. "Some Themes of Counter-Subversion: An Analysis of Anti-Masonic, Anti-Catholic, and Anti-Mormon Literature." *Mississippi Valley Historical Review* 47: 205–24.

Daynes, Kathryn M. 2001. *More Wives than One: Transformation of the Mormon Marriage System, 1840–1910*. Urbana: University of Illinois Press.

Deveaux, Monique. 2003. "A Deliberative Approach to Conflicts of Culture." *Political Theory* 31 (6): 780–807.

Devlin, Patrick. 1965. *The Enforcement of Morals*. Oxford: Oxford University Press.

Donnelly, Nancy. 1989. *The Changing Lives of Refugee Hmong Women*. Seattle: University of Washington Press.

Dressler, Joshua. 1995. *Understanding Criminal Law*. 2nd edn. New York: Matthew Bender/Irwin.

    2002. "Why Keep the Provocation Defense?: Some Reflections on a Difficult Subject." *Minnesota Law Review* 86: 959–1002.

Dryzek, John S. 2000. *Deliberative Democracy and Beyond: Liberals, Critics, Contestations*. Oxford: Oxford University Press.

Dumont, Linda, and Tara De Ryk. 1997. "C-31 Women Protest." *Alberta Sweetgrass*, July: 15.

Dworkin, Ronald. [1977] 1978. *Taking Rights Seriously*. Cambridge, MA: Harvard University Press.

    1985. *A Matter of Principle*. Cambridge, MA: Harvard University Press.

Eisenberg, Avigail and Jeff Spinner-Halev eds. 2005. *Minorities within Minorities: Equality, Rights and Diversity*. Cambridge: Cambridge University Press.

Elster, Jon. 1978. *Logic and Society: Contradictions and Possible Worlds*. New York: John Wiley and Sons.

Engineer, Asghar Ali. 2004. *The Rights of Women in Islam*. Elgin, IL: New Dawn Press.

Estrich, Susan. 1986. "Rape." *Yale Law Journal* 95: 1087–163.

Evans-Pritchard, Deirdre and Alison Dundes Renteln. 1995. "The Interpretation and Distortion of Culture: A Hmong 'Marriage by Capture' Case in Fresno, California." *California Interdisciplinary Law Journal* 4: 1–48.

"Ex-Santa Clara Governor Attempting to Change Tribal Law." 2005. *Associated Press*, Oct. 17.

Firmage, Edwin B., and Richard Collin Mangrum. 1988. *Zion in the Courts: A Legal History of the Church of Jesus Christ of Latter-day Saints, 1830–1900*. Urbana: University of Illinois Press.

Flexner, Eleanor. [1959] 1975. *Century of Struggle: The Woman's Rights Movement in the United States*. Cambridge, MA: Harvard University Press.

Foster, Craig L. 1993. "Victorian Pornography Imagery in Anti-Mormon Literature." *Journal of Mormon History* 19: 115–32.

Foster, Lawrence. 1981. *Religion and Sexuality: The American Communal Experiments of the Nineteenth Century*. Oxford: Oxford University Press.

Fraser, Nancy, and Axel Honneth. 2003. *Redistribution or Recognition? A Political-Philosophical Exchange*. London: Verso.

Freeman, Samuel. 2000. "Deliberative Democracy: A Sympathetic Comment." *Philosophy and Public Affairs* 29 (4): 371–418.

2003. "Introduction: John Rawls – An Overview." In *The Cambridge Companion to Rawls*. Samuel Freeman ed. Cambridge: Cambridge University Press.

Galeotti, Anna Elisabetta. 2002. *Toleration as Recognition*. Cambridge: Cambridge University Press.

Galston, William A. 2002. *Liberal Pluralism: The Implications of Value Pluralism for Political Theory and Practice*. Cambridge: Cambridge University Press.

Gans, Herbert. 1979. "Symbolic Ethnicity: The Future of Ethnic Groups and Cultures in America." *Ethnic and Racial Studies* 2 (1): 1–20.

Geertz, Clifford. 1973. *The Interpretation of Cultures*. New York: Basic Books.

Goldstein, Beth L. 1986. "Resolving Sexual Assault: Hmong and the American Legal System." In *The Hmong in Transition*. Glenn L. Hendricks, Bruce T. Downing, and Amos S. Deinard eds. Staten Island: Center for Migration Studies of New York.

Göle, Nilüfer. 1997. *The Forbidden Modern: Civilization and Veiling*. Ann Arbor: University of Michigan Press.

Gordon, Sarah Barringer. 1996a. "'Our National Hearthstone': Anti-polygamy Fiction and the Campaign against Moral Diversity in Antebellum America." *Yale Journal of Law and Humanities* 8: 295–350.

1996b. "'The Liberty of Self-Degradation': Polygamy, Woman Suffrage, and Consent in Nineteenth-Century America." *Journal of American History* 83: 815–47.

2002. *The Mormon Question: Polygamy and Constitutional Conflict in Nineteenth-Century America*. Chapel Hill: University of North Carolina Press.

Gould, L. Scott. 2001. "Mixing Bodies and Beliefs: The Predicament of Tribes." *Columbia Law Review* 101: 702–72.

Gover, Kevin. 2000. "Remarks of Kevin Gover, Assistant Secretary for Indian Affairs, Department of the Interior, at the Ceremony Acknowledging the 175th Anniversary of the Establishment of the Bureau of Indian Affairs." Sept. 8. Bureau of Indian Affairs web page, www.doi.gov/bia/as-ia/175gover.htm.

Green, Leslie. 1995. "Internal Minorities and Their Rights." In *The Rights of Minority Cultures*. Will Kymlicka ed. Oxford: Oxford University Press.

Green, Rayna. 1980. "Native American Women." *Signs* 6 (2): 248–67.

Greenfeld, Lawrence A., Michael R. Rand, Diane Craven, Patsy A. Klaus, Craig A. Perkins, Cheryl Ringel, Greg Warchol, Cathy Matson, and James Alan Fox. 1998. *Violence by Intimates: Analysis of Data on Crimes by Current or Former Spouses, Boyfriends, and Girlfriends, 1976–1996*. Washington, DC: US Department of Justice, Office of Justice Programs.

Griffin, James. 1986. *Well-Being: Its Meaning, Measurement, and Moral Importance*. Oxford: Clarendon Press.

Grimes, Alan P. 1967. *The Puritan Ethic and Woman Suffrage*. Oxford: Oxford University Press.

Grossberg, Michael. 1985. *Governing the Hearth: Law and the Family in Nineteenth-Century America*. Chapel Hill: University of North Carolina Press.

Gutmann, Amy. 2003. *Identity in Democracy*. Princeton: Princeton University Press.

Gutmann, Amy, and Dennis Thompson. 1996. *Democracy and Disagreement: Why Moral Conflict Cannot Be Avoided in Politics, and What Should Be Done about It.* Cambridge, MA: Harvard University Press.

Hamilton, Alexander, James Madison, and John Jay. 1961. *The Federalist Papers.* Clinton Rossiter ed. New York: New American Library.

Haney Lopez, Ian F. 1998. *White by Law: The Legal Construction of Race.* New York: New York University Press.

Hansen, Klaus J. 1967. *Quest for Empire: The Political Kingdom of God and the Council of Fifty in Mormon History.* East Lansing: Michigan State University Press.

1981. *Mormonism and the American Experience.* Chicago: University of Chicago Press.

Hardy, B. Carmon. 1992. *Solemn Covenant: The Mormon Polygamous Passage.* Urbana: University of Illinois Press.

Harris, Angela P. 1990. "Race and Essentialism in Feminist Legal Theory." *Stanford Law Review* 42: 581–616.

Hart, H. L. A. 1963. *Law, Liberty, and Morality.* Stanford: Stanford University Press.

Hawley, Florence. 1948. *Some Factors in the Indian Problem in New Mexico.* Albuquerque: University of New Mexico.

Held, David. [1987] 1996. *Models of Democracy.* 2nd edn. Stanford: Stanford University Press.

Hill, W. W. 1981. *Ethnography of Santa Clara Pueblo, New Mexico.* Albuquerque: University of New Mexico.

Hirschman, Albert O. 1970. *Exit, Voice, and Loyalty: Responses to Decline in Firms, Organizations, and States.* Cambridge, MA: Harvard University Press.

Hirschmann, Nancy J. 2003. *The Subject of Liberty: Toward a Feminist Theory of Freedom.* Princeton: Princeton University Press.

Hollinger, David. 1995. *Postethnic America: Beyond Multiculturalism.* New York: Basic Books.

hooks, bell. 1981. *Ain't I a Woman: Black Women and Feminism.* Boston: South End Press.

Horder, Jeremy. 1992. *Provocation and Responsibility.* Oxford: Clarendon Press.

Howard-Hassmann, Rhoda E. 2004. "Getting to Reparations: Japanese Americans and African Americans." *Social Forces* 83 (2): 823–40.

Iversen, Joan Smyth. 1997. *The Antipolygamy Controversy in US Women's Movements, 1880–1925: A Debate on the American Home.* New York: Garland Publishing, Inc.

Ivison, Duncan, Paul Patton, and Will Sanders eds. 2000. "Introduction." In *Political Theory and the Rights of Indigenous Peoples.* Cambridge: Cambridge University Press.

Jacobs, Margaret D. 1999. *Engendered Encounters: Feminism and Pueblo Cultures, 1879–1934.* Lincoln: University of Nebraska Press.

Jacobsohn, Gary Jeffrey. 2003. *The Wheel of Law: India's Secularism in Comparative Constitutional Context.* Princeton: Princeton University Press.

Janofsky, Michael. 2001. "Conviction of a Polygamist Raises Fears among Others." *New York Times,* May 24: A14.

Jayawardena, Kumari. 1986. *Feminism and Nationalism in the Third World.* London: Zed Books.

Johnson, James. 2000. "Why Respect Culture?" *American Journal of Political Science* 44 (3): 405–19.

Johnston, James Hugo. 1929. "Documentary Evidence of the Relations of Negroes and Indians." *Journal of Negro History* 14 (1): 21–43.

Jones, Peter. 1994. "Bearing the Consequences of Belief." *Journal of Political Philosophy* 2 (1): 24–43.

Kadish, Sanford H., and Stephen J. Schulhofer. 1995. *Criminal Law and Its Processes: Cases and Materials.* 6th edn. New York: Aspen Law and Business.

Kaplan, John, Robert Weisberg, and Guyora Binder. 1996. *Criminal Law: Cases and Materials.* 3rd edn. New York: Aspen Publishers.

Kateb, George. 1994. "Notes on Pluralism." *Social Research* 61 (3): 511–37.

Kern, Louis J. 1981. *An Ordered Love: Sex Roles and Sexuality in Victorian Utopias – the Shakers, the Mormons, and the Oneida Community.* Chapel Hill: University of North Carolina.

Keyssar, Alexander. 2000. *The Right to Vote: The Contested History of Democracy in the United States.* New York: Basic Books.

Kilbride, Philip Leroy. 1994. *Plural Marriage for Our Times: A Reinvented Option?* Westport, CT: Bergin and Garvey.

Knight, Jack, and James Johnson. 1997. "What Sort of Political Equality Does Deliberative Democracy Require?" In *Deliberative Democracy: Essays on Reason and Politics.* James Bohman and William Rehg eds. Cambridge, MA: MIT Press.

Kukathas, Chandran. 1992. "Are There Any Cultural Rights?" *Political Theory* 20: 105–30.

　　1997. "Cultural Toleration." In *Ethnicity and Group Rights: Nomos XXXIX.* Ian Shapiro and Will Kymlicka eds. New York: New York University Press.

　　2003. *The Liberal Archipelago: A Theory of Diversity and Freedom.* Oxford: Oxford University Press.

Kymlicka, Will. 1989. *Liberalism, Community, and Culture.* Oxford: Oxford University Press.

　　1995. *Multicultural Citizenship: A Liberal Theory of Minority Rights.* Oxford: Oxford University Press.

　　1998. *Finding Our Way: Rethinking Ethnocultural Relations in Canada.* Oxford University Press.

　　2000. "American Multiculturalism and the 'Nations Within.'" In *Political Theory and the Rights of Indigenous Peoples.* Duncan Ivison, Paul Patton, and Will Sanders eds. Cambridge: Cambridge University Press.

　　2001. *Politics in the Vernacular: Nationalism, Multiculturalism, and Citizenship.* Oxford: Oxford University Press.

Laborde, Cecile. 2005. "Secular Philosophy and Muslim Headscarves in Schools." *Journal of Political Philosophy* 13 (3): 305–29.

Laitin, David D. 1986. *Hegemony and Culture: Politics and Religious Change among the Yoruba.* Chicago: Chicago University Press.

Lawrence, Bonita. 2003. "Gender, Race, and the Regulation of Native Identity in Canada and the United States: An Overview." *Hypatia* 18 (2): 3–31.

Laycock, Douglas. 1990. "The Remnants of Free Exercise." *Supreme Court Review*. Chicago: University of Chicago Press.

Lazreg, Marnia. 1994. *The Eloquence of Silence: Algerian Women in Question*. New York: Routledge.

Lee, Cynthia. 2003. *Murder and the Reasonable Man: Passion and Fear in the Criminal Courtroom*. New York: New York University Press.

Lerner, Gerda. 1971. *The Woman in American History*. Menlo Park, CA: Addison-Wesley.

Levy, Jacob T. 2000. *Multiculturalism of Fear*. Oxford: Oxford University Press.

Linford, Orma. 1964. "The Mormons and the Law: The Polygamy Cases, Part I." *Utah Law Review* 9 (1): 308–70.

Lyman, E. Leo. 1986. *Political Deliverance: The Mormon Quest for Utah Statehood*. Urbana: University of Illinois Press.

Lyons, David. 1977. "The New Indian Claims and Original Rights to Land." *Social Theory and Practice* 4 (3): 249–73.

MacFarquhar, Neil. 2006. "A Simple Scarf, but Meaning Much More than Faith." *New York Times*, Sept. 8: A20.

Maguigan, Holly. 1991. "Battered Women and Self-Defense: Myths and Misconceptions in Current Reform Proposals." *University of Pennsylvania Law Review* 140: 379–486.

Margalit, Avishai, and Moshe Halbertal. 1994. "Liberalism and the Right to Culture." *Social Research* 61 (3): 491–510.

Margalit, Avishai, and Joseph Raz. 1990. "National Self-Determination." *Journal of Philosophy* 87 (9): 439–61.

Markell, Patchen. 2003. *Bound by Recognition*. Princeton: Princeton University Press.

Marx, Karl. [1845–46] 1972. "The German Ideology." In *The Marx-Engels Reader*. Robert C. Tucker ed. New York: W.W. Norton.

McConnell, Michael. 1990. "Free Exercise Revisionism and the Smith Decision." *University of Chicago Law Review* 57: 1109–53.

McCullen, Kevin. 1991. "Coloradan Charged with Buying Bride." *Rocky Mountain News*, July 16.

Mendus, Susan. 2002. "Choice, Chance and Multiculturalism." In *Multiculturalism Reconsidered*. David Held and Paul Kelly eds. Cambridge: Polity Press.

Meredith, William, and George Rowe. 1986. "Changes in Hmong Refugee Marital Attitudes in America." In *The Hmong in Transition*. Glenn L. Hendricks, Bruce T. Downing, and Amos S. Deinard eds. Staten Island: Center for Migration Studies of New York.

Mernissi, Fatima. 1982. "Virginity and Patriarchy." In *Women and Islam*. Azizah al-Hibri ed. New York: Pergamon Press.

Mill, John Stuart. [1859] 1978. *On Liberty*. Indianapolis: Hackett.

Miller, David. 2001. "Distributing Responsibilities." *Journal of Political Philosophy* 9 (4): 453–71.

   2002. "Liberalism, Equal Opportunities and Cultural Commitments." In *Multiculturalism Reconsidered: Culture and Equality and Its Critics*. Paul Kelly ed. Cambridge: Polity Press.

2004. "Holding Nations Responsible." *Ethics* 114 (2): 240–68.

Minow, Martha. 1987. "We, the Family: Constitutional Rights and American Families." *Journal of American History* 74 (3): 959–83.

Moghadam, Valentine M. 1994. "Reform, Revolution, and Reaction: The Trajectory of the 'Woman Question' in Afghanistan." In *Gender and National Identity: Women and Politics in Muslim Societies*. Valentine M. Moghadam ed. Atlantic Highlands, NJ: Zed Books.

Mohanty, Chandra Talpade, Anne Russo, and Lourdes Torres eds. 1991. *Third World Women and the Politics of Feminism*. Bloomington: Indiana University Press.

Montesquieu. 1989. *The Spirit of the Laws*. Anne M. Cohler, Basia Carolyn Miller, and Harold Samuel Stone eds. Cambridge: Cambridge University Press.

Moore, Margaret. 2005. "Internal Minorities and Indigenous Self-Determination." In *Minorities within Minorities: Equality, Rights, and Diversity*. Avigail Eisenberg and Jeff Spinner-Halev eds. Cambridge: Cambridge University Press.

Moraga, Cherrie and Gloria Anzaldúa eds. 1981. *This Bridge Called My Back: Writings by Radical Women of Color*. New York: Kitchen Table / Women of Color Press.

Murray, John Courtney. 1993. "The Problem of Religious Freedom." In *Religious Liberty: Catholic Struggles with Pluralism*. J. Leon Hooper ed. Louisville: Westminster / John Knox Press.

Narayan, Uma. 1997. *Dislocating Cultures: Identities, Traditions, and Third World Feminism*. New York: Routledge.

Navarro, Mireya. 2004. "The Most Private of Makeovers." *New York Times*, Nov. 28: Sect. 9, 1–2.

Newman, Maria. 2006. "Leader of Polygamist Sect Agrees to Face Utah Charges." *New York Times*, Sept. 1: A12.

Nobles, Melissa. 2000. *Shades of Citizenship: Race and the Census in Modern Politics*. Stanford: Stanford University Press.

Nourse, Victoria. 1997. "Passion's Progress: Modern Law Reform and the Provocation Defense." *Yale Law Journal* 106: 1331–409.

Nozick, Robert. 1974. *Anarchy, State, and Utopia*. New York: Basic Books.

Nussbaum, Martha. 2000. *Women and Human Development: The Capabilities Approach*. Cambridge: Cambridge University Press.

O'Brien, Sharon. 1989. *American Indian Tribal Governments*. Norman: University of Oklahoma Press.

Okin, Susan Moller. 1998. "Feminism and Multiculturalism: Some Tensions." *Ethics* 108 (4): 661–84.

1999. *Is Multiculturalism Bad for Women?* Joshua Cohen, Matthew Howard, and Martha C. Nussbaum eds. Princeton: Princeton University Press.

2002. "Mistresses of their Own Destiny: Group Rights, Gender, and Realistic Rights of Exit." *Ethics* 112 (2): 205–30.

2005. "Multiculturalism and Feminism: No Simple Questions, No Simple Answers." In *Minorities within Minorities: Equality, Rights and Diversity*. Avigail Eisenberg and Jeff Spinner-Halev eds. Cambridge: Cambridge University Press.

Oliver, Myrna. 1988. "Immigrant Crimes: Cultural Defense – A Legal Tactic." *LA Times*, July 15.

Omi, Michael, and Howard Winant. 1994. *Racial Formation in the United States: From the 1960s to the 1990s*. New York: Routledge.

Ortner, Sherry B. 1974. "Is Female to Male as Nature Is to Culture?" In *Woman, Culture and Society*. Michelle Z. Rosaldo and Louise Lamphere eds. Stanford: Stanford University Press.

1996. *Making Gender: The Politics and Erotics of Culture*. Boston: Beacon Press.

1999. "Introduction." In *The Fate of "Culture": Geertz and Beyond*. Sherry B. Ortner ed. Berkeley: University of California Press.

Ostrom, Carol M. 1996. "Is Form of Circumcision Outlawed? Procedure at Harborview under Review." *Seattle Times*, Oct. 14.

Parekh, Bhikhu. 2000. *Rethinking Multiculturalism: Cultural Diversity and Political Theory*. Cambridge, MA: Harvard University Press.

Parsons, Elsie Clews. 1932. "The Kinship Nomenclature of the Pueblo Indians." *American Anthropologist* 34 (3): 377–89.

Patten, Alan. 2001. "The Rights of Internal Linguistic Minorities." In *Minorities within Minorities: Equality, Rights and Diversity*. Avigail Eisenberg and Jeff Spinner-Halev eds. Cambridge: Cambridge University Press.

Perkins, Rollin M., and Ronald N. Boyce. 1982. *Criminal Law*. 3rd edn. Mineola, NY: Foundation Press.

Phillips, Anne. 2003. "When Culture Means Gender: Issues of Cultural Defence in the English Courts." *Modern Law Review* 66: 510–31.

Philp, Kenneth R. 1977. *John Collier's Crusade for Indian Reform, 1920–1954*. Phoenix: University of Arizona.

Polman, Dick. 1989. "When Is Cultural Difference a Legal Defense? Immigrants' Native Traditions Clash with US Law." *Seattle Times*, July 12: A1.

Posner, Eric A., and Adrian Vermeule. 2003. "Reparations for Slavery and Other Historical Injustices." *Columbia Law Review* 103: 690–747.

Poulter, Sebastian. 1997. "Muslim Headscarves in School: Contrasting Legal Approaches in England and France." *Oxford Journal of Legal Studies* 17 (1): 43–74.

Prucha, Francis Paul. 1984. *The Great Father: The United States Government and the American Indians*. 2 vols. Lincoln: University of Nebraska Press.

"Questions for Sherman Alexie." 1997. *New York Times Magazine*, Jan. 5: 8.

Rasche, Christine E. 1993. "Given Reasons for Violence in Intimate Relationships." In *Homicide: The Victim/Offender Connection*. Anna Victoria Wilson ed. Cincinnati: Anderson Publishing Co.

Rawls, John. [1971] 1999. *A Theory of Justice*. Cambridge, MA: Harvard University Press.

[1993] 1996. *Political Liberalism*. New York: Columbia University Press.

1999. "The Idea of Public Reason Revisited." In *Collected Papers*. Samuel Freeman ed. Cambridge, MA: Harvard University Press.

Rennison, Callie Marie. 2003. *Intimate Partner Violence, 1993–2001*. Washington, DC: US Department of Justice, Buneau of Justice Statistics, Crime Data Brief No. NCJ 197838.

Renteln, Alison D. 1993. "A Justification of the Cultural Defense as Partial Excuse." *Southern California Review of Law and Women's Studies* 2: 437–526.
  2004. *The Cultural Defense.* Oxford: Oxford University Press.
  2005. "The Use and Abuse of the Cultural Defense." *Canadian Journal of Law and Society* 20 (1): 47–67.
Resnik, Judith. 1989. "Dependent Sovereigns: Indian Tribes, States, and the Federal Courts." *University of Chicago Law Review* 56: 671–759.
Rice, Ranee Liamputtong. 2000. *Hmong Women and Reproduction.* Westport, CT: Bergin and Garvey.
Riker, William H. 1982. *Liberalism against Populism: A Confrontation between the Theory of Democracy and the Theory of Social Choice.* Prospect Heights, IL: Waveland Press.
Rosenblum, Nancy L. 1989. "Introduction." In *Liberalism and the Moral Life.* Nancy L. Rosenblum ed. Cambridge, MA: Harvard University Press.
  1997. "Democratic Sex: Reynolds v. US, Sexual Relations, and Community." In *Sex, Preference, and Family: Essays on Law and Nature.* David M. Estlund and Martha C. Nussbaum eds. Oxford: Oxford University Press.
  1998. *Membership and Morals: The Personal Uses of Pluralism in America.* Princeton: Princeton University Press.
Sager, Lawrence G. 2000. "The Free Exercise of Culture: Some Doubts and Distinctions." *Daedalus: Journal of the American Academy of Arts and Sciences* 129 (4): 193–208.
Said, Edward W. 1989. "Representing the Colonized: Anthropology's Interlocutors." *Critical Inquiry* 15 (2): 205–25.
Scheffler, Samuel. 2003. "What is Egalitarianism?" *Philosophy and Public Affairs* 31 (1): 5–39.
Schulhofer, Stephen J. 1990. "The Gender Question in Criminal Law." *Social Philosophy and Policy* 7: 105–37.
  1998. *Unwanted Sex: The Culture of Intimidation and the Failure of Law.* Cambridge, MA: Harvard University Press.
Scott, David. 2003. "Culture in Political Theory." *Political Theory* 31 (1): 92–115.
Sen, Amartya. 1992. *Inequality Reexamined.* Oxford: Oxford University Press.
Sewell, Jr., William H. 1999. "The Concept of Culture." In *Beyond the Cultural Turn.* Victoria E. Bonnell and Lynn Hunt eds. Berkeley: University of California Press.
Shachar, Ayelet. 2001. *Multicultural Jurisdictions: Cultural Differences and Women's Rights.* Cambridge: Cambridge University Press.
Shapiro, Ian. 2003. *The State of Democratic Theory.* Princeton: Princeton University Press.
Shaw, Shannon. 2005. "The Right to Belong." *Santa Fe New Mexican,* Oct. 16: C1.
Sher, George. 1979. "Compensation and Transworld Personal Identity." *Monist* 62: 378–91.
  1980. "Ancient Wrongs and Modern Rights." *Philosophy and Public Affairs* 10 (1): 3–17.
Sherman, Rorie. 1989. "Cultural Defenses Draw Fire." *National Law Journal,* Apr. 17: 28.
Sherman, Spencer. 1986. "When Cultures Collide." *California Lawyer,* Jan. 6: 36, 60.

Shklar, Judith. 1989. "The Liberalism of Fear." In *Liberalism and the Moral Life*. Nancy L. Rosenblum ed. Cambridge, MA: Harvard University Press.

Shweder, Richard A. 2000. "What about 'Female Genital Mutilation'? And Why Understanding Culture Matters in the First Place." *Daedalus: Journal of the American Academy of Arts and Sciences* 129 (4): 209–32.

Simmons, Marc. 1979a. "History of Pueblo-Spanish Relations to 1821." In *Handbook of North American Indians*, vol. IX: *Southwest*. William C. Sturtevant gen. ed. and Alfonso Ortiz vol. ed. Washington, DC: Smithsonian Institution.

    1979b. "History of the Pueblos since 1821." In *Handbook of North American Indians*, vol. IX: *Southwest*. William C. Sturtevant gen. ed. and Alfonso Ortiz vol. ed. Washington, DC: Smithsonian Institution.

Simon, Russell Max. 2005. "Santa Clara Ex-Gov. Tries to Change Marriage Law." *Albuquerque Journal*, Oct. 16: B5.

Simpson, Andra. 2000. "Paths toward a Mohawk Nation: Narratives of Citizenship and Nationhood in Kahnawake." In *Political Theory and the Rights of Indigenous Peoples*. Duncan Ivison, Paul Patton, and Will Sanders eds. Cambridge: Cambridge University Press.

Smith, Rogers M. 1997. *Civic Ideals: Conflicting Visions of Citizenship in US History*. New Haven: Yale University Press.

    2003. *Stories of Peoplehood: The Politics and Morals of Political Membership*. Cambridge: Cambridge University Press.

Sollors, Werner. 1989. "Introduction: The Invention of Ethnicity." In *The Invention of Ethnicity*. Werner Sollors ed. Oxford: Oxford University Press.

Song, Sarah. 2005. "Majority Norms, Multiculturalism, and Gender Equality." *American Political Science Review* 99 (4): 473–89.

    2006. "Religious Freedom v. Sex Equality." *Theory and Research in Education* 4 (1): 23–40.

Spatz, Melissa. 1991. "A 'Lesser' Crime: A Comparative Study of Legal Defenses for Men Who Kill Their Wives." *Columbia Journal of Law and Social Problems* 24: 597–620.

Spinner-Halev, Jeff. 2000. *Surviving Diversity: Religion and Democratic Citizenship*. Baltimore: Johns Hopkins University Press.

    2001. "Feminism, Multiculturalism, Oppression, and the State." *Ethics* 112 (1): 84–113.

    2005. "Autonomy, Association, and Pluralism." In *Minorities within Minorities: Equality, Rights and Diversity*. Avigail Eisenberg and Jeff Spinner-Halev eds. Cambridge: Cambridge University Press.

Spinner-Halev, Jeff, and Elizabeth Theiss-Morse. 2003. "National Identity and Self-Esteem." *Perspectives on Politics* 1 (3): 515–32.

Stanton, Elizabeth Cady, Susan B. Anthony, and Matilda Joslyn Gage, eds. 1881–1922. *History of Woman Suffrage*. 6 vols. New York: Fowler and Wells.

Stocking, Jr., George W. 1968. *Race, Culture, and Evolution: Essays in the History of Anthropology*. New York: Free Press.

Strauss, David A. 1991. "The Law and Economics of Racial Discrimination in Employment: The Case for Numerical Standards." *Georgetown Law Journal* 79: 1648–57.

Strong, Josiah. 1891. *Our Country: Its Possible Future and Its Present Crisis*. New York: Baker and Taylor Co.

Sullivan, Kathleen M. 1992. "Religion and Liberal Democracy." In *The Bill of Rights in the Modern State*. Geoffrey R. Stone, Richard A. Epstein, and Cass R. Sunstein eds. Chicago: University of Chicago Press.

Sullivan, Kathleen M. and Gerald Gunther. 2004. *Constitutional Law*. 15th edn. New York: Foundation Press.

Sunstein, Cass. 2001. *Designing Democracy: What Constitutions Do*. Oxford: Oxford University Press.

Taylor, Charles. 1985. *Philosophical Papers*. Cambridge: Cambridge University Press.
    1994. "The Politics of Recognition." In *Multiculturalism: Examining the Politics of Recognition*. Amy Gutmann ed. Princeton: Princeton University Press.
    1995. *Philosophical Arguments*. Cambridge, MA: Harvard University Press.

Thao, T. Christopher. 1986. "Hmong Customs on Marriage, Divorce, and the Rights of Married Women." In *The Hmong World*. B. Johns and D. Strecker eds. New Haven: Council on Southeast Asian Studies, Yale Center for International and Area Studies.

Tocqueville, Alexis de. [1835] 1966. *Democracy in America*. J. P. Mayer ed. New York: Harper Perennial.

Tomasi, John. 1995. "Kymlicka, Liberalism, and Respect for Cultural Minorities." *Ethics* 105 (Apr.): 580–603.

Tribe, Laurence H. 1988. *American Constitutional Law*. 2nd edn. New York: Foundation Press.

Trimarchi, Anthony. 1989. "US Judge Refuses to Jail Wife-Killer." *Asian Outlook* (May–June): 29.

Tsawb, Yaj Txooj. 1986. "Outline of Marriage Rites." In *The Hmong World*. B. Johns and D. Strecker eds. New Haven: Council on Southeast Asian Studies, Yale Center for International and Area Studies.

Tully, James. 1994. "Diversity's Gambit Declined." In *Constitutional Predicament: Canada after the Referendum of 1992*. Curtis Cook ed. Montreal: McGill-Queen's University Press.
    1995. *Strange Multiplicity: Constitutionalism in an Age of Diversity*. Cambridge: Cambridge University Press.

Van Wagoner, Richard S. 1989. *Mormon Polygamy: A History*. 2nd edn. Salt Lake City: Signature Books.

Vang, Kao N. 1982. "Hmong Marriage Customs: A Current Assessment." In *The Hmong in the West: Observations and Reports*. Bruce T. Downing and Douglas P. Olney eds. Minneapolis: Southeast Asian Refugee Studies Project, Center for Urban and Regional Affairs, University of Minnesota.

Volpp, Leti. 1994. "(Mis)identifying Culture: Asian Women and the 'Cultural Defense.'" *Harvard Women's Law Journal* 17: 57–101.

Waldron, Jeremy. 1992. "Superseding Historic Injustice." *Ethics* 103 (1): 4–28.
    [1992] 1995. "Minority Cultures and the Cosmopolitan Alternative." In *The Rights of Minority Cultures*. Will Kymlicka ed. Oxford: Oxford University Press.

Wanderer, Nancy A., and Catherine R. Connors. 1999. "Culture and Crime: Kargar and the Existing Framework for a Cultural Defense." *Buffalo Law Review* 47: 829–73.

Warner, Carolyn M., and Manfred W. Wenner. 2006. "Religion and the Political Organization of Muslims in Europe." *Perspectives on Politics* 4 (3): 457–79.

Waters, Mary C. 1990. *Ethnic Options: Choosing Identities in America*. Berkeley: University of California Press.

Weber, Bruce. 1999. "Reggae Rhythms Speak to an Insular Tribe." *New York Times*, Sept. 19: A1.

Weber, David. 2007. "Mashpee Wampanoag Indians Receive Federal Recognition." *Boston Globe*, Feb. 15. www.boston.com/news/local/massachusetts/articles/2007/02/15/mashpee_wampanoag_indians_receive_federal_recognition/.

Wedeen, Lisa. 2002. "Conceptualizing Culture: Possibilities for Political Science." *American Political Science Review* 96 (4): 713–28.

Weil, Patrick. 2004. "A Nation in Diversity: France, Muslims and the Headscarf." www.openDemocracy.net. Mar. 25.

Weisbrod, Carol, and Pamela Sheingorn. 1978. "Reynolds v. US: Nineteenth-Century Forms of Marriage and the Status of Women." *Connecticut Law Review* 10 (4): 828–58.

White, George. 1991. "Hmong Case to be Settled with Pleas This Afternoon." *Louisville Times/Lafayette News*, Nov. 13.

Williams, Bernard A. O. [1962] 1997. "The Idea of Equality." In *Equality: Selected Readings*. Louis P. Pojman and Robert Westmoreland eds. Oxford: Oxford University Press.

Wilson, Terry. 1992. "Blood Quantum: Native American Mixed Bloods." In *Racially Mixed People in America*. Maria P. P. Root ed. Newbury Park, CA: Sage Publications.

Wolf, Eric R. 1982. *Europe and the People without History*. Berkeley: University of California Press.

Wolff, Jonathan. 1998. "Fairness, Respect, and the Egalitarian Ethos." *Philosophy and Public Affairs* 27 (2): 97–122.

Wolin, Sheldon S. 2004. *Politics and Vision: Continuity and Innovation in Western Political Thought*. Expanded edn. Princeton: Princeton University Press.

Yen, Marianne. 1989. "Refusal to Jail Immigrant Who Killed Wife Stirs Outrage; Judge Ordered Probation for Chinese Man, Citing His 'Cultural Background.'" *Washington Post*, Apr. 10: A3.

Young, Iris Marion. 1996. "Communication and the Other: Beyond Deliberative Democracy." In *Democracy and Difference: Contesting the Boundaries of the Political*. Seyla Benhabib ed. Princeton: Princeton University Press.

Index